Making
Change Work

Making Change Work

How to create behavioural change in organizations to drive impact and ROI

Emma Weber
Patricia Pulliam Phillips
Jack J Phillips

KoganPage

LONDON PHILADELPHIA NEW DELHI

First published in Great Britain and the United States in 2016 by Kogan Page Limited

2nd Floor, 45 Gee Street	1518 Walnut Street, Suite 900	4737/23 Ansari Road
London EC1V 3RS	Philadelphia PA 19102	Daryaganj
United Kingdom	USA	New Delhi 110002
www.koganpage.com		India

© Emma Weber, Patricia Pulliam Phillips and Jack J Phillips, 2016

ISBN   978 0 7494 7760 8
E-ISBN   978 0 7494 7761 5

British Library Cataloguing-in-Publication Data

A CIP record for this book is available from the British Library.

Library of Congress Cataloging-in-Publication Data

Names: Weber, Emma, author. | Phillips, Patricia Pulliam, author. | Phillips, Jack J., 1945- author.
Title: Making change work : how to create behavioural change in organizations to drive impact and ROI / Emma Weber, Patricia Pulliam Phillips, Jack J. Phillips.
Description: 1st Edition. | Philadelphia, PA : Kogan Page, 2016. | Includes bibliographical references and index.
Identifiers: LCCN 2016008407 (print) | LCCN 2016011623 (ebook) | ISBN 9780749477608 (paperback) | ISBN 9780749477615 (e-ISBN) | ISBN 9780749477615
Subjects: LCSH: Organizational change. | Personnel management. | Organizational behavior. | BISAC: BUSINESS & ECONOMICS / Management. | BUSINESS & ECONOMICS / Human Resources & Personnel Management. | BUSINESS & ECONOMICS / Organizational Development.
Classification: LCC HD58.8 .W4326 2016 (print) | LCC HD58.8 (ebook) | DDC 658.4/06–dc23
LC record available at http://lccn.loc.gov/2016008407

Typeset by Graphicraft Limited, Hong Kong
Print production managed by Jellyfish
Printed and bound by CPI Group (UK) Ltd, Croydon, CR0 4YY

CONTENTS

ACKNOWLEDGEMENTS

A big thank you to Patti and Jack Phillips for collaborating with me on this venture.

Bringing your depth of skill and experience in the ROI Methodology to the project has made for a rich and robust end-to-end approach to change. Thanks for being excited by the idea in the first place and sticking with it when the deadlines were tight. I look forward to continuing our work together.

Sincere thanks to Sharmila Shearing and team at UNSW Innovations, and also to Kristine Gatt from WCD – Workers' Compensation Solutions. Your case study contributions to the book have been deeply appreciated. Thank you.

A heartfelt thanks to Karen McCreadie. Your word mastery is second to none and your crafting on this project has been essential to its fruition. We would not have made it without you!

Thanks and credit to the whole team at Kogan Page, especially Philippa Fiszzon, Lucy Carter, Nancy Wallace and Megan Mondi – thank you for working with me for a second time on a project close to my heart. Thanks too for your patience and for keeping us on track. It's a real pleasure to be working with you.

Any work I deliver in the field of Turning Learning into Action is a true team effort. Especially on this project – a huge thank you to Jess Sayer, whose combination of creativity and organization skills behind the scenes enabled much of this work to be delivered.

Thanks also to Carole Orbell for your design skill with images for the book. It looks so much better for your input and care.

Thanks to the wider Lever – Transfer of Learning team who are crafting our approach to change on a daily basis, delighting our clients and deepening our learning in the field.

Finally, thank you to my mentors, friends and family who continue to support me on my ventures, especially my love Damien, and the gorgeous Belle for your support and patience while I wrote, reviewed and edited into the night.

Emma

It has been a privilege to work with Emma on this publication. Her work to help organizations move from knowing to doing is second to none. It is by making change work that organizations can drive operational excellence, customer relationships, innovation and sustainability. Investment in change can have a significant payoff by aligning change initiatives to the needs of the business and building a strategy to transfer learning into action.

As with all of our publications, this publication was the work of many. Particularly Karen McCreadie, who took drafts from multiple authors and made them flow as if written by one: you are a master at your craft. We would also like to thank the team at Kogan Page. It has been a privilege to work with you. Your professionalism in developing this book is greatly appreciated. Many thanks also go to our team at the ROI Institute. Your ability to manage our schedules and support us in our work is invaluable.

Finally, we want to thank Emma for inviting us to contribute to this book. We value your partnership and your friendship. You are truly one who can make change work.

Patti and Jack

PART ONE
Why change?

The need for results from change

Right now, somewhere in the world another change initiative just died. It was probably introduced with enthusiastic fanfare – a new IT system that would make the business more efficient and employees' and customers' lives easier or a new process that would streamline operations and improve productivity. The news of the impending change initiative was probably not met with quite the same enthusiasm from those affected as the person responsible for leading and implementing the change (change agent). And to be fair it's hardly surprising.

Most of us who have worked in an organization anywhere in the world will have experienced some new change initiative or another. Some of us may even have some memorabilia to prove it – a T-shirt with the project name on the front and 'We did it' on the back (that no one wore because 'we didn't do it') or a 'Mission Ignite' coffee mug where someone scored out 'Ignite' and replaced it with 'Impossible' with a permanent marker! We can probably all remember the initiative 'that started so well' but ended so badly or just petered out. Even those that seem destined to deliver, with clear objectives and detailed implementation plans, can so easily derail and all that is left to prove it was ever started is the implementation document that is now used as a hefty bookend.

In 1995 John P Kotter, the renowned change management thinker, revealed in an article for the *Harvard Business Review* that only 30 per cent of change initiatives are successful (1995). He later went on to publish what many regard as the seminal work in the field (1996). In 2002 David Miller reported in the *Journal of Change Management* that 70 per cent of change programmes fail. In 2005, Malcolm Higgs and Deborah Rowland reported in the same industry magazine that 'Only one in four or five change programmes actually succeed.' In 2006 McKinsey & Company surveyed 1,546 business executives from around the world to ascertain the new updated statistics for successful change implementation. Lo and behold only 30 per cent of change initiatives were considered a success (Isern and Pung, 2006).

Incredibly, all the independent research into the effectiveness of change initiatives over the past several decades, whether from the Gartner Group, Harvard Business School or McKinsey & Company and beyond, consistently illustrates the ironic truth that change doesn't actually change that much (Keller and Aiken, 2008). All the time, money and energy poured into change initiative after change initiative doesn't actually matter most of the time. It should matter, otherwise why start the change process in the first place? Even though we have known these dismal figures since the mid-1990s the failure rate of change initiatives is still stubbornly stuck at 70 per cent (Leonard and Coltea, 2013). In fact, Towers Watson bumped that figure up to 75 per cent when the ability to sustain change was factored in (2013).

And the changing pace and complexity of business mean that the situation is only getting worse. According to IBM's 2008 Global CEO Study 83 per cent of CEOs and senior leaders expected substantial change – up from 65 per cent two years earlier. Unfortunately those reporting they had successfully managed change in the previous two years rose only 4 per cent, up from 57 per cent to 61 per cent. This 'Change Gap' or the disparity between the expected change and the ability to manage it nearly tripled between 2006 and 2008 (IBM, 2008a, 2008b). The same study two years later identified the escalating complexity of operating in an increasingly volatile and uncertain world as the primary challenge. And a surprising number of CEOs reported that they still felt ill-equipped to succeed in this drastically different world (IBM, 2010). In 2012 the challenge was still change – how to adequately manage and capitalize on the convergence of the digital, social and mobile spheres, connecting customers, employees and partners to organizations and to each other in new ways (IBM, 2012).

Today the challenges are even more pressing. We live in a VUCA world – volatile, uncertain, complex and ambiguous. Change is a constant and increasingly permanent aspect of modern business – and we are not adapting quickly enough. Too few of us possess genuine change capability and so are struggling under the weight of escalating change initiatives and expectations.

The pressure on CEOs and senior leaders to continuously deliver shareholder value is relentless. For most businesses that pressure means a necessary preoccupation with short-term results and a continuous drive for growth and elevated performance. Indeed it is this drive for better financial results, either increased revenue or cost savings, that is behind most change initiatives.

There is little doubt that modern business is encountering more change than ever. Research collaboration between the Association for Talent Development (ATD, formerly ASTD) and i4cp found that only 17 per cent of business and learning professionals surveyed rate their organization as highly effective in managing change initiatives. That's not very encouraging when most organizations are facing a minimum of three major changes per year (ASTD, 2014).

Essentially what all this means is that not only is our ability to successfully implement change notoriously poor across the board but our need to implement more change successfully is escalating at an alarming rate. Clearly we need a solution.

But before we unpack that solution in more detail it's worth getting a handle on just how urgent the need for answers really is.

The cost of failed change

There are three main costs when it comes to failed change initiatives:

- financial cost;
- human cost;
- competitive cost.

Financial cost

Think about the last change initiative you were involved in... consider all the meetings, analysis, and presentations you were privy to. Think about the various options that were explored before a decision was made to opt for one change initiative over another. All this took time and therefore money. And that was before any change was even announced. Whether you are installing a new database or order system or moving premises or instituting a new quality initiative, change is always expensive.

Dr John McManus and Trevor Wood-Harper showed that the estimated cost of IT project failure across the European Union was a staggering €142 billion. Professor Chris Clegg of the University of Sheffield conducted research into the same area and discovered that as much as £58 billion is wasted in IT-related change in the UK every year (McManus, 2004).

An investigation by the *Independent* found that a significant number of IT change initiatives undertaken by the UK government suffered severe delays, ran millions of pounds over budget or had been cancelled with the total cost estimated to be £26 billion. Parliament's spending watchdog described the projects as 'fundamentally flawed' and blamed ministers for 'stupendous incompetence' in managing them (Savage, 2010).

In 2005 the US Air Force initiated the Expeditionary Combat Support System to assist in resource planning. Despite costing $1.1 billion, no significant capabilities were ready on time and it would have cost $1.1 billion more just to get a quarter of the original scope. Needless to say the project was cancelled.

It almost seems unfair to call out these examples – in truth there is no shortage of war stories about the epic waste of money caused by failed change initiatives. Often IT changes are easier to quantify and therefore get more media attention but failed change of all types is financially costly. But unfortunately it's not just the financial cost that's so frustrating.

Human cost

If 7 out of every 10 change initiatives fail then a huge number of people may only have experienced failure. That has serious repercussions on employee morale and engagement. It's hardly surprising that the mere mention of any change initiative is universally met with heavy sighing and copious eye-rolling along with veiled mutterings of 'Oh no, not again'.

Failed change is soul destroying. And if we look at Gallup employee engagement figures there is little doubt lack of engagement is a problem for many organizations. During 2010–2012 Gallup conducted a comprehensive study into the US workforce and discovered that just 30 per cent of the 100 million full-time employees were engaged, 52 per cent were disengaged and 18 per cent were actively disengaged. This means that some 70 million US workers are 'not engaged' or 'actively disengaged' and are emotionally disconnected from their workplaces, which makes high performance and productivity unlikely. In fact Gallup estimates that these actively disengaged employees cost the United States between $450 billion and $550 billion every year in lost productivity, stating disengaged workers are 'more likely to steal from their companies, negatively influence their co-workers, miss workdays, and drive customers away' (Gallup, 2013a). And, in case you are reading this and thinking, 'Oh, that's OK, I live in Australia, UK, Europe...' according to Gallup's 142-country study into global workplace engagement North America and Canada are at the top of the list! Australia and New Zealand come in second with engaged employees accounting for 24 per cent of the workplace, while only 14 per cent of Western Europe's workforce is engaged. According to the report, 'Currently, 13 per cent of employees across 142 countries worldwide are engaged in their jobs – that is, they are emotionally invested in and focused on creating value for their organizations every day. As in Gallup's 2009–2010 global study of employee engagement, actively disengaged workers – ie those who are negative and potentially hostile to their organizations – continue to outnumber engaged employees at a rate of nearly 2:1 (Gallup, 2013b).

Clearly there is more to engagement and disengagement than change but one of the major influencing factors in employee engagement is the degree to which employees see their organization successfully implementing change. You don't need to be Einstein to appreciate that being part of change initiatives that constantly fail or peter out to nothing is demotivating for the people involved. Change usually means 'on top of normal workload' so employees are constantly expected to make the changes as well as do what they normally do each day. Investing that extra time and effort – even grudgingly – to then see it all fall in a heap is extremely frustrating for people. It's little wonder they disengage and grind out their day so they can go home and watch their favourite TV show or simply leave. Repeated failed change initiatives undoubtedly increase staff turnover.

Continuous failed initiatives also extract a high credibility cost for managers and leaders which can erode trust and make leadership extremely difficult. Successful leadership requires followership. After all, if no one follows then we can hardly be called a leader at all. When a manager or senior team is constantly initiating changes that fail or are only partially successful then their standing in the business is negatively impacted. It creates the 'Palm Tree Effect' (Miller, 2011). The leader announces yet another change initiative so the employees simply adopt the characteristics of a palm tree in a storm. They bend over to accommodate the storm but once the storm has passed the tree springs right back to its original position as if nothing has happened. Even if the leader is new and enthusiastic, if the organization has a legacy of failed change initiatives it can be extremely difficult to break down the cynicism and persuade people to stop behaving like a palm tree!

Competitive cost

Being able to manage change successfully is now more important than ever. We need to stay competitive and find effective ways to adapt to the ever-changing market conditions.

Even in the last decade technology has transformed business. We have increased connectivity and social media have turned traditional marketing on its head. We can now know what our customers think about us almost as fast as they think it. Our ability to store and analyse data has created

'Big Data' – the ability to use all sorts of digitized data, from traditional text, numbers and graphics to new data such as sensor data, to predict market changes and explore opportunities faster than ever before.

The complexity of modern business also means we need to constantly adapt. Often that can mean leaving tried and tested approaches or abandoning long-term lucrative products and services that have lost their appeal with customers. Or ramping up investment in high-potential products where our market share is currently low but could be significant. We need to ensure we know about these changes to market conditions early so we can take steps early to adapt instead of sticking our head in the sand and lamenting the speed of change.

Obviously all these costs also carry an opportunity cost. We only have finite resources, be they money, human capital, hours or creativity. When we invest in another change initiative the money could have been used elsewhere. The time and energy required by employees could also have been used elsewhere, which could in turn have allowed the business to pull away from the competition. In fact in some cases it has been found that shareholders or taxpayers would have been better off if the organization had simply given them the budget spent on the change initiative.

How to build successful change management capability

Change is constant and whatever the reason for change it is clear that the organizations that will prosper are the ones who embrace it when it's needed regardless of their market position or dominance.

Gone are the days when we can recruit legions of consultants to project manage the change only to see it fall in a heap upon their departure. Gone are the days where we can ignore change in the hope it will go away, or sit by and hope someone else deals with it. Today we are being called on to develop change capability within our business. If we understand change and have a proven practical process to implement change successfully then we will develop an ongoing competitive advantage, save money and improve engagement and morale. We will have a way to ensure that we only initiate the right change initiatives based on thorough analysis and clear outcome and we will be able to steer that change through to a quantifiable return on investment.

One of the biggest concerns highlighted by the IBM Global CEO Study was the fear that there were not enough personnel in the business armed with the capability to manage change successfully. This book therefore offers you a real opportunity to differentiate yourself in your business and future career so that you can consistently demonstrate your capacity to successfully manage and deliver change.

Successful change happens when the change agent:

- defines stakeholder needs, reflecting opportunities for change;
- develops specific, measurable objectives reflecting those needs and using the objectives to design the change initiative and direct its implementation;
- implements a transfer strategy to ensure successful behavioural change occurs;
- evaluates the change initiative, ensuring it leads to desired results and identifying opportunities to adjust if necessary.

Each of these bullet points is expanded on below.

Define stakeholder needs

Far too many change initiatives are initiated out of desperation, lacking alignment with what the stakeholders inside the organization really need. The 'throw everything at the wall and see what sticks' approach is expensive, time consuming, and prohibits productivity in employees. It is therefore crucial that stakeholder needs are thoroughly defined before change is really considered so that the outcome of the change is clear to all the stakeholders. By clarifying the stakeholder needs – whether to make more money, save more money, avoid costs, or do some greater good – defining the specific measures that need to improve ensures that change solutions are aligned to a clear objective.

In Chapter 2 we will explore an alignment model – the V Model – that helps organizations identify opportunities and the change that has to occur to take advantage of those opportunities and meet the stakeholder needs. This alignment approach sets up the change initiative so that it targets change that matters from the outset. It answers the most fundamental question: Why change?

Develop measurable objectives

Objectives represent an intended outcome. They serve as the blueprint for the construction of change initiatives. Frequently referred to as goals, objectives define in specific, measurable terms how change will occur, when it will occur, and how success will be measured. By developing objectives that reflect stakeholder needs the change agent (or leader of the change) not only reassures stakeholders that their needs are heard, but that there is a clear path to addressing those needs.

In addition to serving as a blueprint for the construction of change initiatives, objectives serve as a management tool. Clear objectives provide the basis for ongoing measurement and monitoring. They allow the change agent and other stakeholders to keep up with success, and, in the case where success is lacking, they signal the change agent to pivot from the current path. Objective setting is discussed in more detail in both Chapter 2 and Chapter 7.

Implement a transfer strategy

A transfer strategy ensures change occurs. Chapter 2 onwards is dedicated to the unpacking of the transfer strategy.

There is a vast amount written on change and the subject is discussed and debated in conferences around the world. What is however almost always missing – hence the persistent dismal results – is the behavioural change piece. Successful change of any type ultimately requires people to do something different. Whether that is to use a new IT system or answer the telephone differently or to fulfil an order differently, someone somewhere has to change their behaviour and behavioural change is not automatic or necessarily easy. It's also difficult to manage and control. But without behavioural change the organization doesn't change, and therefore the measures that matter do not improve, leaving the organization with yet another missed opportunity.

As a result most people focus on the easy bit – the systems, processes and procedures, the documentation and design of the change. They pour their focus into planning and communicating the change before the initiative, and as soon as it starts the energy drains away as the 'human element' kicks in. Change only happens when people change, which means that we need to implement a change transfer strategy to support people with that process. We need a way of holding people to account so they will do what they say they will do and make the behavioural adjustments to allow the change to 'stick'.

The transfer strategy we will unpack in detail is called Turning Learning into Action™ (TLA). Initially designed to transfer learning back into the workplace following training initiatives, it is just as effective with change because it holds people to account after the change has been initiated to ensure they do actually change their behaviour, which will in turn deliver the expected outcome.

Evaluate results

What results will come from the investment in change initiatives? This is the big question, and this is where evaluation comes into play. Investing in any change initiative is costly. How much to invest is determined by the opportunity. But not knowing what return comes from that investment is misguided. Evaluation is the thread that runs through the fabric of change. Collecting, analysing and reporting data are integral.

All too often, however, change agents view evaluation as an unnecessary next step. Evaluation is the third phase of the alignment model described in Chapter 2, and Chapters 6, 7, 8 and 9 present the evaluation process in more detail. The output of the evaluation process described in this book is a chain of impact that occurs as the change initiative rolls out. This chain of impact describes success at multiple time frames from multiple perspectives. It provides change agents and all stakeholders with the information they need to make decisions about the initiative and offers opportunities for making adjustments for future programmes and projects that help sustain the change.

Change is not negative

While at a learning conference in Malaysia organized by the International Federation of Training and Development Organisations (IFTDO) we listened to a presentation by Peter Cheese, CEO of the CIPD, and he raised a very interesting issue.

Almost all the change methodology is geared around the various stages of change, adapted from psychiatrist Elisabeth Kübler-Ross's seminal work on the five stages of grief. Kübler-Ross identified the specific stages that people go through when diagnosed with a terminal illness and are facing death, including: Denial, Anger, Bargaining, Depression and Acceptance.

Industrial psychologists then recognized that there was a correlation between the grief people experience when they hear they are going to die and the stages people pass through when confronted with change, and subsequent models have added additional stages such as shock, adapting and testing to make it easier to use in an organizational setting.

There is little doubt this work has helped us to understand the mechanics of change better but it has also deeply embedded change as a negative experience in the international psyche. We hate change, probably at least in part because it reminds us of death! Change and death have become inextricably linked when they shouldn't be. Change doesn't have to be negative at all. In fact it can be positive, rewarding and fulfilling. It's time we changed the perception of change and this book will help us do that through a new methodology that will transform results.

And let's face it, the alternative is not attractive – if we do nothing then we will continue to waste vast sums of money and countless thousands of hours on change initiatives that are destined to fail before they begin or should never have been started in the first place. Employees will remain disengaged and frustrated which means we will never unlock their discretionary effort and step-change their performance.

The methodology in this book means you can successfully change anything. But perhaps most importantly you only successfully change what needs to be changed and will show you demonstrable results. Finally, you have an opportunity to make change work.

References

ASTD and i4cp Whitepaper (2014) Change agents: the role of organizational learning in change management [online] https://www.td.org/Publications/Research-Reports/2014/Change-Agents-the-Role-of-Organizational-Learning-in-Change-Management

Gallup (2013a) The state of the American workplace: employee engagement insights for US business leaders, *Gallup* [online] http://www.gallup.com/services/178514/state-american-workplace.aspx

Gallup (2013b) The state of the global workplace: employee engagement insights for business leaders worldwide, *Gallup* [online] http://www.gallup.com/services/178517/state-global-workplace.aspx

Higgs, M and Rowland, D (2005) All changes great and small: exploring approaches to change and its leadership, *Journal of Change Management*, 5 (2), pp 121–51 [online] http://www.tandfonline.com/doi/abs/10.1080/14697010500082902?journalCode=rjcm20

IBM (2008a) Global CEO Study: The Enterprise of the Future *IMB* [online] https://www-03.ibm.com/industries/ca/en/healthcare/files/2008_ibm_global_ceo_study.pdf

IBM (2008b) Making Change Work, *IBM* [online] http://www-935.ibm.com/services/us/gbs/bus/pdf/gbe03100-usen-03-making-change-work.pdf

IBM (2010) Global CEO Study: Capitalizing on Complexity, *IBM* [online] http://www-01.ibm.com/common/ssi/cgi-bin/ssialias?infotype=PM&subtype=XB&htmlfid=GBE03297USEN

IBM (2012) Global CEO Study: Leading through Connections, *IBM* [online] http://www-935.ibm.com/services/us/en/c-suite/ceostudy2012/

Isern, J and Pung, C (2006) Organizing for successful change management: a McKinsey global survey, *McKinsey Quarterly*, June

Keller, S and Aiken, C (2008) The inconvenient truth about change management: why it isn't working and what to do about it, *McKinsey & Company* [online] http://www.academia.edu/8368956/The_Inconvenient_Truth_About_Change_Management_Why_it_isnt_working_and_what_to_do_about_it

Kotter, J P (1995) Leading change: why transformation efforts fail, *Harvard Business Review* March–April, p 1

Kotter, J P (1996) *Leading Change*, Harvard Business School Press, Boston

Leonard, D and Coltea, C (2013) Most change initiatives fail – but they don't have to, *Gallup Business Journal* [online] http://www.gallup.com/businessjournal/162707/change-initiatives-fail-don.aspx

McManus, J (2004) *Risk Management in Software Development Projects*, Routledge, London

Miller, D (2002) Successful change leaders: what makes them? What do they do that is different? *Journal of Change Management*, **2** (4), pp 359–68 [online] http://www.tandfonline.com/doi/abs/10.1080/714042515

Miller, D (2011) *Successful Change: How to implement change through people*, Changefirst Ltd, Haywards Heath

Savage, M (2010) Labour's computer blunders cost £26bn, *Independent* [online] http://www.independent.co.uk/news/uk/politics/labours-computer-blunders-cost-16326bn-1871967.html

Towers Watson (2013) Only one-quarter of employers are sustaining gains from change management initiatives, Towers Watson survey finds, *Towers Watson* [online] https://www.towerswatson.com/en/Press/2013/08/Only-One-Quarter-of-Employers-Are-Sustaining-Gains-From-Change-Management

Business alignment
The V Model

02

Logic would tell us that change happens for a reason. However, change initiatives frequently take place when the reason is not clear at all. This chapter explores why this is and how to rectify the situation through a thorough business alignment process.

Clarity drives results and helps to facilitate the desired change. Clarifying the need for change prior to investing in it is the first essential step toward ensuring the change process aligns with the needs of the business. From there, the change agent develops objectives that reflect those clearly defined business needs, designs and then implements the initiative so as to deliver on those objectives. Measuring the success of the change initiative is a natural outflow of the business alignment process. By utilizing the business alignment model (the V Model) you will help to ensure the reason for change is clear and the outcomes are successful. But before we unpack the model in more depth, it's worth exploring the theory of change that serves as the basis for alignment.

Theory of change

Theories of change represent logical models that help develop solutions to complex problems by providing a comprehensive picture of inputs as well as immediate, intermediate and long-term outcomes (Anderson, 2005). Theories of change, or programme theory, 'enable evaluators to eliminate rival hypotheses and make causal attributions more easily' (House, 2001). They offer a basis for argument when proposing an initiative and when reporting results of that initiative.

The basis for the alignment model presented in this chapter evolved from the learning and development field and has since been employed in human resources, organizational development, marketing, quality, and other areas from which change is initiated and in which change occurs (Phillips and Phillips, 2013).This framework aligns five categories, or levels, of needs with results that occur as organizations implement change initiatives. Together the five levels of results represent a chain of impact, or theory of change, that occurs as people react to change, learn through the change process, and apply what they learn. As a consequence, key business measures improve. By converting the improvement to money and comparing the monetary output to the cost of the change initiative, an organization can determine the return on investment (ROI) on a given change process. Each level in this chain of impact represents a different type of data. Table 2.1 presents the framework and describes the type of data collected at each level.

In simple terms, when an organization has an opportunity to improve and it embarks on a change initiative to do so, the five levels create clarity in terms of what it needs to do and the expected outcomes.

Level 0: Inputs and indicators

Inputs and indicators represent the investment in change. These measures describe the cost of the change including how many people are involved, how much the process costs the organization per person, and how much time is involved in the change process, among other inputs.

Inputs and indicators do not represent results. They represent the activity of change. They are the starting point for the chain of impact that will occur as the change initiative gets under way.

Level 1: Reaction and planned action

As change rolls out, an early indicator of the potential success comes from the reaction of participants to the change.

Measures such as their perception of the initiative's relevance to their job, the importance of the change to the job, their intent to engage in the change process, and their motivation to change are key predictors of future success.

Level 2: Learning

Learning data indicate the ability of participants in the change process to do what is required to successfully implement the change. These measures may

TABLE 2.1   Chain of impact: types and levels of data

MEASUREMENT FOCUS	LEVEL	TYPICAL MEASURES
Inputs into the programme including indicators representing scope, volumes, costs, and efficiencies.	**0** **INPUTS AND INDICATORS**	✔ Types of topics/content. ✔ Number of programmes ✔ Number of people ✔ Hours of involvement ✔ Costs
MEASUREMENT FOCUS	LEVEL	TYPICAL MEASURES
Reaction to the programme including the perceived value of the programme.	**1** **REACTION AND PLANNED ACTION**	✔ Importance ✔ Usefulness ✔ Appropriateness ✔ Intent to use ✔ Motivational
MEASUREMENT FOCUS	LEVEL	TYPICAL MEASURES
Learning how to use the content and materials, including the confidence to use what was learned.	**2** **LEARNING**	✔ Skills ✔ Knowledge ✔ Capacity ✔ Competencies ✔ Confidences ✔ Contacts
MEASUREMENT FOCUS	LEVEL	TYPICAL MEASURES
Use of content and materials in the work environment, including progress with implementation.	**3** **APPLICATION**	✔ Extent of use ✔ Task completion ✔ Frequency of use ✔ Actions completed ✔ Success with use ✔ Barriers to use ✔ Enablers to use
MEASUREMENT FOCUS	LEVEL	TYPICAL MEASURES
The consequences of the use of the content and materials expressed as business impact measures.	**4** **BUSINESS IMPACT**	✔ Productivity ✔ Revenue ✔ Quality ✔ Time ✔ Efficiency ✔ Customer Satisfaction ✔ Employee Engagement
MEASUREMENT FOCUS	LEVEL	TYPICAL MEASURES
Comparison of monetary benefits from the programme to programme costs.	**5** **ROI**	✔ Benefit Cost Ratio (BCR) ✔ ROI (%) ✔ Payback period

SOURCE: ROI Institute, Inc.

be indicators of knowledge acquisition, competence, new skills, awareness of the need for change, or confidence to drive the change. Learning outcomes are important. They describe whether or not the people expected to change their behaviour in some way know what they need to know to make change happen.

Level 1 and Level 2 data are interrelated. As individuals learn about the change and learn from the change initiative, their reactions to the initiative will evolve. A reaction is based on information at hand. As individuals understand why change is occurring, how it will occur, and what results will come from it, their reaction usually changes. They are likely to become more confident, more competent, and more comfortable that the change is a positive intervention.

Level 3: Application

Application data describe success in terms of people doing what they need to do to make change happen. Measures may include success with actions taken, behaviours changing, processes being followed, and policies being executed. It is at this application level that the behavioural change becomes evident. Measures at this level indicate how people are engaging in the organization differently than they did in the past. Additionally, these data describe the barriers against and enablers toward successful change from a system perspective.

Level 4: Impact

Level 4 Impact data represent the improvement in business measures that occur as a result of the change initiative. Here measures of output, quality, cost, time, customer satisfaction, job satisfaction, work habits, and innovation are taken to determine the extent to which the change initiative positively impacts and contributes to the organization.

Level 5: ROI

The final category of data is return on investment (ROI). ROI is a fundamental business measure that describes in a single metric the success of an initiative in economic terms. To calculate ROI, improvement in business impact measures is converted to money. That monetary value is then compared to the cost of the initiative. The output is expressed either as a benefit–cost ratio (BCR) or as a percentage. The formulas are shown below.

$$BCR = \frac{\text{Programme Benefits}}{\text{Programme Costs}}$$

$$ROI\ (\%) = \frac{\text{Net Programme Benefits}}{\text{Programme Costs}} \times 100$$

These five levels of data describe the complete story of success. They are the logic that serves as the basis for the argument that a change initiative pays off. They are the theory of change that serves as the basis for aligning change initiatives to the business.

Business alignment

Change should always begin with an end in mind. This requires a clear focus on the ultimate outcome. Outcomes must be specifically defined in order to position the initiative to drive the desired results. This focus includes pinpointing all the details to ensure that the change process is properly planned and executed. In the end, evaluation of the change process describes the success of the change and the degree to which outcomes were met. By beginning with the end in mind, designing change initiatives for results, and evaluating accordingly, business alignment occurs. Using the five-level framework described earlier is the connection between organization needs and the results that occur. Figure 2.1 presents the business alignment model, or V Model. It is called the V Model because visually it looks like a V and when used to navigate change initiatives it helps to ensure that 'Value' is derived from the change process.

As shown in the model, alignment occurs in three phases:

1 defining stakeholder needs (Initial Analysis);

2 developing measurable objectives (Business Alignment);

3 evaluating results (Evaluation).

The alignment model creates the framework for change. Having experienced many change initiatives, the crucial factor that drives a successful change is figuring out what needs to be done to actually implement that change. Beyond knowing about the change and learning what needs to be done, we need to map a course through the change to ensure it actually happens on the ground. To complement the alignment model we will explore how implementation needs to be paired with a change transfer strategy such as Turning Learning into Action™ (TLA). Successful change usually requires

FIGURE 2.1   Business alignment V Model

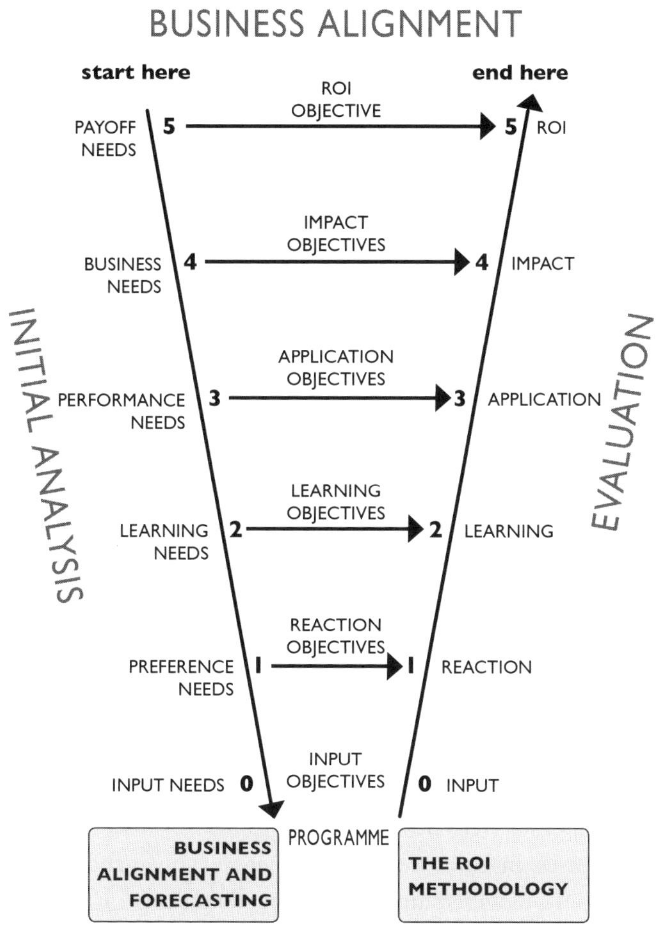

BUSINESS ALIGNMENT

INITIAL ANALYSIS

EVALUATION

start here

end here

PAYOFF NEEDS	**5** — ROI OBJECTIVE →	**5** ROI
BUSINESS NEEDS	**4** — IMPACT OBJECTIVES →	**4** IMPACT
PERFORMANCE NEEDS	**3** — APPLICATION OBJECTIVES →	**3** APPLICATION
LEARNING NEEDS	**2** — LEARNING OBJECTIVES →	**2** LEARNING
PREFERENCE NEEDS	**1** — REACTION OBJECTIVES →	**1** REACTION
INPUT NEEDS	**0** INPUT OBJECTIVES	**0** INPUT

PROGRAMME

BUSINESS ALIGNMENT AND FORECASTING

THE ROI METHODOLOGY

behavioural change; it requires people to do something differently and behavioural change simply does not happen without a transfer strategy that supports those involved to make those changes.

Let's explore the alignment framework in more detail.

Defining stakeholder needs

Stakeholder needs are defined as five types: payoff needs, business needs, performance needs, learning needs, and preference needs. A final type of need is the input needs. This set of needs reflects the inputs into the change initiative. Each level of need aligns with the level in the chain of impact illustrated in Table 2.1.

Payoff needs

As shown on the left side of the business alignment model, stakeholder needs assessment begins with identifying the potential payoff for the organization. Potential payoff represents the opportunity for the organization to make money, save money, avoid costs, or do greater good – which would eventually lead to making money, saving money, or avoiding costs. Assessing payoff needs allows you to answer the crucial first question: 'Is this problem or opportunity worth pursuing?' The answer to this question can be obvious or not so obvious.

Obvious opportunities are those that are objectively defined. For example, if turnover of critical talent is at 35 per cent, which is above the benchmark set by the organization, there is an obvious payoff opportunity. Or if the organization is seeing excessive product returns – 30 per cent higher than the previous year – the payoff opportunity is obvious. Other opportunities are not so well defined. For example, if the organization wants to become a great place to work, the payoff is inherent, but not obvious.

The potential payoff in monetary terms for either type of opportunity will result in either profit increases or cost savings. Cost savings come by way of cost reduction or cost avoidance. Figure 2.2 presents the payoff opportunities. Profit increases are generated by programmes that improve sales, increase market share, introduce new products, open new markets, enhance customer service, or increase customer loyalty. These should pay off with increases in sales revenue. Other revenue-generating measures include increasing memberships, increasing donations or obtaining grants – all of which, after taking out the cost of doing business, leave a profitable benefit.

FIGURE 2.2   Payoff opportunities

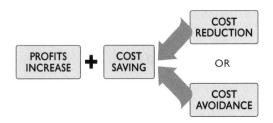

Business needs

Determining specific business needs is linked to the previous step in the needs analysis, determining the potential payoff. When determining the business needs, specific measures are pinpointed so that the business situation can be clearly assessed. The term 'business' is used in governments, non-profits, non-governmental organizations, and educational institutions, as well as in private sector firms. Initiatives in all types of organizations show value by improving productivity, quality and efficiency, and by saving time and reducing costs.

A business need is represented by a business measure. These business measures are often categorized as hard data and soft data. Hard data are objectively based, easy to measure, and relatively easy to convert to money. For example, a measure reflective of hard data is sales. The number of sales made or revenue generated is easily counted. Soft data are more subjective in nature. A soft data measure is one that is measurable along a scale or continuum based on perception, or one where the quality changes depending on the situation. For example, customer satisfaction is considered a soft measure. Soft data are also more difficult to convert to money. In either case, business measures are readily available in any organization. They can be identified through department records, HR databases, service records, annual reports and benchmarking data, to name a few.

Performance needs

If the payoff opportunity represents a problem, identifying performance needs focuses on the cause of the problem. If it represents an opportunity, this step focuses on the changes necessary to take advantage of that opportunity. This step may require a variety of analytical techniques that utilize tools from problem solving, quality assurance, and the performance improvement fields. Diagnostic tools such as statistical process control, brainstorming, nominal group technique, simulations, and problem analysis can also be used to identify performance needs.

It is at this stage that solutions are considered. As performance gaps become apparent, so do potential solutions, including major overhauls in the organization. At the same time, the system is assessed to determine what risks exist if change should occur. Assessment at this level is critical as it begins to define how the change will look in terms of employee behaviours, actions, and interactions.

Learning needs

As solutions to performance needs are defined, so are learning needs. Learning ensures that those people engaged in the change initiative are well prepared to make whatever behavioural change is necessary to drive business results. Learning needs are measured in a variety of ways. Subject matter experts may have the greatest insight into what people need to know to change their behaviours, processes, or actions. Sometimes job and task analyses are used to identify learning needs. Demonstrations, tests, and management assessments are also useful to determine what knowledge gaps exist that could prevent the change from being successful.

Preference needs

This level of needs analysis is based on preferences, which drive the initiative requirements. Essentially, individuals prefer certain processes, schedules, or activities for the structure of the change initiative. The preferences define how the particular initiative will be implemented. If the initiative is a solution to a problem, this step defines how the solution will be installed. If the initiative addresses an opportunity, this step outlines how the opportunity will be addressed, taking into consideration the preference needs of those involved in the initiative.

Input needs

This final level of analysis represents the specifics in terms of project planning. Data here represent who is involved, how many people are involved, along with the cost and timing of the initiative. The results of analysis at this level represent the investment the organization will make in change.

Developing measurable objectives

Developing specific objectives at different levels for change initiatives provides important benefits. First, they provide direction to the participants directly involved in making the initiative work. Objectives define exactly what is expected at different time frames and show the ultimate outcomes of the initiatives. Objectives provide guidance for the change agents and facilitators of activities so that they understand the ultimate goal and impact of the initiative. They also provide information and motivation for the initiative designers and developers as they see the implementation and impact outcomes. In most initiatives, multiple stakeholders are involved and will influence the results. Specific objectives provide goals and motivation for the stakeholders so that they see the gains that should be achieved. Objectives provide important information to help the key sponsor groups clearly understand how the landscape will look when the change initiative is successful. Finally, from an evaluation perspective, objectives provide a basis for measuring the success of the initiative.

Input objectives

All initiatives should have a project plan. This plan describes the expected number of people involved, the timeline for implementation, and the costs for each step in the change cycle. These input objectives describe in detail the intended inputs and activities associated with the change initiative.

Reaction objectives

For any initiative to be successful, various stakeholders must react favourably – or at least not negatively – toward the initiative. Ideally, the stakeholders should be satisfied with the initiative and see its value. They should be motivated to move forward or change their behaviours. This motivation and 'buy-in' to the change creates a win–win relationship for all stakeholders.

Developing reaction objectives should be straightforward and relatively easy. The objectives reflect immediate and long-term satisfaction and explore issues important to initiative success. They also form the basis for evaluating the chain of impact. In addition, they emphasize planned action, when feasible and useful.

Learning objectives

Every initiative involves at least one learning objective and usually more. With major change initiatives, the learning component is incredibly important. To ensure that the various stakeholders learn what they need to know to make the initiative successful, learning objectives are developed.

Learning objectives are critical to measuring change because they communicate the expected outcomes of learning required to drive change and define the desired competence or performance necessary for initiative success.

Application objectives

Application objectives define what is expected and often to what level of performance. Application objectives are similar to learning objectives but reflect actual actions or implementation of activities required to drive the change. They also involve specific milestones, indicating when part or all of the process is implemented.

Application objectives are critical because they describe the expected intermediate outcomes. They describe how things should be or the state of the workplace after the initiative is implemented.

Impact objectives

Change initiatives should drive one or more business impact measures. Impact objectives represent key business measures that should be improved as the application and implementation objectives are achieved. Business impact objectives are critical to measuring business performance because they define the ultimate expected outcomes of the initiative. They describe business-unit performance that should be connected to the initiative. Above all, impact objectives emphasize achieving bottom-line results that key client groups expect and demand.

ROI objective

The fifth level of objectives for initiatives is the acceptable return on investment (ROI): the monetary impact. These objectives define the expected payoff from the initiative and compare the input resources (the cost of the initiative) to the value of the ultimate outcome (the monetary benefits). An ROI objective is typically expressed as an acceptable return on investment percentage that compares the annual monetary benefits minus the cost, divided by the actual cost, and is multiplied by one hundred. A 0 per cent ROI indicates a break-even initiative. A 50 per cent ROI indicates that the cost of the initiative is recaptured and an additional 50 per cent 'earnings' (50 cents for every dollar invested) is achieved.

For some initiatives, the ROI objective is larger than might be expected from the ROI of other expenditures – such as the purchase of a new company, a new building, or major equipment. However, the two are related, and the calculation is the same for both.

For many organizations, the ROI objective for a change initiative is set slightly higher than the ROI expected from other 'routine investments' because of the relative newness of applying the ROI concept to these types of initiatives. For example, if the expected ROI from the purchase of a new company is 20 per cent, the ROI from a new team leader development initiative might be in the 25 per cent range. The important point is that the ROI objective should be established up front and in coordination with the change sponsor.

Evaluating results

The final phase of the alignment model is evaluation. While the evaluation model will be described in more detail in Chapters 7, 8, 9 and 10, it is important to introduce it here.

Evaluation is the final step toward demonstrating alignment between a change initiative and the needs of the business. Through evaluation, one can determine if needs are met, objectives are achieved, and what opportunities for improvement exist. The model shown in Figure 2.3 represents the ROI Methodology,™ developed by Jack Phillips and Patti Phillips and the trademark process of ROI Institute, Inc.

FIGURE 2.3   ROI Methodology™ Process Model

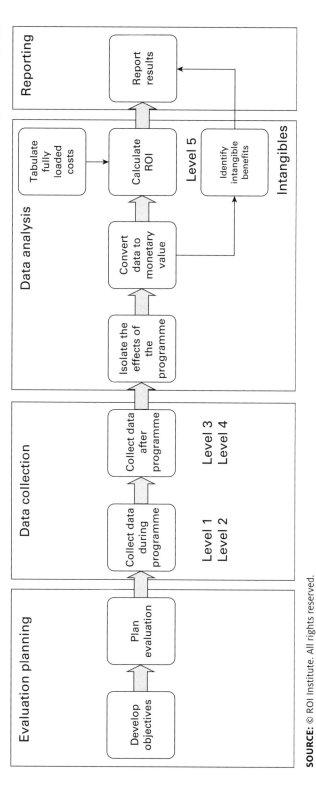

This approach to evaluating change initiatives generates six types of data: reaction, learning, application, impact, ROI, and intangible benefits. It describes success with change in terms that resonate with all stakeholders.

Identifying stakeholder needs, developing measurable objectives, and evaluating results represent three phases of business alignment. Each phase is grounded in the theory of change that reflects the chain of impact that occurs as people are involved in change initiatives. But to ensure change occurs and evaluation results demonstrate success, organizations must implement a transfer strategy such as TLA.

CASE STUDY   Southeast Corridor Bank

The following case study describes the application of the alignment process in a regional bank located in the United States. By clarifying the payoff opportunity and identifying the specific business needs, Southeast Corridor Bank (SCB) was able to implement a change initiative that paid off.

Stakeholder needs

SCB, a regional bank operating in four US states with 60 branches, had grown from a one-state operation into a multi-state network through a progressive strategic campaign of acquisitions. As a result, SCB faced merger and integration problems including excessive employee turnover.

Payoff needs

The company's annual employee turnover was 57 per cent, compared with an industry average of 26 per cent. Based on external studies in the banking industry the cost of this turnover was estimated to be between 110 per cent and 125 per cent of annual salary. The potential payoff for addressing this need was approximately US $3 million.

In addition to the monetary value of excessive turnover, the organization was seeing additional operational problems such as extra time needs for staff and supervisors to deal with the turnover and the resulting disruptive situations with customers.

Business needs

SCB monitored turnover by two categories, defining employee departures as either voluntary separations or terminations for performance. Departures due to retirement or disability were not included in the definition. A termination for performance involved an important problem that might have been rectified if the performance deficiency had been recognized or prevented early.

The turnover rate was monitored by job group, region, and bank branch. Branches had the highest rate of voluntary turnover, averaging 71 per cent, or 336 employees in the previous year. This statistic far exceeded any expectations and the industry averages of turnover acquired from other financial institutions and the American Bankers Association. Turnover was also considered excessive in a few entry-level administrative job classifications in regional and corporate offices.

While the external research indicated turnover costs ranging from 110 per cent to 125 per cent of the annual salary for an employee, the senior executive team suggested a lower value for this particular group, at only 90 per cent (0.9 times an employee's annual pay). This cost, while lower than the research indicated, still caused executives concerns. Additionally, the specific area in which turnover was the greatest had tremendous impact on customer relationships. This more specific business need became the focus for the organization.

Performance needs

To determine the cause of the turnover and how to address performance needs, the organization implemented the nominal group technique. This process was selected because it allowed unbiased input to be collected efficiently and accurately across the organization. Focus groups were planned with 12 employees in each region, for a total of six groups representing all the regions. In addition, two focus groups were planned for the administrative staff in corporate headquarters. This approach provided approximately a 10 per cent sample, which was considered a sufficient number to pinpoint the problem.

Focus group participants consisted of employees from areas in which turnover was the highest. They described why their colleagues were leaving, not why they themselves would leave. Data were taken from individuals in a carefully structured format during two-hour meetings at each location, using third-party facilitators, and was integrated and weighted so the most important reasons were clearly identified. This process had the advantages of low cost and high reliability. Only two days of external facilitator time was needed to collect and summarize the data for review.

Findings showed that the 10 most important reasons for turnover in the bank branches were:

1 lack of opportunity for advancement;
2 lack of opportunity to learn new skills and new product knowledge;

3 pay level not adequate;

4 not enough responsibility and empowerment;

5 lack of recognition and appreciation of work;

6 lack of teamwork in the branch;

7 lack of preparation for customer service problems;

8 unfair and unsupportive supervisors;

9 too much stress at peak times;

10 not enough flexibility in work schedules.

A variety of solutions was identified to address the performance needs. However, a skill-based pay solution offered the most opportunity. This programme would address the top five reasons for turnover. It was designed to expand the scope of the jobs, with increases in pay for acquiring skills, and to provide a clear path for advancement and improvement. Bank teller positions were redesigned from narrowly focused teller duties to expanded jobs with a new title: Banking Representative I, II or III depending on the skills and tasks. This process changed the way bank tellers were paid, how they advanced in the organization, how their performance was measured and managed, and how the branch would work with customers.

Learning needs

To ensure the process worked, tellers, managers, and others in the organization had to learn why the initiative was taking place and how it would support employees. Managers needed to learn how to provide tellers opportunities to develop skills and how to manage their performance to ensure advancements, if tellers wanted to pursue such advancement. Tellers had to acquire the knowledge and skills that would position them to perform new and more challenging jobs so they could progress.

Preference needs

Project leaders knew that in order for learning to occur, the solution would have to be presented in a way that motivated and challenged the employees. They also knew that developmental opportunities would have to be offered on a routine basis. Opportunities would assist employees in acquiring relevant knowledge and skills so they could advance – not only achieving higher levels in the organization, more responsibility, and greater recognition, but better serving customers.

Objectives

The skill-based pay programme was rolled out to all bank branches. Although the system had definite benefits from the employee's perspective, there were also benefits for the bank. Not only was turnover expected to lessen, but actually staffing levels were expected to be reduced in larger branches. In theory, if all employees in a branch could perform all the duties, fewer employees would be needed. Prior to this change initiative, minimum staffing levels were required in certain critical jobs, and those employees were not always available for other duties.

In addition, the bank anticipated improved customer service. The new approach would prevent customers from having to wait in long lines for specialized services. For example, in the typical bank branch, it had not been unusual to see long lines for such special functions as opening a checking account, closing out a Certificate of Deposit (CD), or taking a consumer loan application, while such activities as paying bills and receiving deposits often required little or no customer waiting time. With each employee able to perform all the tasks, shorter waiting lines would not only be feasible, but expected.

The programme was designed around a set of specific objectives. The objectives were intended to guide design and implementation, but also served as the target for results. Table 2.2 presents the objectives. As shown, the objectives represent the chain of impact that occurs as peopled are involved in programmes and projects. Because of the nature of the programme, it was important to demonstrate the impact and ROI.

To support this new arrangement, the marketing department referred to the concept in its publicity about products and services. Included with the checking account statements was a promotional piece labelled 'In our branches there are no tellers'. This document described the new process and stated that all branch employees could perform all branch functions and therefore provide faster service and reduce customer wait time.

Evaluation

Measuring the success of the initiative required collecting data at multiple levels.

Level 1: Reaction

Level 1, Reaction, was measured during meetings with the employees and during regularly scheduled training sessions. This measurement provided input on employee acceptance of the new arrangement and different elements of the programme. Using brief surveys, data were collected on a five-point scale. As expected, the results were positive, averaging 4.2 composite rating.

TABLE 2.2 Skill-based pay programme objectives

Reaction	On a scale of 1–5 (1 disagree; 5 agree), participants rate the following 4.0 out of 5 regarding the skill-based pay programme.
	● I am motivated to develop knowledge and skills that will help me take on additional responsibilities.
	● I perceive the skill-based pay programme as a challenge.
	● I intend to take on the challenges presented by the skill-based pay programme in order to progress in the company.
	● I view the skill-based pay programme as a rewarding opportunity.
	On a scale of 1–5 (1 disagree, 5 agree), participants rate the following 4.0 out of 5 regarding training programmes targeting knowledge and skills relevant to job progression.
	● The programme is relevant to the job that I am pursuing.
	● The programme should be useful to me as I progress toward advancement in the company.
	● I intend to apply the knowledge and skills learned in the programme, even though I have not yet been promoted.
Learning	On a scale of 1–5 (1 disagree; 5 agree), participants rate the following 4.0 out of 5.
	● I understand why the skill-based pay programme is being implemented.
	● I understand what is required of me to be successful with the programme.
	● I understand how promotion decisions are made.
	● I understand the timing of various aspects of the programme.
	For each training programme attended that targets job progression, participants will:
	● Acquire knowledge/skills as measured by that programme.
	● Demonstrate abilities with skill pertinent to promotional level as measured by supervisor assessment.

TABLE 2.2   *Continued*

Application	• 100% participation in programme.
	• Increase in number of requests for training (45 per month baseline).
	• Review meetings with managers regarding developmental plan taking place.
	• Increase in actual promotions (139 per year baseline).
Business impact	• Reduce branch employee turnover (baseline: 71%; 336 per year).
	• Reduce branch staffing levels (baseline: average 480 total).
	• Customer satisfaction.
	• Job satisfaction.
	• Deposits.
	• Loan volume.
	• New accounts.
	• Transaction volume.
	• Cross-selling.
ROI	• 25% based on first year actual plus second year forecast.

Level 2: Learning

Level 2, Learning, was measured in two different ways. For each learning opportunity offered to tellers, skill acquisition and knowledge increase were measured. Informal self-assessments were taken for many of the programmes. A few critical skills required actual demonstration to show that employees could perform the skill (eg documentation, compliance, and customer services). When learning measurements revealed unacceptable performance, participants were provided an opportunity to repeat training sessions or take more time to practise. In limited cases, a third opportunity was provided. After one year of operation, only two employees were denied a promotional opportunity, due to their performance in training programmes.

Level 3: Application and implementation

Level 3, Application and implementation, revealed success with the programme, although at 95 per cent participation the target of 100 per cent was not quite reached. The remaining 5 per cent indicated they were content with the Banking

TABLE 2.3   Application results

	Application progress	
	Target	1 year results
Participation in programme	100%	95%
Requests for training	45 per month	86 per month
Review situations	N/A	138
Actual promotions	139	257

Representative I classification and were not interested in learning new skills. Requests for training averaged 86 per month. The follow-up evaluation also revealed that 138 progress reviews were conducted; this review was the formal way of demonstrating the skills required for promotion. Lastly, promotions increased from 139 per year to 257 per year, indicating the process was working. Table 2.3 compares targets for the objectives to post-initiative results.

Level 4: Impact

Nine categories of business impact measures were monitored and are shown in Table 2.4 along with the definitions. In all, nine categories of data were expected to be influenced to some degree by this project, although the first four were considered to be the primary measures.

In almost any situation, multiple influences affect specific impact measures such as those listed, so an important concern in evaluating the impact results was how to isolate the actual impact of the skill-based pay project from other influences. This topic is discussed in more detail in Chapter 9. While a variety of techniques was considered, the method used for this project was estimates from branch managers and the branch staff. In brief group meetings, the branch staff members were provided the actual results of turnover reduction and discussed the other factors that could have contributed (two were identified). They were asked to discuss the linkage between each factor and the actual turnover reduction. Since these were estimates, an error adjustment was made, by asking participants to indicate the level of confidence in their estimate using a scale of 0 to 100 per cent, with 0 per cent meaning no confidence and 100 per cent meaning certainty. For the staffing levels, actual improvements were judged by the branch managers using a similar process to isolate the effects of the new initiative.

TABLE 2.4   Impact measures

Impact measures	
1. Branch employee turnover (monthly)	Avoidable turnover. Total number of employees leaving voluntarily and for performance reasons divided by the average number of employees in the branch for the month. This number is multiplied by 12 to develop the annual turnover rate.
2. Staffing level	The total number of employees in the branch, reported monthly.
3. Customer satisfaction	Customer reaction to the job changes (faster service, fewer lines) measured on a 1–5 scale.
4. Job satisfaction	Employee feedback on selected measures on the annual feedback survey process.
5. Deposits	Savings, checking, and securities deposits by type and product.
6. Loan volume	Consumer loan volume by loan type.
7. New accounts	New accounts opened for new customers.
8. Transaction volume	Number of face-to-face transactions, paying and receiving, by major category.
9. Cross-selling	New products sold to existing customers.

Table 2.5 presents the Level 4 results. As shown the decrease in turnover attributable to the initiative was 120. Staffing level reduction due to the initiative was 17 in total.

Increases in deposits, loan volume, new accounts, transactions, and cross-selling were minimal and were influenced by many variables other than the new programme. Consequently, no attempt was made to isolate the effect on these items or to use the improvements in the ROI analysis. However, they were listed as intangible benefits, providing evidence that they have been affected by the turnover reduction programme.

TABLE 2.5   Level 4 Impact results

Turnover	Staffing levels
• Prior year 71% (336)	• Prior year 480
• One year post 35% (162)	• One year post 463
• Difference 174	• Difference 17
• Contribution factor 84%	• Contribution factor 100%
• Confidence estimate 82%	• Confidence estimate 100%
• Adjusted contribution 120	• Adjusted contribution 17

Survey cards completed at the end of a transaction and deposited at the entrance to the branch provided a sample of customer reactions. The customers appreciated the new approach, liked the service delivered, and indicated that they would continue to use the branch. The annual employee job satisfaction survey showed that employees were pleased with the improvements in advancement opportunities, the chance to use skills, performance-based pay, and other related changes. Improvements in these measures were important intangible benefits.

Level 5: ROI

The ROI target was 25 per cent for the first year, plus bank executives wanted to see an ROI forecast that included year two benefits. To calculate the ROI for the skill-based pay initiative, Level 4 Impact measures were converted to monetary value and compared to the cost of the programme.

The value of turnover was determined to be 90 per cent, or 0.9 times the salary of employees leaving the organization. Average annual salary of branch staff below manager level was $18,500. This meant the cost of one turnover statistic was $16,650 ($18,500 × 0.9). With a reduction of 120 turnovers, the cost saving to the bank was $1,998,000. Based on these results, the bank forecasted benefits for year two to be $3,996,000.

To convert staffing levels to monetary value, the actual salaries for the job that had been eliminated were used. Only a few branches were affected. The actual number was multiplied by the average salary of the branch staff. Average salary for the target group was $18,500. The reduction due to the skill-based pay initiative was 17. Total savings to the bank for the first year were $314,500. The year two forecast was $629,000. Table 2.6 summarizes the calculations for the monetary benefits of the programme.

TABLE 2.6   Monetary benefits of the programme

Turnover	Staffing levels
• Prior year 71% (336)	• Prior year 480
• One year post 35% (162)	• One year post 463
• Difference 174	• Difference 17
• Contribution factor 84%	• Contribution factor 100%
• Confidence estimate 82%	• Confidence estimate 100%
• Adjusted contribution 120	• Adjusted contribution 17
• Unit amount $16,650	• Unit amount $18,500
• Annual benefits $1,998,000	• Annual benefits $314,500
• Two-year benefits $3,996,000	• Two-year benefits $629,000

The total cost of the programme for the first year included the initial analysis, programme development, participant time, branch manager time, salary increases resulting from promotions, administration and operation costs, and the evaluation costs. The total first year costs totalled $857,195. When comparing the first-year benefits of $1,998,000 for turnover reduction and $314,500 for staffing reductions, the year 1 ROI was:

$$BCR = \frac{\$2,312,500}{\$857,195} = 2.70$$

$$ROI\ (\%) = \frac{\$2,312,500 - \$857,195}{\$857,195} \times 100 = 170\%$$

Thus one year results far exceeded the 25 per cent target.

The total costs for year two were expected to be $433,200. Including the projected benefits for year two, the total benefit for turnover reduction was $3,996,000 and the total benefit for staffing level reduction was $629,000. The two-year ROI was expected to be:

$$BCR = \frac{\$4,625,000}{\$1,290,395} = 3.58$$

$$ROI\ (\%) = \frac{\$4,625,000 - \$1,290,395}{\$1,290,395} \times 100 = 258\%$$

This case study described the alignment process in action. By clarifying stakeholder needs, aligning an initiative to those needs and positioning the initiative through the development of objectives, and evaluating it accordingly, the argument that the skill-based pay initiative drove meaningful results stands strong.

However, following the alignment process alone does not always ensure success. Often success only comes from implementing a transfer strategy alongside alignment that promotes successful application and implementation of initiatives. But, before we unpack TLA in more detail it's worth taking a closer look in Chapter 3 at why so many change initiatives fail to change behaviour.

Summary of key points

- Change happens for a reason. However, change initiatives frequently take place when the reason is not clear.

- This can be rectified by a thorough business alignment process prior to the change.

- Clarifying the need for change prior to investing in change is the first essential step toward ensuring the change process aligns with the needs of the business.

- Next the change agent develops objectives that reflect those clearly defined business needs.

- The change intervention is then designed and implemented to deliver on those objectives.

- Measuring the success of the change initiative is a natural outflow of the alignment and we recommend you use the business alignment model (the V Model) to ensure the reason for change is clear and the outcomes are successful.

- The V Model aligns five categories, or levels, of needs with results that occur as organizations implement change initiatives ('Inputs and Indicators', 'Reaction and Planned Actions', 'Learning', 'Application', 'Impact' and 'ROI'.)

- The five levels of results represent a chain of impact that occurs as people react to change, learn through the change process, and apply what they learn.

- As a consequence, key business measures improve. By converting the improvement to money and comparing the monetary output to the cost of the change initiative, an organization can determine the return on investment (ROI) on a given change process.

- By beginning with the end in mind, designing change initiatives for results, and evaluating accordingly, business alignment occurs.

- Business alignment is a three-stage process:
  1 defining stakeholder needs;
  2 developing measurable objectives; and
  3 evaluating results.

- Defining stakeholder needs includes:
  - payoff needs;
  - business needs;
  - performance needs;
  - learning needs;
  - preference needs; and
  - input needs.

- Developing measurable objectives includes:
  - input objectives;
  - reaction objectives;
  - learning objectives;
  - application objectives;
  - impact objectives; and
  - ROI objectives.

- Through evaluation, one can determine if needs are met, objectives are achieved, and what opportunities for improvement exist.

- Business alignment between the change and the needs and objectives of the business is crucial for successful change. But if behavioural change is needed and expected from the change initiative, a transfer strategy must also be included so that people are held accountable for the change and supported through the change process.

References

Anderson, A (2005) An introduction to theory of change, *The Evaluation Exchange* (Harvard Graduate School of Education, Boston) [online] http://www.hfrp.org/evaluation/the-evaluation-exchange/issue-archive/evaluation-methodology/an-introduction-to-theory-of-change [accessed October 15, 2015]

House, E (2001) Unfinished business: causes and values, *American Journal of Evaluation*, **22**, p 311.

Phillips, P P and Phillips, J J (2013) *Measuring the Success of Organization Development: A step-by-step guide for measuring impact and ROI*, ATD Press, Alexandria, VA

Current failures of behavioural change

03

It's likely that you already know that most change initiatives fail to deliver on their promise; otherwise you wouldn't have bought this book. You've almost certainly experienced it in your working life. This chapter explores why change so often falls short – especially when behavioural change is required as part of the change initiative.

According to Edelman's 15th Annual Global Trust Barometer 51 per cent of respondents believe that the pace of change in business is now too fast (Edelman, 2015). And the top three drivers for that change were identified as:

1 technology;
2 business growth targets;
3 greed/money.

Clearly we need to adapt to changing technology and embrace opportunities for improvement. It's also important to push for greater growth and certainly the pressure on senior leaders to do so is now intense. But change is still failing. There may be more of it and we may think we know why it's necessary but that isn't improving the success rate. Every year, we still waste a colossal amount of time and money on change initiatives with nothing to show for it except a depleted bank account and a deeply disgruntled workforce.

While this may seem simplistic often the all-singing and all-dancing approach to change initiatives lacks the follow-through to behaviour change at an individual level. Change initiatives rarely get people to actually change their behaviour because of four key factors. There is:

- no ownership of the change;
- little understanding of what's needed after the change;
- loss of control for those involved in the change;
- little appreciation of the difference between reinforcement and reflection.

No ownership of the change

Change is almost always initiated from the top down. It is senior leaders and executives that are traditionally most familiar with the performance and financial results of a department or business. It is therefore almost always senior leaders and executives that decide change of some type is needed to improve that performance or results.

If the business is lucky then a more thorough assessment of what's not working well enough is instigated. And of course the alignment model can be used to break down the exact requirements of the change. This assessment is essential to identify the real challenge and therefore isolate exactly what needs to change and who needs to be involved in that change. If the business is not so lucky a senior leader or group of senior executives will jump to conclusions about the cause of the problem and therefore what to do about it.

The change is then passed on down the business toward the people who are expected to make the behavioural change – each level quite content that they have done their bit and can breathe easy that they have identified the problem and have taken decisive action.

But of course thinking we know what needs to change and knowing what needs to change can be two very different things. Plus, even if the challenge has been identified correctly we all know that knowing what to change is one thing but seeing that change through to successful implementation and sustaining it is quite another. Getting people to do something different is not that easy.

Usually those involved in a potential change initiative have ownership of the process up to a point. For senior leaders they often feel their role is to identify the need for change and authorize that change. The HR professionals may be involved in designing that change, especially if the change involves a training initiative. And the manager assigned to make that change happen often feels their role is complete when they have informed those that need to change what they need to change, or the people involved have all been put through a training programme.

Companies will often take great pains to clearly communicate the 'why' behind the change – which is essential. However, it's a false belief that selling the 'why' hard enough will be enough to create the ownership. Besides, the corporate 'why' may not be important to the individual and may need to be interpreted or translated into a personal 'why' for the person who is expected to change their behaviour.

In most cases, there is rarely a coherent, integrated approach where everyone involved shares the ownership of change from start to finish. As a result, the 'little things' that have such a profound effect on successful change imple-mentation can too easily slip through the cracks between various stakeholders' responsibilities. No one owns the change and so it simply doesn't get done, is only partially implemented or simply peters out. Often the burning platform that triggered the change initiative is replaced by another burning platform and the emphasis, time, money and urgency switch elsewhere.

The change initiatives the authors are very familiar with are training initiatives. Corporate training is almost always initiated to change employee behaviour. Whether the training is designed to encourage employees to plan their day more constructively, coach their direct reports or operate a new IT system the desired outcome is getting the existing workforce to do something different or do something they already do differently. And yet time and time again we see Learning & Development (L&D) KPIs such as 'bums on seats' or 'spend per capita' or 'training days delivered' or some other attendance-based measure. Granted, in a world of compliance and operational oversight there are situations where ensuring everyone in a business has received the safety briefing or taken the 'manual handling' course is essential for safety and liability but most training is initiated to deliver a specific behavioural outcome or improvement. If that outcome or improvement does not materialise then the training has failed.

In fact, the dismal statistics around failed change and learning transfer, ie how much training is successfully transferred back into the workplace, are remarkably similar. In one of the earliest and most detailed examinations of the learning transfer problem the authors noted that 'American industries annually spend more than $100 billion on training and development; not more than 10 per cent of the expenditure actually results in transfer to the job' (Baldwin and Ford, 1988). These findings were then reconfirmed nine years later (Ford and Weissbein, 1997). Authors Broad and Newstrom wrote: 'Most of the investment in organizational training… is wasted because most of the knowledge and skills gained (well over 80 per cent by some estimates) are not fully applied by these employees on the job' (2000).

And change initiatives, including training, can only really be considered a success if the behavioural change is then evident in the business. Of course this is extremely difficult to achieve – as the statistics demonstrate – because there is no real ownership of the change process. Although many individuals along the way may take ownership of a small piece of the puzzle there is no ultimate 'buck stops here' ownership to ensure the outcomes the change was initiated to deliver are actually delivered. And as we all know, without ownership nothing gets done.

Think about the last time you were waiting at the baked goods section of your local supermarket. Imagine you stopped a shop assistant to ask about the ingredients in the croissant. The shop assistant didn't know but went to the front desk and made an announcement: 'Customer at bakery needing assistance; will someone please go to bakery.' Chances are your desire for a croissant disappeared after about five minutes of waiting. No one came because no one was accountable. Had the shop assistant said, 'Will Jackie Oliver please go to bakery' instead, you would have had all your croissant-related enquires answered in a flash. Without ownership nothing actually happens. Everyone just assumes that someone else is on the case even when no one is on the case. Unless we have a role in the change process and are accountable for that role we just won't do it.

The importance of ownership needs to be considered at two different levels. The first is ownership of the change initiative which may come down to the change agent or nominated stakeholder. And second is the individual ownership of the person who needs to actually change. Much is written about the bigger-picture role but the source of much of the change failure is in lack of ownership at an individual level. The gap therefore that needs to be bridged is to create ownership for change across both groups.

In the end there are often just too many stakeholders who have different agendas and as there is no single agreed consensus regarding the objectives of the change programme, no one takes ownership of the behaviour change so often required for success. Instead each stakeholder skews the assessment protocol to suit their own objectives so they can say, 'Hey, I don't know why it failed but I did my bit.' Without genuine ownership of the outcomes it's easy to see why so many change initiatives fail to deliver on their promise.

Little understanding of what's needed after the change

Often the drive for change is urgent. This urgency means that there is often a great deal of focus on the current reality (before the change) and what therefore needs to happen, but there is much less focus during the change and virtually nothing after it.

In a study of Fortune 500 CEOs regarding the measures of success required by executives two of the authors (Phillips and Phillips) discovered that business contribution, notably business impact, was their number one desired measure of change initiatives. The change in this context was training initiatives and what CEOs specifically wanted to see as a result of the investment.

Each CEO was asked three questions:

1 'What do you currently measure in terms of your training?'

2 'What do you think you should measure in the future?'

3 'How do you rank each measure in terms of its importance?'

Figure 3.1 shows the results of the study. Ironically the top three things that the CEOs identified as currently being measured – number of people trained, cost per hour of training and employee opinion – were considered the least important three things to measure in the future. And the bottom three things that the CEO identified as not currently being measured also happen to be the top three things that they need measured.

This is logical. Most businesses are already under pressure in terms of what they need to do and what results they need to deliver – they simply wouldn't initiate change unless they believed that the change would improve performance and results. And yet the same study showed that only 8 per cent of CEOs received impact data after the change despite 96 per cent wanting to see that data. In a search for key words for this study, executives provided written comments about the need for business alignment, business contributions, and business connections (Phillips and Phillips, 2010, 2012).

Before the change, the problem the business faces is usually clarified, unpacked and analysed. At least it should be. The alignment model acts as a framework for how to do this in the most effective and useful way. The resulting insights then direct the nature of the change initiative – at least they should do. To some extent the activity before the change is the easy part. It's relatively easy to see the gap between where the business is right now and where the business needs to be. When properly identified, the problem will immediately throw up potential solutions to that problem such as an IT upgrade or employee training. Whatever the proposed solution is, however, it will almost always require people in the business to behave differently and do certain tasks or roles differently.

Once chosen the solution is sourced and either the IT system is installed, the training is designed or the change initiative – whatever that may be – is prepared for implementation.

What occurs during the change depends on the type of change. In some cases an event such as the installation of an IT system will herald the beginning of the change process in earnest, in others it may simply be a date where a switchover to a new way of working is requested or following a training event, but once the change initiative is under way there is still usually a fair amount of momentum around the process.

FIGURE 3.1   Results of Jack and Patti Phillips's research

THE EXECUTIVE VIEW			
MEASURE	WE CURRENTLY MEASURE THIS	WE SHOULD MEASURE THIS IN THE FUTURE	MY RANKING OF THE IMPORTANCE OF THIS MEASURE
a INPUTS 'Last year, 78,000 employees received formal learning.'	(90) 94%	(82) 85%	6
b EFFICIENCY 'Formal learning costs $2.15 per hour of learning consumed.'	(75) 78%	(79) 82%	7
c REACTION 'Employees rated our training very high, averaging 4.2 out of 5.'	(51) 53%	(21) 22%	8
d LEARNING 'Our programmes reflect growth in knowledge and skills of our employees'	(31) 32%	(27) 28%	5
e APPLICATION 'Our studies show that at least 78% of employees are using the skills on the job'	(11) 11%	(59) 61%	4
f IMPACT 'Our programmes are driving our top five business measures in the organization.'	(8) 8%	(92) 96%	1
g ROI 'Five ROI studies were conducted on major programmes yielding an average of 68% ROI.'	(4) 4%	(71) 74%	2
h AWARDS 'Our learning and development programmes won an award from the American Society of Training and Development'	(38) 40%	(42) 44%	3

Phillips, J.J. and Phillips, P.P. (2010) Measuring for Succcess: What CEOs Really Think About Learning Investments. Alexandria, VA: ATD Press

However, that momentum can soon drain away, especially as competing demands are made on people's time and energy. When it's easier to do something the old way, or use the old system or forget about the coaching conversation with staff, they will – especially when no one is watching or they are under pressure.

Whether your change initiative will be a success is actually almost all down to what happens after its official launch or start date. All the focus is on the change itself and how to get the ball rolling but very little time is then spent on how to keep that ball rolling, assess the process and ensure behavioural change in the workplace. Although this is understandable because it's easy to control the plans and tactics before the change, the benefit of the change only happens after the launch.

Loss of control for those involved in the change

Change initiatives are often extremely good at dissecting what needs to change and why. Those involved can usually make a strong case for change and systems, and processes and procedures can be invented and installed to help facilitate that change, but the simple, often overlooked fact is that people don't like change.

We were reminded of this fact by a colleague who told the story of a large organization that had invested heavily in creating new state-of-the-art premises to facilitate hot-desking – all supported by a sophisticated booking app. The office space was amazing, specifically designed to create collaboration and have multiple workspace options suited to different types of working environment including stand-up desks, white boards, discussion corners, meeting rooms, etc. Depending on your workload or who you needed to work with the following day team members could check the schedule and book a desk next to a specific colleague to improve productivity. However, when the people moved into this innovative space, they quickly established a routine of using the same desk, in the same space every day. It's human nature.

Human beings have a very strong control orientation. We are control freaks – some more so than others but all of us like to feel as though we have some control over our lives. This control gives us a sense of comfort and certainty but change by definition alters that perception and that doesn't always feel good. This is why we so often resist change – it makes us feel uncomfortable and diminishes our feeling of control. When a top-down change initiative is implemented without consultation or input from those expected to change then it's little wonder the initiative fails and the people involved fail to actually change. Often those individuals are not being lazy or deliberately difficult; they are simply reacting to what the change brings and the perceived loss of control over their environment.

Change or evolution may have made us the most dominant species on the planet but that evolution is gradual. The change we face day in day out is often sudden, significant and disarming. Unfortunately the hardware that we have to deal with this hasn't actually changed that much since we emerged from the caves. Or as professor of organizational behaviour at the London Business School, Nigel Nicholson suggests, 'You can take the person out of the Stone Age, but you can't take the Stone Age out of the person' (1998).

Far too often change initiatives fail to account for our need to feel in control. Professor of psychology at Harvard, Ellen Langer was one of the first scientists to identify our deep need for control back in the 1970s. Along with a colleague at the time, Judith Rodin, she conducted some now-famous experiments in a nursing home. One group of participants were encouraged to make more decisions for themselves and exercise more control over their own lives such as when they could see visitors, when to watch movies and what movies to watch. This group also chose a house-plant to care for and could decide where the plant was to stay in their room and when to water it. The second group received no such encouragement to take more control of their choices and environment. Although they also got a house plant, they were given the house plant by staff and told the nursing staff would take care of it.

Eighteen months later the first group were more cheerful, active and alert based on a variety of tests Langer and Rodin had administered to both groups prior to the start of the experiment. The first group was also healthier. In fact less than half as many of the more engaged group had died over the period as compared to the unengaged group (Langer, 2010).

Most change initiatives require people to change their behaviour. But often that change can rob those people of a sense of control, which is derailing the process before it begins. The only really effective way to get someone to change is to involve them and get them to want to change.

And to do that effectively we need to understand motivation.

Understanding motivation

When science first examined motivation the consensus of opinion was that there were two main motivational drives. The drive to survive – also known as the biological imperative – and the 'carrot and stick' approach to motivation.

Our motivation to survive is intrinsic; it comes from within and motivates us to take the necessary steps to stay alive. So we eat when we are hungry, drink when we are thirsty and sleep when we are tired. The biological imperative is a motivational baseball bat – there is no finesse. Plus it's not particularly useful as a motivational tool. It can however be activated in a change situation as people involved become agitated and wonder if they are going to be 'surplus to requirements'. Announcements of change can trigger this 'fight or flight' response which is clearly not that helpful. Again, people feel 'out of control' and that is never conducive to successful change. When people are scared or unsure you may get compliance but you will never unlock discretionary effort and fast-track change.

Reward and punishment are the other commonly understood motivational tools. These are extrinsic in that the motivation is coming from outside the individual by way of a promise of a new office or a financial bonus if targets are met. According to these motivational forces the only way we can get people to change is to reward those that do what we want them to do and punish those that don't.

Unfortunately they are still remarkably ineffective. Social science has proven that using reward and punishment doesn't always work. In fact they can often encourage the very behaviour you are seeking to avoid!

Change initiatives can trigger the survival instinct and diminish an individual's sense of control – that's not great news for successful change. It is possible to scare people into changing and we can also reward them into changing but these tricks will only work short term in certain situations. They are not a long-term option. If an individual is only changing their behaviour because they are scared they will lose their job if they don't, or have been promised a bonus if they do, then as soon as the cheque has cleared the bank or the immediate threat has passed they will simply return to their own, more comfortable behaviour.

When it comes to changing a person's behaviour we have long relied on reward and punishment but neither works very well when it comes to changing behaviour and improving performance.

There is however a third motivation drive and Ellen Langer touched on it when she identified our need for control. Identified in the mid-1980s by Edward Deci and Richard Ryan, Self-Determination Theory (SDT) helps to explain just how hard it is for people to change their behaviour through change initiatives – unless they are specifically supported to do so over the longer term (Pink, 2009).

Intrinsic motivation is always much more powerful than extrinsic. Finding ways to get someone to do something is always much harder, more time consuming and expensive than simply finding people who want to do what you want them to do anyway! What Deci and Ryan proposed was a recipe for activating intrinsic motivation, and the ingredients are:

- autonomy;
- competence;
- relatedness.

Autonomy

In order to feel motivated and engaged we need to feel some measure of control over our situation. When the boss announces the latest change initiative most people don't feel a measure of control. Far from it, they know the boat is about to get rocked and that makes them very nervous and naturally resistant to the change right from the start.

This absolutely must be managed for change to be successful.

Competency

Competency refers to our ability to demonstrate competence in a particular task. Psychologist Mihaly Csikszentmihalyi who introduced us to the concept of 'flow' is effectively talking about a level of competency (2002). When we are good at something and are consumed by the activity of doing it we are said to be in 'flow'. When in 'flow', the reward for the task is doing the task itself.

Csikszentmihalyi even conducted a series of experiments to demonstrate just how important a feeling of competence is to wellbeing. Having identified areas where individuals experienced competence the participants were then asked to refrain from those activities. The task itself could be anything from running to washing dishes – but the results were almost immediate. Participants became sluggish, began complaining of headaches and had difficulty concentrating. Csikszentmihalyi noted that 'After just two days of deprivation… the general deterioration in mood was so advanced that prolonging the experiment would have been unadvisable.'

We need to feel that we know what we are doing and have a level of competence in our role otherwise we can quite quickly begin to exhibit symptoms that are remarkably similar to depression.

Again in a change context it is easy to see why change initiatives are so frequently met with heavy sighing and eye-rolling – the people involved are scared that they are going to be asked to do something that they can't do or don't want to do and stop doing what they can do and are currently good at. This can feel very uncomfortable and explains why so many are so keen to revert to old ways so quickly.

Relatedness

The final ingredient is relatedness – people need other people. We are social creatures and how motivated we are in the workplace is often profoundly influenced by who we work with, the work groups we are involved in and how the team works and interacts together. When we are connected to other people we like, respect or care about we are intrinsically motivated.

Again, think what happens to relationships when change initiatives are announced and implemented. The fear is that strong working relationships and friendships will be broken up and people moved around the business or moved into different physical locations in the business.

When people are able to express autonomy, competence and relatedness they are intrinsically motivated and are much more likely to be creative, enthusiastic and productive. When these needs are inhibited intrinsic motivation plummets and progress can be non-existent. Change almost always challenges autonomy, competence and relatedness and if we don't appreciate the human element of change we will be destined to repeat the dismal statistics for another 30 years.

Little appreciation of the difference between reinforcement and reflection

We've come a long way in our understanding of behavioural change. Back in the 1940s psychologist Kurt Lewin proposed that there were three distinct stages to successful change. He referred to these stages as unfreeze, change and freeze (or refreeze). In other words the first stage was to 'thaw' the old way of doing something, then support the change and then freeze that new behaviour as the default behaviour. And his theory has been the basis of our understanding of how people change successfully ever since.

The second part of the process is making the change and experimenting with the new way of working or the new required behaviour. This is the uncomfortable part for most people because their autonomy, competence and relatedness are being challenged. As a result the pull back to old behaviours can be significant and has to be managed constructively.

The last part is refreezing of the new behaviour so it becomes the default choice rather than the old behaviour. Once achieved, autonomy, competence and relatedness are often restored and the change becomes successfully embedded in the business.

Whatever the change, it almost always requires learning. And that learning is always needed from adults. As a result our appreciation for change has been improved still further by greater understanding of how adults learn best. In 1984 American educational theorist David A Kolb published his adult learning model (Figure 3.2). Kolb's learning theory sets out four distinct stages in the learning cycle and builds on the work of Kurt Lewin as well as Carl Jung, Carl Rogers, John Dewey and Jean Piaget (Kolb, 2015).

FIGURE 3.2   Kolb adult learning principles

Today, this model is widely acknowledged as one of the most important in explaining how adults learn effectively. The change process itself is an endless loop of change, activity, observation, reflection and change. This cycle was implied and indeed intended by Lewin but his terminology implied a more sequential process that ended at 'freezing'. However, he also saw the change process as continuous, where old behaviours would be deconstructed, new behaviours introduced and supported and then the people involved could tweak those behaviours to make them more productive and effective in situ.

Kolb certainly made the cyclical nature of change more obvious with his adult learning model. Kolb's influence on adult learning was profound, and learning and change initiatives began to incorporate time to reflect so that those expected to make the behavioural change could think about what they were being asked to do, relate it back to their own experiences and assimilate the change.

Today reflection is recognized as a vital component to adult learning as it encourages the learner to assimilate the change and make it personal and relevant to their own life and work situation. If a manager is being asked to change their behaviour and take on the role of coach with his or her work team it is only when they have had the experience of using coaching skills to elicit a better outcome for the employee, manager and business that the information, possibly passed over via a training programme, will make any real impact.

Prior to the real-world situation the information was abstract and one-dimensional so it was easy to dismiss it or ignore the directive. If the manager is supported and encouraged to apply that information to a real situation at work and can see how positively the interaction turns out then they are much more likely to incorporate coaching techniques as part of their ongoing management arsenal. It is this reflection stage that helps to facilitate change and yet often it is ignored in favour of reinforcement. Instead of allowing people time to think about the change, engage with it and play around with it in their heads they are simply told and retold about the importance of the change. Reflection is very different from reinforcement and should never be ignored or underestimated.

Of course when a new change initiative comes too quickly on the heels of the last one we simply don't have time to reflect and the chance of success plummets still further. Plus this constant focus on change can create 'perpetual loading' – a situation where companies constantly pile one change on top of another. Often these changes are complex, overlapping and far reaching. As a result employees get worn down and experience 'change fatigue' which further erodes the chance of success. In a study published in the *Harvard Business Review* 86 per cent of employees complained that their employer didn't allow them enough time for reflection and regeneration after stressful periods of change (Bruch and Menges, 2010).

Of course, part of the challenge with reflection is that it can look like we're not doing anything! Action is king in modern business and it's certainly 'doing', action and results that get people promoted, not necessarily thinking and reflecting! More than 25 years ago management guru Henry Mintzberg wrote in the *Harvard Business Review*: 'Study after study has shown that managers work at an unrelenting pace, that their activities are characterized by brevity, variety, and discontinuity and that they are strongly orientated to action and dislike reflective activities' (Mintzberg, 1990). If that was true then, it's exponentially so now.

In most businesses the decision to embark on change initiatives is taken by management. Focus groups and discussion forums may be used to involve the broader business community but in many cases a decision is made without consultation or involvement of the people who will have to actually change their behaviour in some way. Right off the bat there is no ownership.

All the attention is focused on before and during the change, including weighty documents and business cases for the change. No one is paying attention further down the line to what happens as the change unfolds.

Little effort is put into how best to support people to unfreeze existing behaviours, try the new ones and then refreeze the new ones as the default setting. Without this intervention and support people just won't change, or they will for a while and gradually drift back to their old behaviour.

The only really effective way to change people is to encourage them and support them to want to make the changes themselves. And yet a great deal of the change that occurs in business is simply 'inflicted' on employees without any input from them or any understanding about why it's necessary. It's hardly surprising that people resist the change. They feel out of their depth, they lose their sense of autonomy, competence and relatedness and this can make the change unpleasant and uncomfortable.

Plus we can't force people to change; we can't ask, yell at them, plead with them, cajole or punish them to change. We can't give them information and expect that they will automatically connect the dots and change work habits and processes that they have probably been using for years. And we certainly can't remind people to change simply by bombarding the participant with endless reminders, e-mails or PowerPoint decks on the importance of the change initiative. What's needed is a structured process of intervention and support that allows the individual to choose the aspects of the change they want to implement first, gives them time to reflect on the outcome of those behaviours and holds them accountable for making the change. And that process is achieved through Turning Learning into Action™ (TLA).

Although as the name would suggest TLA was originally designed as a learning transfer methodology, it is also extremely potent as a behavioural change methodology. In the learning and development context a training programme is created, a bunch of people attend then go back to work and do what they used to do. This happens all the time. Sometimes the people involved get busy and forget to transfer their learning into the workplace but often it's just because no one is holding them accountable for the change. TLA provides that 'after event' support and intervention to ensure that what is learned is implemented. And the same process can significantly alter change results. A change is announced, and those affected are told of the transition date and given the briefing or training needed to make the change. The date comes and goes but little happens. There may be a flurry of early activity as people try the new IT system or use the new sales script but when the individual is in a hurry or under pressure they will often revert to the old behaviour. As a result the change fails or just peters out. Why? Because no one is supporting those individuals in the workplace after the change event or process is complete and no one is ensuring they make the behavioural change necessary to ensure it is a success.

If we are to successfully implement change we need to appreciate the four factors that are currently derailing our change initiatives. These factors can be mitigated, but only if we appreciate their impact before we begin and pay attention to the process before, during and especially after the change. In the next chapter we will explore the TLA process in more detail together with its application.

Summary of key points

- According to Edelman's 15th Annual Global Trust Barometer 51 per cent of respondents believe that the pace of change in business is now too fast. The top three drivers are technology, business growth targets and greed/money.

- These drivers are fuelling change. Consequently there is now more change than ever and we may think we know why it's necessary but that isn't improving the success rate.

- Every year, we still waste a colossal amount of time and money on change initiatives with nothing to show for it except a depleted bank account and a deeply disgruntled workforce.

- Often the all-singing and all-dancing approach to change initiatives lacks the follow-through to behaviour change at an individual level. Change initiatives rarely get people to actually change their behaviour because of four key factors.

- The first – no ownership of the change. Change is almost always initiated top-down and there is no involvement or buy-in from those who actually need to change.

- Companies may clearly communicate the 'why' behind the change but it's a false belief that selling the why hard enough will be enough to create the ownership.

- There is rarely a coherent, integrated approach where everyone involved shares the ownership of change from start to finish.

- As a result, the 'little things' that have such a profound effect on successful change implementation can too easily slip through the cracks between various stakeholders' responsibilities.

- No one owns the change and so it simply doesn't get done, is only partially implemented or simply peters out. Often the burning platform that triggered the change initiative is replaced by another burning platform and the emphasis, time, money and urgency switch elsewhere.

- The importance of ownership needs to be considered at two different levels. The first is ownership of the change initiative which may come down to the change agent or nominated stakeholder. And second, the individual ownership of the person who needs to actually change.

- Much is written about the change agent role but the source of much of the change failure is in lack of ownership at an individual level. The gap therefore that needs to be bridged is to create ownership for change across both groups.

- The second factor is little understanding of what's needed after the change.

- Often the drive for change is urgent. This urgency means that there is often a great deal of focus on the current reality (before the change) and what therefore needs to happen but there is much less focus during the change and virtually nothing after it.

- The activity before the change is the easy part. It's relatively easy to see the gap between where the business is right now and where the business needs to be.

- What occurs during the change depends on the type of change but once the initiative is under way there is still usually a fair amount of momentum around the process.

- However, that momentum can soon drain away. When it's easier to do something the old way, or use the old system or forget about the coaching conversation with staff, people will, especially when no one is watching or they are under pressure.

- Whether your change initiative will be a success is actually almost all down to what happens after its official launch or start date. All the focus is on the change itself and how to get the ball rolling but very little time is then spend on how to keep that ball rolling, assess the process and ensure behavioural change in the workplace.

- The third factor is loss of control for those involved in the change.

- The simple, often overlooked fact is that people don't like change.

- Often the individuals who don't embrace the change are not being lazy or deliberately difficult; they are simply reacting to what the change brings and the perceived loss of control over their environment.

- Most change initiatives require people to change their behaviour. But often that change can rob those people of a sense of control, which is derailing the process before it begins.

- The only really effective way to get someone to change is to involve them and get them to want to change.

- Change almost always challenges autonomy, competence and relatedness and if we don't appreciate the human element of change we will be destined to repeat the dismal statistics for another 30 years.

- The fourth factor is there is little appreciation for the difference between reinforcement and reflection.

- The change process itself is an endless loop of change, activity, observation, reflection and change.

- Today reflection is recognized as a vital component to adult learning as it encourages the learner to assimilate the change and make it personal and relevant to their own life and work situation.

- It is this reflection stage that helps to facilitate change and yet often it is ignored in favour of reinforcement. Instead of allowing people time to think about the change, engage with it and play around with it in their heads they are simply told and retold about the importance of the change. Reflection is very different from reinforcement and should never be ignored or underestimated.

- In a study published in the *Harvard Business Review*, 86 per cent of employees complained that their employer didn't allow them enough time for reflection and regeneration after stressful periods of change.

- What's needed is a structured process of intervention and support that allows the individual to choose the aspects of the change they want to implement first, gives them time to reflect on the outcome of those behaviours and holds them accountable for making the change.

- That process is achieved through Turning Learning into Action™ (TLA).

- TLA provides that 'after event' support and intervention to ensure that what is learned is implemented. And the same process can significantly alter change results.

References

Baldwin, T T and Ford, K J (1988) Transfer of Training: A review and directions for future research, *Personal Psychology* **41** (1) pp 63–105

Broad, M and Newstrom, J W (2000) *Transfer of Training: Action-packed strategies to ensure high payoff from training investments*, Perseus Books

Bruch, H and Menges J I (2010) The Acceleration Trap, *Harvard Business Review* [online] https://hbr.org/2010/04/the-acceleration-trap/

Csikszentmihalyi, M (2002) *Flow: The psychology of happiness: The classic work on how to achieve happiness* Paperback Rider, London

Edelman (2015) 15th Annual Global Trust Barometer: Trust and Innovation [online] http://www.edelman.com/insights/intellectual-property/2015-edelman-trust-barometer/trust-and-innovation-edelman-trust-barometer/

Ford, K J and Weissbein, D A (1997) Transfer of Training: An updated review and analysis, *Performance Improvement Quarterly* **10** (2) pp 22–41

Kolb, D A (2015) *Experiential Learning: Experience as the sourve of learning and development*, 2nd edition, Pearson, New Jersey

Langer, E J (2010) *Counterclockwise: A proven way to think yourself younger and healthier*, Hodder, London

Mintzberg, H (1990) The manager's job: folklore and fact, *Harvard Business Review* [online] https://hbr.org/1990/03/the-managers-job-folklore-and-fact/ar/1

Nicholson, N (1998) How hardwired is human behavior? *Harvard Business Review* [online] https://hbr.org/1998/07/how-hardwired-is-human-behavior/

Phillips, J J and Phillips, P P (2010). *Measuring for Success: What CEOs really think about the learning investment*, ASTD Press

Phillips, P P and Phillips, J J (2012) *10 Steps to Successful Business Alignment*, ASTD Press

Pink, D H (2009) *Drive: The surprising truth about what motivates us*, Penguin, New York

PART TWO
TLA process and theory

The TLA process and applications

04

The reason so many change initiatives fail is because ultimately their success depends on individual human beings actually changing their behaviour. But behavioural change is not easy, automatic or necessarily natural. We are incredibly wedded to the status quo. When we have done a process or achieved a result one way for years it can be confronting to be asked to change that behaviour. We almost want it to fail so we can turn around and say, 'See, I told you it wouldn't work, we'll just go back to the way we used to do it.'

Turning Learning into Action™ (TLA) is a proven behavioural change methodology that solves the problem through a series of specific, structured and accountable one-on-one conversations that occur at various intervals after the change has been launched. It is this post-launch phase intervention that supports the individuals to experiment with the change, reflect on the outcome and bed the change down into new normal behaviour. Here we explain how TLA came about, the results that can be achieved and how TLA is a lever for change. We will also unpack the three stages of TLA so you know what is required to duplicate solid change results.

TLA evolution and results

TLA has come a long way since its beginnings in April 2004. The first trial of the process took place with just 12 people. A month later, even before the results were in, the large premium automotive client ordered the programme for 120 more people that year. Clearly this was working.

The following year we analysed the results of a group of 15 sales agents who received TLA following some sales training versus a group who did not receive the follow-up. We assessed their average sales per month before the programme and again after the programme and compared the results to the norm within the business. The norm in this case was average monthly sales before and after May. We made this split to take into account seasonal differences in automotive sales.

The average sales consultant achieved an uplift of 16.2 per cent in their average sales per month between the five months prior to the training and the five months following the training and TLA. Like so much training, the company was seeking a behaviour change in the sales executives – they wanted them to use a different sales process and change their approach to the potential buyers. This can be tricky, especially for salespeople because they tend to have set ways of working that have been honed and fine-tuned over the years. It is essentially part of their habitual behaviour and personality that they believe 'gives them the edge'. Changing behaviour in this context is notoriously difficult and yet those who went through the TLA process had a sales uplift of 43.8 per cent over the same period.

These were extraordinary results.

By 2007 we were delivering TLA in tandem with training programmes for another large automotive client in Australia – this time for 400 mid-level managers across the organization over an 18-month period. We were then asked to deliver TLA to 240 people in the UK following four large training events of about 60 people at a time held over a month. The training was outstanding and our job was to ensure that all 240 people transferred the learning back into their workplace.

By the end of the year we had detailed results from the 400-person programme in Australia and the 240-person programme in the UK. The TLA process had been implemented in each case by two completely different teams each trained in the same methodology and yet the results were almost identical (Table 4.1).

Two programmes:

1 Plan to Win, large luxury automotive company, sales managers, UK – 240 people;

2 Large Australian automotive company, sales, service and parts managers attending a leadership training programme – 400 people.

Net Promoter Score (NPS), developed by Frederick F Reichheld to illustrate customer satisfaction, is now widely used across all industries. According to Reichheld, an NPS of 75 per cent to 80 per cent-plus means the business has generated world-class loyalty (2003). In other words the customers of the businesses that are reporting an NPS in excess of 75 per cent are very happy customers – so happy that they will gladly recommend that business to other people. In the UK and Australian TLA programmes we tested we achieved an NPS of 78 per cent and 73 per cent respectively.

TABLE 4.1   Two programmes in large automotive companies in the UK and Australia

	UK – 240 people	Australia – 400 people
Sector	Automotive	Automotive
Audience	Sales managers	Sales managers, service managers, regional managers, parts managers
Timescale	Over 4 months	Over 18 months, phased
Number of coaches	10	4
Training	Soft management / leadership skills	Soft management / leadership skills
	Net promoter score (NPS) for the programme	**Net promoter score for the programme**
Based on your recent telephone coaching experience how likely would you be to recommend this to a colleague?	78%	73%
To what degree were expectations of coaching as a transfer of training tool met? (Score scale of 1 low to 5 high). Scored either 4 or 5	86%	83%
To what degree have the objectives you set at the end of the training programme been met? (Score 1, not met, to 5, fully met) Score of either 4 or 5	88%	87%

TABLE 4.1   *Continued*

	UK – 240 people	Australia – 400 people
Did you see change in particular aspects of your behaviour in response to coaching? – if yes, to what extent has this been achieved? Score 4 or 5 out of a scale of 1–5	78%	83%
To what degree do you believe the objectives in the action plan would have been met without coaching? (1, not met – 5, fully met)	Score 1 or 2 – 47% Score 3 – 32% Score 4 or 5 – 21% * * 70% of these respondents in the next question rated it 5 – essential for helping them follow through on the action plan (as this is a reverse scored question the assumption could be made that the reversed nature had been missed).	Score 1 or 2 – 49% Score 3 – 38% Score 4 or 5 – 13%
How useful was the coaching in ensuring that you followed through on your action plan? (Scale 1, unnecessary, to 5, essential)	85%	82%

Today TLA is being delivered in nine languages across the United States, Europe and Asia as well as Australia and New Zealand. It is solving the transfer of learning challenge for businesses across multiple sectors and is also being used to solve the behavioural change shortfall that so frequently derails change initiatives.

TLA as a lever for change

Businesses buy training or invest in a change initiative because they want to see some sort of performance improvement, be that financial or operational. The initial wins for TLA were in the area of training support and learning transfer. However, as the benefits of a robust TLA methodology were observed in this field and training participants were then supported through the change process to transfer the learning from the training back to the working environment, it became apparent that using the methodology to support broader change initiatives was also both beneficial and desperately needed. Regardless of the required outcome, that outcome will only be realized if certain people in the business embrace that change and actually change the way they do their job. That change will always bring with it challenges and obstacles that the individual and the business have to overcome if the change is to deliver on its promise.

TLA is therefore the potential leverage point that will allow individuals to surmount those challenges and improve performance over the long term.

Have you ever watched a pole vaulter at the Olympic Games? As the athlete stands at the start of her run-up the pole is straight and taut. It looks unwieldy and awkward. The athlete then begins her run-up and plants the pole into the ground; the pole bends and elevates the athlete upwards, over the bar. As she clears the obstacle, she releases the pole and lands safely back down on the protective mat. The pole straightens on release and falls back to the mattress too – having done its job.

Actually, pole vaulting was not originally a sport but rather a sensible and practical way to pass over natural obstacles in marshy places such as provinces of the Netherlands, along the North Sea and the Fens in parts of the UK. Often people needed to cross these marshy areas without getting wet feet and without walking countless extra miles over bridges, so a stack of jumping poles was kept at every house and used for vaulting over the canals. Traditionally vaulting was about distance rather than height and was used to cut short travel time and allow people to get to where they were going faster.

TLA does the same thing by utilizing the same combination of structure and flexibility. Each TLA conversation starts with structure which acts like the pole vaulter's pole and provides strength and purpose to the conversation. It allows the person in the change process to use the power inherent in that structure to catapult themselves up and over their particular change challenge and help to break down their natural resistance to change.

Trained TLA facilitators know the framework they will use before they start the process (structure), but they never know where that path will lead or what the specific needs of the individual are. It is this flexibility that prompts additional exploration and allows the individual to navigate the obstacle in the same way the vaulter navigates the bar. It's the exploration through questions that really matters because they hold the context of the conversation, allowing for flexibility with the answers without being so flexible that the conversation degenerates into an opportunity for the person immersed in change to vent and complain without getting into action.

The conversation is then wrapped up with more structure as we then get the individual's commitment about what they are actually going to do, and what change they are going to make before the next TLA conversation. The individual is accountable for this process and is choosing what to do next. As such he or she is taking responsibility and ownership of the change. This is when the pole vaulter's pole straightens and falls to the ground while the vaulter lands safely on new ground. He or she has used the structure and flexibility to get to where they want to go faster, even if they were not sure they even wanted to go in the first place.

Without this lever for change the behaviour change sought is rarely realized or demonstrated in the business. As Archimedes once said, 'Give me a lever long enough and a fulcrum on which to place it, and I shall move the world.' TLA is the lever that facilitates successful change.

Change requires reflection

The notion that reflection is central to learning and therefore successful behavioural change goes back to Greek philosophers such as Socrates and Plato. The Socratic Method is often referred to as a teaching method that focuses on asking instead of telling. Socrates himself challenged others, including Plato, to question their beliefs and reflect on learning to establish how it did or did not make sense to them as individuals. Sophocles also suggested that we learn by observing what we do in practice and adjusting our behaviours to improve the outcome. John Locke, the English Enlightenment thinker, philosopher and physician, believed that knowing was simply the product of reflection on experience and sensations.

The word 'experience' derives from the Latin word *experientia*, which means trial, proof or experimentation. In other words the way someone gets experience and therefore masters change successfully is by making the change in the real world and using the results as feedback to fine-tune future behaviour.

The process of gathering experience therefore follows the Kolb adult learning model. And at every level change is learning – whether it's a family grappling with the change of having a new baby and all the learning that entails, or the implementation of a new software system. Change needs to happen and learning needs to happen. Initially the person being asked to change engages in a particular activity or approach and the results of that action are noted. Sometimes the activity will be successful and sometimes it will not be successful but it is the experience and the outcome that drive learning and adaptation. Ironically people learn the most when the outcome is not as the individual had anticipated. Under those conditions he or she is much more likely to engage in the crucial ingredient for learning and change – reflection. We rarely stop and reflect on why we've been successful or why something worked out; instead we take the win and quickly move on. However, when something doesn't work we are much more likely to stop and think about why. It is because of that reflection that we are then able to fine-tune our approach, see the failings and try again. This trial-and-error process develops expertise and it's only possible with reflection.

For reflection to really deliver the results that it is capable of delivering it must, however, be specific, structured and accountable (Figure 4.1). This can seem counterintuitive because the word 'reflection' has a dream-like quality to it. It conjures up images of relaxing in flower-filled meadows staring idly up to the clear blue sky. But that's daydreaming and whilst enjoyable it's entirely different from what is required in order to support people to change.

FIGURE 4.1   The principles of effective reflection

Turning Learning into Action™ facilitates specific, structured and accountable reflection through a series of one-on-one conversations after the change initiative has begun in earnest. When people are briefed on the change they may or may not have time to reflect on how the change is going to impact on them in their daily life. However, without structured follow-up little headway is made. The people affected by the change know from past experience that if they just keep their heads down and drag their feet long enough the change will probably peter out. Even if it doesn't they also know, from the legacy of failed change they've been privy to, that they will probably be able to fudge compliance just enough to get away with not actually changing much at all.

This is why business alignment is so important when embarking on the change. When everyone involved in the change is crystal clear why the change is being initiated in the first place and is equally clear on the needs and outcomes that are expected from the change it's much harder for the change to be derailed.

If, on the other hand, there is a specialized follow-up process after the change gets under way and those affected by the change know that the action plans they create about what they are individually going to do are actually going to matter and be followed up on then behavioural change becomes much more likely. The follow-up conversation focuses the individual on moving forward and creates a framework where he or she must keep their agreements with themselves or explain why. The agreements they have made will create the change on an individual level which will feed up to the change required at an organizational level. When the individual has made commitments and reflects on how he or she is progressing and is held accountable, then real change is not only possible but almost inevitable.

Creating the environment for change

Unless we set out to create behavioural change and appreciate the intricacies of personal behavioural change then nothing much will ever happen. It's not that people are lazy, unmotivated or difficult, it's that personal behavioural change is not automatic or easy. Nor is there a one-size-fits-all approach to personal transformation.

According to Charles Jennings at the 2012 AITD (Australian Institute of Training and Development) conference there are certain dynamics that support learning and certain dynamics that support change. He quotes that the dynamics that support learning are:

1 experience (formal or informal);
2 conversations/socializing;
3 practice;
4 reflection (debrief).

Building on this we need to consider the dynamics that support change which are:

1 reflection (debrief);

2 making a decision to change;

3 accessing the iceberg – getting under the behaviour to feelings, thoughts, values, beliefs, fears and needs;

4 self-accountability.

The quickest way to support change is to help someone access what's causing their behaviours in the first place rather than the behaviours themselves. It's therefore important to unpack behaviours so as to access the thoughts, feelings, beliefs, values, needs and fears that an individual has around those behaviours. That simply does not happen in a traditional change environment. Instead people are told to change, encouraged to change, reasoned into change, frightened into change or cajoled into change. None of which are terribly effective.

No one is helping those expected to change to reflect on the information they have received, make a decision to change, understand why they currently do the things they do so they can appreciate the need for change, and embrace self-accountability to make the necessary alterations.

Effective self-accountability is the hardest of these factors to execute well. We know that change happens from the inside out. Addiction programmes all advocate that the individual with the addiction must acknowledge they have a problem before any real progress can be made. So we understand the concept of self-accountability but the terminology ('self') almost gives others permission to step back from that accountability process and so they just leave it to the individual to be self-accountable, which doesn't work! Accountability is key to change but there seems to be a level of confusion around the difference between holding an individual accountable (which conjures up images of hitting people over the head with a stick and forcing them into change) and holding people accountable to themselves, which is where a new level of power and awareness can kick in.

And without this awareness behaviour just doesn't change!

Stages of TLA

In its simplest form TLA is a staged process that facilitates behavioural change. Whether that is following a training event where the learning needs to be demonstrated in the business, or during a change initiative where people are being asked to alter their behaviour and work processes in some way. There are three distinct stages of TLA (Figure 4.2):

- preparation;
- action;
- evaluation.

FIGURE 4.2   Three component parts of TLA

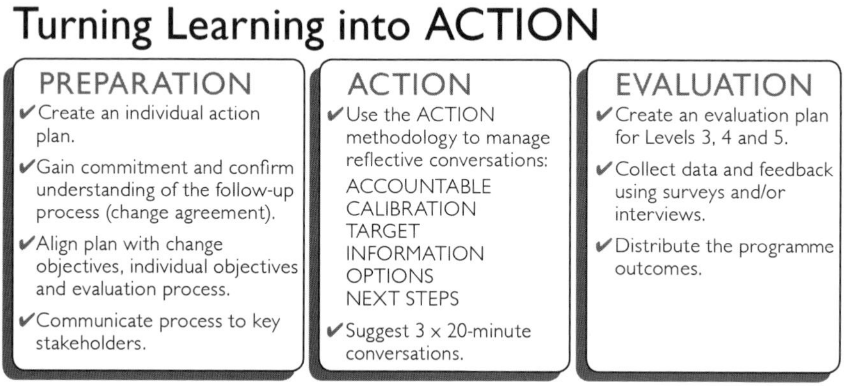

Turning Learning into ACTION

PREPARATION	ACTION	EVALUATION
✔ Create an individual action plan.	✔ Use the ACTION methodology to manage reflective conversations:	✔ Create an evaluation plan for Levels 3, 4 and 5.
✔ Gain commitment and confirm understanding of the follow-up process (change agreement).	ACCOUNTABLE CALIBRATION TARGET INFORMATION OPTIONS NEXT STEPS	✔ Collect data and feedback using surveys and/or interviews.
✔ Align plan with change objectives, individual objectives and evaluation process.	✔ Suggest 3 × 20-minute conversations.	✔ Distribute the programme outcomes.
✔ Communicate process to key stakeholders.		

The initial stage of TLA is preparation. This is, as the name suggests, when the person being asked to change is in some way preparing to change. It could be part of a change briefing, launch or training connected with the change. Regardless of whether the TLA is delivered by specially trained individuals inside the business or external facilitators the preparation includes setting expectations and creating the TLA Action Plan. It is this action plan that will guide the behavioural change to ensure it occurs in the workplace and becomes the new norm. As such the TLA Action Plan reflects the individual's written commitments to change. Obviously those charged with making changes to their behaviour frequently say and do anything to present the appearance of 'getting on board'. Some may at this stage have no intention of actually following through. At this preparation stage it doesn't matter; what matters is that everyone involved in the change creates an individual action plan and we will explain why in due course.

The next stage of TLA is action and it explores what actually happens in the workplace, during and after the change initiative. The action stage focuses on supporting people involved to reflect on their experiences of the change during scheduled TLA action conversations which take place after the change is 'launched'. These conversations give the individual an opportunity to discuss their experience of the change. Did they do the task differently? Did they change their behaviour and if so how did that work out? Whilst this dialogue gives the individual a platform to discuss the change, as the stage name would suggest the emphasis of these conversations is on action and what the individual is actually going to do, or do differently in the workplace and what changes or behavioural tweaks they are going to make between the follow-up conversations to progress each of their stated objectives from their TLA Action Plan. There are typically three scheduled TLA conversations with each individual, set several weeks apart to allow the person to make the changes while being held accountable to do so.

Regardless of whether a fully-trained change manager, L&D professional or external TLA specialist is conducting those conversations it's important to understand they are a very specific and targeted type of conversation. These are not casual chats or opportunities to vent but rather focused interactions designed to support action and change so that the individual can bed down the change into their normal working life. If these conversations are carried out by a trained internal manager or L&D professional it will require them to 'change their hat' from their normal role and communication style.

Once individuals have followed through on their TLA Plan it's time for stage three – evaluation. Evaluation looks at the results and gathers data regarding what people have actually done since the start of the change initiative and between the TLA conversations. This is why we need to be really clear from the start about what we are going to measure.

Change needs to be aligned to the business needs and aspirations and the alignment model in Chapter 2 is, we believe, the most comprehensive way to do this. There needs to be a clear sense of the problem that the change is seeking to solve and the expected results the change will deliver – this is why business alignment is so crucial to successful change.

Too often the 'let's throw everything at the wall and see what sticks' approach is used when it comes to purchasing training or starting change initiatives. Driven from a place of desperation to 'just do something' change programmes are started without enough step-by-step analysis into what outcome the business is seeking from the initiative. Evaluation is always significantly easier when we are clear about the destination from the start and are confident that it's the right destination (Figure 4.3). This means that we need to start with our end evaluation in mind so that we can set not just learning objectives but application objectives and business objectives for what the programme is going to achieve.

Change for the sake of change is pointless, time consuming and leads to disengagement and 'change fatigue'. We absolutely must see it through to

FIGURE 4.3   Aim for the REAL destination of change

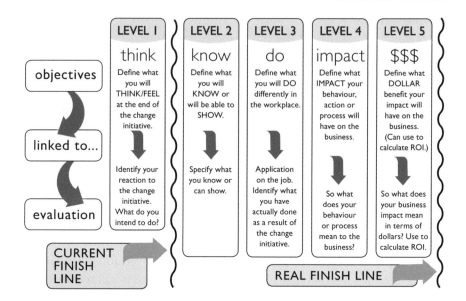

behavioural change and improved results otherwise we need to stop initiating change. Change can therefore only really be considered successful if the behavioural change that it was initiated to create is visibly demonstrated in the business and is delivering the expected performance improvement or elevated result.

The TLA process which will be unpacked and explored in greater detail in the rest of the book allows people to try out the behavioural change, and experiment with it in a supported environment rather than being expected to 'flick a switch' and move seamlessly from behaviour A to behaviour B. The latter is unrealistic and stressful for those involved, which makes it even more likely to fail. We will also discuss how this can work for large-scale projects and how to make it workable in a scalable way. Tailoring the change initiative with the post-change TLA process allows individuals to test the behaviour, monitor the results and reflect on how the new behaviours or action turned out and how useful the new experience was. It is this process of trial, error and reflection that facilitates real learning and behavioural change. Knowledge and information become wisdom and experience only when they have been applied in the real work situation. Turning Learning into Action™ empowers the individual to take control of the change process and increase their value and productivity for individual and collective success. In the following chapter we will unpack the first stage of TLA – preparation.

Summary of key points

- Behavioural change is not easy, automatic or necessarily natural. We are incredibly wedded to the status quo. When we have done a process or achieved a result one way for years it can be confronting to be asked to change that behaviour.

- Turning Learning into Action™ (TLA) is a proven behavioural change methodology that solves the problem through a series of specific, structured and accountable one-on-one conversations that occur at various intervals after the change has been launched.

- It is this post-change intervention that supports the individuals to experiment with the change, reflect on the outcome and bed the change down into new normal behaviour.

- Regardless of the required outcome that outcome will only be realized if certain people in the business embrace that change and actually change the way they do their job. There are always challenges and obstacles that the individual and the business have to overcome if the change is to deliver on its promise.

- TLA is therefore the potential leverage point that will allow individuals to surmount those challenges and improve performance over the long term.

- TLA uses a combination of structure and flexibility to facilitate change at the individual level.

- Each TLA conversation starts with structure which provides strength and purpose to the conversation. It allows the person in the change process to use the power inherent in that structure to catapult themselves up and over their particular change challenge and help to break down their natural resistance to change.

- Trained TLA facilitators know the framework they will use before they start the process (structure), but they never know where that path will lead or what the specific needs of the individual are. It is this flexibility that prompts additional exploration and allows the individual to navigate the obstacles.

- Without this lever for change the behaviour change sought is rarely realized or demonstrated in the business.

- Change only really occurs when those involved can reflect on their experience of the change, and use this as a feedback loop to refine ongoing effort.

- Initially the person being asked to change engages in a particular activity or approach and the results of that action are noted. Sometimes the activity will be successful and sometimes it won't but it is the experience and the outcome that drive learning and adaptation.

- Turning Learning into Action™ facilitates specific, structured and accountable reflection through a series of one-on-one conversations after the change initiative has begun.

- The follow-up conversation focuses the individual on moving forward and creates a framework where he or she must keep their agreements with themselves or explain why.

- When the individual has made commitments and reflects on how he or she is progressing and is held accountable then real change is not only possible but almost inevitable.

- The quickest way to support change is to help someone access what's causing their behaviours in the first place rather than the behaviours themselves. It's therefore important to unpack behaviours so as to access the thoughts, feelings, beliefs, values, needs and fears that an individual has around those behaviours.

- That simply does not happen in a traditional change environment.

- No one is helping those expected to change to reflect on the information they received, make a decision to change, help them to understand why they currently do the things they do so they can appreciate the need for change, and embrace self-accountability to make the necessary alterations.

- There are three distinct stages of TLA: preparation, action and evaluation.

- The initial stage of TLA is preparation. This is, as the name suggests, when the person being asked to change is in some way preparing to change. It could be part of a change briefing, launch or training connected with the change. This stage includes setting expectations and creating the TLA Action Plan.

- It is this action plan that will guide the behavioural change to ensure it occurs in the workplace and becomes the new norm.

- The next stage of TLA is action and it explores what actually happens in the workplace, during and after the change initiative.

- The action stage focuses on supporting people involved to reflect on their experiences of the change during scheduled TLA conversations which take place after the change is 'launched'.

- These conversations give the individual an opportunity to discuss their experience of the change and decide what they are actually going to do, or do differently in the workplace, and what changes or behavioural tweaks they are going to make between the follow-up conversations to progress each of their stated objectives from their TLA Action Plan.

- There are typically three scheduled TLA conversations with each individual involved in the change process set several weeks apart to allow the person to make the changes while being held accountable to do so.

- Stage three – evaluation – looks at the results and gathers data regarding what people have actually done since the start of the change initiative and between the TLA conversations. Evaluation also links to the alignment model for an in-depth way to measure the effectiveness of the change.

- Change for the sake of change is pointless, time consuming and leads to disengagement and 'change fatigue'. We absolutely must see it through to behavioural change and improved results otherwise we need to stop initiating change.

- TLA makes that possible by allowing people to try out the behavioural change, and experiment with it in a supported environment rather than being expected to 'flick a switch' and move seamlessly from behaviour A to behaviour B.

- It is this process of trial, error and reflection that facilitates real learning and behavioural change.

- Turning Learning into Action™ empowers the individual to take control of the change process and increase their value and productivity for individual and collective success.

Reference

Reichheld, F F (2003) The one number you need to grow, *Harvard Business Review* [online] https://hbr.org/2003/12/the-one-number-you-need-to-grow/ar/1

Preparation

05

In this chapter we will explore the preparation stage. This includes the anatomy of change so we can better appreciate what we are up against, the importance of the right mindset going into change and the all-important TLA Action Plan that forms the source document on which the follow-up conversations are constructed.

As the name would suggest the preparation stage of TLA is focused on what the people involved need to know and expect from the change initiative and the follow up TLA process. Effectively, it sets the TLA process up for success.

Often people can think that preparation before the change is basically a euphemism for 'revving up the troops'. One of us (EW) was at a client's site helping them with the preparation phase and the key stakeholder boldly announced to the group that I had arrived to motivate everyone and get them revved up to make change. This particular stakeholder had been absent from the meeting discussing what would happen in this preparation session so it was important to set the record straight – albeit delicately. Revving people up for change was the exact opposite to what was going to happen in the preparation session. Instead it was important to challenge the group to think about the fact that they did actually have a choice. The new software was being implemented and ultimately it was down to them as individuals as to whether they supported the business moving forward with this new system or got involved reluctantly, kicking and screaming towards change. They had a choice. It wasn't something they had to do – they could choose to do it or not but it had to be an individual commitment and an individual choice.

Often one of hardest aspects of change is the inherent uncertainty it brings. People can very easily become anxious and uncomfortable with the change simply because they don't know why it's happening or what to expect. Plus they are nervous about how the change will impact them personally and whether they are capable of what is being asked of them. It is this emotional response, even though many would deny it is an emotional response, that ignites their resistance.

Giving them the ownership for choosing to opt into the change positively or experience it negatively gave them back some feeling of power over the process and self-accountability began to kick in. Obviously the software was going ahead so there wasn't really a choice but giving those involved a sense that there was allowed them to take some control and ownership over the change.

The anatomy of change

It's therefore always wise to reassure people about the nature of change and how it actually occurs for human beings. The process of successful change has been written about for many hundreds of years. In the 18th century Goethe stated: 'Progress has not followed a straight ascending line, but a spiral with rhythms of progress and retrogression, of evolution and dissolution.' Since then a variety of change models has been proposed including Kurt Lewin's model we touched on earlier, McKinsey's 7-S model, John Kotter's 8-step change model through to Elisabeth Kübler-Ross's model, which initially looked at stages of grief but was later expanded to mirror how people transition through any form of change. Behavioural scientists James Prochaska, John Norcross and Carlo DiClemente also concur with Goethe. Having reviewed every major change methodology at the time they concluded that behavioural change spirals through phases (2007).

Even when those involved in change feel that they are making progress there is almost always a lapse as the individual will stumble and retreat back to old behaviours. As a result change is not linear, it is not a step-by-step forward process. Instead it can feel more like the individual is taking two steps forward and three back followed by three forward and two back. And unfortunately this non-linear progress can also feel remarkably like failure.

If, however, this is fully explained to the people most affected by the change so they know what to expect, when these experiences arrive they are not as thrown by them. It's a little like deciding to go for laser eye surgery. One of us has a friend who decided to have laser eye surgery with her husband. He was definitely more excited about the procedure than she was. In fact as the day came closer and closer she started to have some serious doubts and talked up the convenience of contact lenses and how she actually didn't mind wearing glasses. The day of the procedure arrived and the nurse sat both of them down and explained exactly what was going to happen. She even warned them about the sounds they would experience and the smell! The nurse told them both how long it would take and what to expect once the procedure was over. It wouldn't be like the TV 'makeover' shows where the patient opens her eyes and can miraculously see – that actually doesn't happen. They were instructed to get to their hotel as quickly as possible and then rest for at least 12 hours as it could take that long before their eyes settled and they could see clearly. Plus they needed to expect that their eyes would be sore; it shouldn't be too painful but it was definitely going to feel uncomfortable and a little weird. This was all normal and they were then to come back for a final check-up in the morning. Had the nurse not been so thorough in setting the scene and managing their expectations our friend may still be wearing contact lenses. But she knew what to expect so when she did detect a weird smell during the procedure she wasn't distressed by it, and when her eyes nipped back at the hotel she wasn't panicked by that either. When after five hours her husband could see clearly and she couldn't she still wasn't worried because she had been told these variations may occur. By morning she had 20/20 vision and they donated their glasses to charity.

Imagine how upsetting or stressful that experience would have been had the nurse said nothing! The same is true of any change. If we know what to expect and recognize the signs and symptoms of change as and when they arrive, rather than being upset or put off by them, then we are much more likely to follow through and experience the full benefit of change. Behavioural change is rarely an on/off phenomenon – it's a gradual process. More often than not lapses are the rule rather than the exception, and knowing that up front can make change much less daunting and much more likely to stick.

There is always a readjusting period when the old way is packed away and a new way is put in its place. But when we have done a process or task a certain way for years this will take time and it can often feel odd. Say I asked you to fold your arms right now... Go on – take a moment and just fold your arms. Chances are you've folded your arms the same way all your life. Now – fold them the other way. Again, put the book down for a moment and fold your arms the other way. So if you naturally tuck your right hand under the top of your left arm, with your left hand clutching the top of your right arm, then tuck your left hand under the top of your right arm with your right hand clutching the top of your left arm. It feels weird, doesn't it? So weird that it may take you several moments to work out how to do it.

That is the nature of change; it may feel strange at first but if we persevere and don't expect perfection from the outset then it will soon start to feel more normal until the new behaviour becomes the default behaviour. Making sure that those involved in change know what to expect can massively help to alleviate many of the feelings of uncertainly that push people back to old behavioural habits.

Remember Self-Determination Theory (SDT) from Chapter 3, which provides a more complete picture of human motivation? If someone doesn't want to change, reward and punishment may work initially but both are unsustainable over the long term. Besides, reward and punishment tend to facilitate compliance and 'gaming' of the change so the individuals may do just enough to look like they've changed or find ways to manipulate the change but that is not successful change. The best way to create change is to get those involved to want to change for their own reasons by activating their intrinsic motivation. Although intrinsic motivation is far superior to extrinsic motivation it does rely on autonomy, competence and relatedness – all of which are challenged by the change process.

This is also backed up and expanded upon by David Rock, who proposes the SCARF model to explain our behavioural reactions to change. Delving into the field of social science Rock suggests that there are two themes emerging from this field. First, much of our social behaviour is governed by the need to minimize threat and maximize reward (Gordon, 2000). And second, several domains of social experience draw upon the same brain networks used for primary survival needs (Lieberman and Eisenberger, 2008). Or as Rock puts it, 'social needs are treated in much the same way in the brain as the need for food and water [in the body]'.

The SCARF model therefore summarizes these two themes by providing a framework that captures the common factors that can activate a reward or threat response in social situations. Change, especially organizational change, is a social situation. Change is rarely solitary in a work setting and almost always involves your work colleagues and team members. SCARF is an acronym which involves the five domains of human social experience:

S – Status: Where you feel you are in the pecking order.

C – Certainty: Perception of how well you can predict the future.

A – Autonomy: A feeling of having choices and having control over events.

R – Relatedness: A feeling of being safe with other people and experiencing trust.

F – Fairness: A feeling of fair connections and fair exchanges.

These five domains activate either the 'primary reward' or 'primary threat' circuitry (and associated networks) of the brain (Rock, 2008, 2009) For example, if a change initiative is viewed as a perceived threat to an individual's status then this perception will activate their primary threat circuitry which will make change difficult. Moving forward with the change will literally feel threatening and they will resist it. If, however, the change is positioned as elevating the individual's status then it could activate the primary reward circuitry, making successful change more likely.

If the change initiative makes people believe they have no choice then again they will feel threatened and resist. If, however, the change can be positioned as a choice that they have control over then the primary threat circuitry is bypassed and progress is possible. This is why it was so important to reposition the preparation discussion we mentioned earlier, where the key stakeholder told the assembled group that the change was happening and everyone needed to get revved up about it. That approach decimated their autonomy and negatively impacted the possibility of success before we'd even begun.

Understanding that the feelings of uncertainty and discomfort are a normal and universally experienced part of the change process can help to reduce the inherent pressure so that each individual involved can find their own pace and rhythm toward change.

Everyone experiences the same or similar feelings when trying to change behaviour and often just knowing that can make a massive difference to our willingness and ability to persevere and see the change through to successful implementation.

The need for the right mindset

As we've said, almost all change requires learning of some sort. We need to learn a new process or a new behaviour or how to use a new order-processing system or database. Unfortunately by the time we are involved in company-sponsored change initiatives we are adults and that can make change even more difficult.

If you have children or have spent any time around children you will probably have noticed their sponge-like qualities – they literally soak up information at an alarming rate. The sheer number of questions they ask can make a TV quizmaster look lazy. Children have a very visceral, trial-and-error, devil-may-care attitude to learning. They don't stress about it or overanalyse it – they just do it, over and over again until they get it right. When a child becomes mobile, they tend to start shuffling around on their backside or they crawl and drag themselves around the house. It's not long before they figure out that they can pull themselves upright by grabbing sofas, legs or chairs. They will then skirt around the room, using props to hold them up. Then one day they let go of the prop and wobble into the middle of the room. Usually a parent is at the other end encouraging the child to take a few more steps. Of course the first attempt never works that well. The child plonks down on their bottom but still the parents clap and cheer as though they've just witnessed the breaking of the four-minute mile. This evolutionary process can go on for weeks, often months, but the encouragement and enthusiasm from both child and parent never waver. The parent, assuming they are a good parent, never gets bored (at least they never show it), and they never berate the child for their lack of progress. It's just positive encouragement all the way.

Contrast that to how adults learn. By the time we reach adulthood we have evolved through various developmental levels including the one that makes us acutely aware of what we look like. This developmental level kicks in during the teenage years and social conditioning and peer pressure become very important influencers of decision making. Learning stops being about learning and starts being about what everyone else is doing, how we look, how we are perceived and how to manage our persona. Of course failure doesn't look good and it doesn't feel that wonderful either. As a result, by the time we are adults we will do just about anything to avoid situations where failure is even an option and sadly learning new information so we can change behaviour is one of those situations.

We are encouraged to try but if we try and fail that's so much worse than never having tried in the first place. The child instinctively understands the phrase, 'If at first you don't succeed, try, try and try again.' Whereas the adult more accurately resonates with, 'If at first you don't succeed, destroy all the evidence that you ever tried in the first place.'

Stanford University psychologist Carol Dweck became obsessed with this difference in mindset and 'obsessed with understanding how people cope with failures'. Her early research involved giving children a series of puzzles to solve. Immediately she noticed the difference between how children and adults tend to view failure. Dweck had expected to find that, like adults, some children coped well with failure and some didn't, but what she found was that children just don't view failure in the same way as adults. When the children couldn't solve the puzzles they didn't even see that as failure; instead it was a challenge. It was fun and they loved the process of trying to figure out the answer.

As a result of her research Dweck proposes that it is our mindset that determines our ability to handle failure and therefore determines our ability to change. Everything in life comes down to mindset and she believes that there are only two – fixed and growth.

When an individual has a fixed mindset they believe that their skills, abilities and natural talent are down to a genetic quirk of fate. If their father was good at maths they will be good at maths, if their mother was a brilliant pianist then they will be able to play the piano. What they are capable of is essentially carved in stone at birth – determined by their genetic makeup and environment. For someone with a fixed mindset, if they are not especially talented at something there is nothing they can do about it. Of course, this mindset is extremely toxic. It allows the individual to abdicate responsibility because they 'either have it or they don't'. Plus it sets up competition and forces the individual to constantly prove themselves worthy. As Dweck says, 'If you have only a certain amount of intelligence, a certain personality, and a certain moral character – well, then you'd better prove that you have a healthy dose of them. It simply wouldn't do to look or feel deficient in these most basic characteristics' (2007).

On the other hand when an individual has a growth mindset they do not believe that their relative attributes are carved in stone. Instead they believe that what we are born with is the starting line not the finish line and as such they can improve, enhance and add to those attributes with effort, practice and perseverance. An individual with a growth mindset believes that their potential is unknown and the development of that potential is down to what they are prepared to do to manifest it.

We are all born with a growth mindset. Children are not fazed by learning and change, they are not threatened by it and embrace it without fear. But over time that changes and failure becomes something to avoid; fear becomes distorted into cynicism as a way to avoid even trying.

We are actually trained in the fixed mindset from a very early age. In school we are praised for being smart, which of course implies that not being smart is a sin. We are congratulated for winning and rarely for effort, which means we learn to 'game' the winning and minimize the effort. Have you ever watched a football game for 10-year-olds? The kids are just having fun but the parents are yelling instructions from the sidelines, desperate for their child to put in a good performance and secure the victory! We are encouraged to produce perfect work first time so we can receive a gold star or smiley face. All of these messages confirm what we are beginning to suspect – failure is unacceptable. Eventually we decide the easiest and surest way to avoid failure is to stop actually trying. We become paralysed by the need to maintain a façade of perfection, competence and expertise and as such we actively stop the learning process dead in its tracks. And without learning or the willingness to learn change becomes virtually impossible.

There is a great TEDx presentation by Peter Bregman that talks about the power of uncertainty and admitting that we don't know the answers. Being able to admit that we don't know is actually part of the growth mindset and it's an extremely potent weapon in the process of change.

Bregman's first job was as an outward bound instructor. In his presentation he recalls the time when we was first appointed as the course director – responsible for a two-day retreat for 150 teenagers. He'd designed a comprehensive activities plan and shared his plan with the eight instructors that were helping him to manage and coordinate the group. Unfortunately, his coordinators were less enthusiastic about his plan and voiced their concerns that it would not work with 13- and 14-year-olds. But Bregman was confident he knew what he was doing so pushed it through. Then, as he states, 'four Greyhound buses drove up to the camp and all hell broke loose'. The teenagers immediately started arguing with the instructors and they had no qualms about sharing their thoughts on just how boring the programme was. Bregman didn't know what to do. So he found an empty room and freaked out. After composing himself and realizing that he actually didn't have any idea how to fix the situation he assembled his instructors, apologized for not listening to them and admitted he was stumped as to how to rectify the situation.

To his utter amazement one by one the instructors started offering really innovative solutions. One lady, who had originally been his most vocal opponent, stood up and said she had a background in theatre. She suggested rounding up all the kids who were interested in acting and they would create and put on a show about the issues facing teenagers, which they would then perform to the rest of the group the following evening. Another instructor said that there was a bunch of Polaroid cameras in the resource supplies so she could take the kids who were interested in photography into the surrounding woodland and create some instant photography montage. One by one the instructors suggested solutions that he would never have thought of and the retreat was rescued (Bregman, 2012).

Bregman suggests that this was the most important early lesson of his career. By having the courage to apologize and admit he didn't have all the answers he created an opportunity for positive change.

Understanding the process of change and knowing what to expect can help people relax into the change. Encourage those involved in change to experiment, admit when they don't know and foster a mindset of openness and curiosity – all valuable skills for successful change. People need to appreciate that they will feel anxious and awkward as the change progresses but that they will be supported and it will be a safe environment for them to test out their new skills and, with help, make the transition. Just knowing that no one is expecting perfection straight off the bat can allow people to relax and make the change at their own pace (within reason).

The TLA Action Plan

Once people understand change and know what to expect during the process it's time to create the TLA Action Plan and explain the transition between the launch of the change initiative and the individual follow-up conversations (Figure 5.1).

FIGURE 5.1   Transition between the training event and TLA

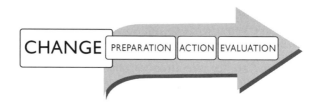

Anyone who has been involved in corporate training programmes will already be familiar with action plans – usually completed at the end of the training event. Often these are rushed as the trainer, keen to deliver useful content, runs out of time. Even if enough time is allocated to the action plan and what the training participant intends to do differently back in the workplace as a result of the training, they are rarely effective. The participants have probably disengaged and are thinking about what they are going to have for dinner, not what they are going to do when they get back to work. Besides, they know that, nine times out of ten, no one will follow up on the action plan. They know therefore that they can safely write just about anything because no one will check or hold them accountable to their commitments (Weber, 2014).

As a result, when people involved in change first hear about the TLA Action Plan they will probably assume that it's the same type of action plan that they are already familiar with in the training environment. One of the key differences between the TLA Action Plan and regular action plans is that this one will actually be followed up on through a series of one-on-one conversations to help transition through the change.

TLA can be delivered externally or internally by either recruiting an external TLA specialist or having key internal HR personnel and/or managers trained in the TLA methodology. If the organization invests heavily in change initiatives or training programmes then the latter option may be more cost-effective over time. This approach integrates change capability into the business. By doing so, it propels effective change and transfer of learning that occurs as the organization invests in new processes and programmes. We will explore the advantages and disadvantages of both options in Chapter 13.

Regardless of who is best suited to deliver TLA the process begins during the change briefings or toward the end of any training that occurred around the change. The objective of the preparation stage is to have all those involved and expected to make behavioural change finish the stage with a created TLA Action Plan.

People need to appreciate that they are not expected to make the change without support and just because the change has been launched doesn't mean they can now go back to 'business as usual' and quietly ignore it! The TLA Action Plan reframes the weeks and months after the change and therefore helps to shift the momentum and energy away from a 'launch date' and onto the forthcoming action planning session.

How to create the TLA Plan

The truth is people are usually pretty cynical about action plans for all the reasons already mentioned. But they are an essential part of effective change. What separates the TLA Action Plan from traditional action plans is genuine follow-up. Most of us have had the experience of creating an action plan knowing that as soon as we are out of the room it will be stuffed in a folder, never to see the light of day again. With TLA everything that the individual documents on the action plan will be followed up on through a series of specific, structured and accountable one-on-one conversations after the change begins. We will also discuss the nuances that enable this to be an effective document for follow-up. The TLA Plan is therefore the source document which will ignite and steer the change process for each person affected by the change at an individual level.

We always recommend allowing 45–60 minutes for the TLA planning session. Typically this is held towards the end of the launch, training or communication phase of the change. It needs to happen when individuals are at the point where they know the bigger picture for the change and what is required from them. Everyone in the change briefing or training programme must have enough time to really engage with the change process, know what's being asked of them and how that translates into their everyday working life. There needs to be a clear distinction between the change initiative, change launch date or theory of the change, and the creation of the TLA Action Plan so that those expected to change their behaviour appreciate the change is not going to disappear or peter out but they are going to be held accountable for it. As such TLA is often most effective when it is delivered by someone other than the leader or initiator of the change. That 'other' person can be an HR manager, L&D professional or manager from within the business, or it can be a trained TLA facilitator from outside the business. When the leader of the change initiative and the TLA facilitator are different people then those affected by the change are better able to make a clear division between the change and the follow-up TLA process to bring that change about one individual at a time.

Each person must complete a TLA Action Plan which includes:

- their **Target(s)**;
- what **Success** looks like for them in relation to the change initiative;
- **Calibration** – where they consider themselves right now in relation to their chosen target(s);
- **Why** the target is important for them;
- their chosen **Next Steps** to achieve the target.

Target

The target, as the name would suggest, is what the individual commits to implementing or actioning in relation to the change initiative and by when.

Most modern change initiatives involve the alteration of behaviour across a number of areas, whether that is learning a new IT system, changing the process the sales team use to close sales, or an alteration to quality standards and assessment. The target allows the individual to regain some control over the situation and identify what changes to what processes or behaviours they want to initiate first. Remember we need to feel as though we exercise at least some measure of control over our own lives in order to feel energized and engaged. Getting the individual to choose what they want to change first helps them to regain some sense of control over the process and also further attaches them to those outcomes because of something known as the endowment effect. Behavioural science has proven time and time again that people are much more invested in things they had a hand in creating.

Ideally the TLA Action Plan should include three goals or targets, chosen by the individual around the change initiative. The targets need to be realistic and achievable but also represent a bit of a stretch for the individual – so not too easy, not too hard. If the target is too easy then there will be no impetus behind achieving it, and even if they do achieve it, it won't feel like a real win, so no progress will have really been made. If it's too hard then the individual will assume it's impossible from the start and won't even try.

The target needs to reflect what the individual thinks will give them benefit back in the workplace. Some of the actions may be fairly literal and task-focused or others may be about communication or relationships that need to change to make the overall project successful. Although the desired outcome is to facilitate behavioural change, usually in a specific direction, it's important to acknowledge whatever the individual identifies as a target. For example the change initiative could be the transition from one database to another. The intended alteration in behaviour is to encourage and support people who need to use the new system to actually use it but if someone identifies a target of, say, creating more workspace, then it's highly likely that target will impact the ability of that person to use the new system. If they physically can't get on the system or there are too many people trying to access it then addressing this issue is going to ultimately assist in the behavioural change.

It's important to understand that each TLA Action Plan is a personal document unique to the individual and each person needs to be encouraged to view it as their personal success map. More often than not the targets will relate to the change initiative but it's not essential. If other issues are taking up 'head space' for those completing their plan then it's always best to encourage the person to put those issues on the plan so that they can be dealt with. Ignoring them and simply encouraging them to refocus on the change will rarely work, whereas helping them to address whatever is holding them back in the change initiative or outside will usually fast-track progress and engagement.

Sometimes during this target-setting phase people are tempted to say 'Let's give them example targets of things other people have done or the type of things we need or want to happen.' While it's tempting, giving people examples can help to shape their thinking and become too prescriptive. Essentially we want the person involved in the change to think about what is important to them to achieve ownership of the process.

Each individual affected by the change will reflect on what is important to them and what is causing them problems. They know this far better than the TLA facilitator does so acknowledge that and allow them to take ownership of the targets. Solving issues – even issues that have no obvious bearing on the change you are seeking – will help them do a better job and will ensure that they are then freed up to do other things on their TLA Plan that may be more relevant to the change initiative.

It's also worth noting here that some people get really hung up on creating SMART targets – Specific, Measurable, Attainable, Realistic and Time-bound. What's more important is to capture the essence and the calibration (more on that in a moment) of the target and then probe more deeply in the follow-up conversation. If an individual wants to create SMART targets they can but it's not necessary. If an individual enjoys adding SMART detail to their targets they can but if they don't enjoy it, making them adhere to SMART will simply drain all the energy and motivation from the process.

Appendix 1 illustrates what a strong TLA Action plan looks like.

Success

For the success part of the TLA Action Plan individuals need to imagine their ideal future in relation to the change. What we are aiming for here is for each person to imagine their working life and environment after the change has been successfully implemented and they are familiar and comfortable with the new behaviours. Get each person to consider how they will know when they have been successful in implementing their chosen target. What will they see happening around them? What will people be saying about their new ability, skill or performance? How will they feel?

In success the participant is encouraged to use their senses to describe the desired outcome. In other words get them to imagine what they would see, hear and feel so that they can get a deeper appreciation of what success for them would be like. This acknowledges different learning styles and ensures that each person taps into their favoured motivational modality.

Calibration

Calibration asks each person to rate, on a scale of 1 (low) to 10 (high) where they consider themselves to be today against each target they identified.

This approach provides a very insightful and useful measurement of the gap they feel they need to bridge in order to meet the target. And it is particularly useful for change that focuses on altering soft skill behaviour. Say the company wants all their managers to use coaching techniques with their direct reports. In order to work out if any progress is made over time we first have to establish a baseline for how often they coach their people and how successful they are at coaching people currently. Without a tool like calibration even the initial self-assessment can be complicated. Besides, it's really a matter of personal opinion.

Calibration dispenses with the complexity and challenges inherent in self-assessment and instead asks each person to rank their coaching skills on a scale from 1 to 10. More often than not they will give an almost immediate response. They will automatically reflect on that question, think about their current experience, the outcome of events and situations that have already called on their coaching skills and arrive at a number between 1 and 10. Their subconscious mind provides an answer, their conscious mind may not always be able to explain the number or articulate why but on some level the individual was giving a measured albeit unconscious or instinctive response.

The beauty of calibration is that it actually doesn't matter how the person arrived at that number or even if the change manager or their line manager thinks it's an accurate reflection of their current skill level. What matters is that the participant has graded themselves on their coaching skill at the point of creating their TLA Action Plan. This is now the benchmark on which to measure progress throughout the follow-up conversations.

There are those who may argue that the measurement of the baseline needs to be much more scientific than calibration but for the purpose of helping someone change it doesn't. Spending too long trying to establish the baseline or getting too hung up on some mathematical formula can very easily drain any energy or impetus that may exist around the change. By asking each person to record their gut instinct on where they are at the moment against that behavioural change allows us to create a baseline in seconds. If someone assigns their current skill level at six, that's the baseline. They may tell the facilitator that they believe they can get that to a nine and will also probably be able to state how they envisage doing that. It doesn't matter what the metric was. And it doesn't even matter if they call it a six and the facilitator thinks they are probably more a three or an eight. What matters is that the individual assigned a starting place from which they and the TLA facilitator can measure subsequent progress.

This type of gut response is known as 'thin slicing' and refers to our subconscious ability to find patterns in situations and behaviour based on a very narrow slice of experience (Gladwell, 2005). When asked to rate or calibrate their current skill level on a score of 1–10 each person will instinctively thin-slice their knowledge and experience and arrive at a number.

Calibration is therefore about trusting that first response so we can get into action. It is simple, easy to use and quickly establishes a baseline for the objective. If someone identifies their current coaching skill level as a six and feels that they can elevate that to a nine then they have effectively identified the gap between where they are now and where they want to be. Closing this gap will therefore be the focus of the follow-up conversations.

Why

Next is 'Why' the individual has chosen their targets in the first place. By being encouraged to really engage with the target and their vision of success they are better able to connect to the motivation behind that target. This part of the TLA Plan asks, 'Why do you want to achieve this? What does it mean to you personally? Why is that important to you?'

Nothing is achieved without effort. Regardless of the target everyone also experiences setbacks and roadblocks as they navigate the change. These challenges can very easily derail progress – especially if the individual is not even sure why they are making the change. Unless we bring the 'Why' into conscious awareness and get the individual to connect to it, it becomes too easy to give up and move on to a new target.

It's also important to understand that each person's 'Why' may be very different and does not necessarily relate to the change initiative. For example, going back to the coaching skills example, one manager's 'Why' may be anything from wanting to creating ownership within his team, reducing the pressure on himself to work long hours, to improving the engagement scores for him as a manager so he can further his career, gaining a promotion. They have varying levels of connectedness with the company's bigger-picture aim for implementing a coaching approach to management, but when the individual can find a personal reason, one that's important to him, for making the change, he is much more likely to stay energised through the process and so persevere with the change when it would be easier to quit.

The TLA Plan is a very personal document and it details why something is important to the individual creating the plan, not necessarily why the change is important to the business, boss or department. It's the individual's own 'Why' that is critical and it is this motivation that will keep the person on track.

One of the simplest ways to uncover someone's 'Why' is to continuously ask, 'And why is that important to you?' For each target the individual has identified they must state why it's important, whatever answer springs to mind. They then ask, 'And why is that important?' and so on until the individual arrives at the real reason that the target is important. This drives back to the real heart of the matter, allowing people to really connect to that reason so they can then reconnect to it if and when motivation starts to slide.

Take the example from earlier, where management have implemented a change initiative to ensure that their senior managers use coaching techniques with the staff to improve communication and elevate productivity. The relevant managers have all been given one-on-one coaching themselves to appreciate its value and taught how to use the same techniques on others. In the TLA action planning session one of the managers creates a target of improving the working relationships with his staff.

The manager would then be encouraged to drill down into that target to get to a more personal and meaningful 'Why' by answering the following question:

Q: Why is that important to you?

A: Improving the working relationships will make life easier.

Q: Why is that important to you?

A: Because some of the relationships are challenging and I'd like them to improve.

Q: Why is that important to you?

A: Because it will improve efficiency and productivity in the department.

Q: Why is that important to you?

A: Because I may then get promoted.

Q: Why is that important to you?

A: Because I'd like to move to a bigger house so my family has a better home.

By repeatedly asking the 'Why' question the purpose transforms from making life easier at work to providing for his family. There is no right or wrong answer; it's just a simple method to help the individual connect to what is genuinely important to them rather than necessarily what's important for the business or the boss. This process usually also highlights a person's beliefs and values, which can be very helpful during the coaching process.

Change is a personal journey; for someone to want to take that journey and stay focused on the destination they usually have to identify a personal reward. Only when someone can genuinely see the personal and professional advantages of embracing change will they engage with the process and actually make the behavioural change. The higher the level of ownership of the target the greater the likelihood of change and forward momentum.

Giving each individual control over the targets they choose and the space to drill down into those targets to find personal meaning also acknowledges that each person is the expert in their own job and life so they will be far better placed to identify how that change could best serve them than the facilitator or business is. Even if the target they identify turns out to be wrong, they will discover that themselves during the TLA conversations and as such will be much more involved and engaged in the process. No one likes to be told what to do so it's far more beneficial to assume each person is best suited to identify the biggest win or the best outcomes for their own situation.

Next steps

Anyone who is familiar with action plans will already know about the Next Steps section. This part of the TLA Plan seeks to establish what action the individual can take toward the target within the next 48 hours.

It is important for the momentum of the change that those expected to change their behaviour break through the resistance and inertia quickly and get into some type of positive action. The more time passes between the launch of the change and those involved engaging with it personally and doing something, the less likely the change will take root. Engaging each person in what they plan to do next and what they will do before the first TLA follow-up conversation ensures that they stay in motion toward their stated targets.

The importance of Next Steps was demonstrated by psychologist Professor Richard Wiseman who conducted two large-scale studies into the psychology of motivation, involving 5,000 participants from around the world (2009). Participants were tracked for between six months and a year as they attempted to achieve a wide range of goals ranging from a career change to weight loss. By the end of the experiment only 10 per cent had achieved what they set out to achieve. Of those 10 per cent all broke their aspiration or goal down into a series of sub-goals and next steps so as to create a step-by-step action plan. This acted as a road map for the journey toward change whilst also helping to remove the fear and overwhelm often felt when making change. Next Steps are about making that initial, often tentative step toward change. Getting into action is the key; even if that action is small it starts the process of change and gathers momentum. Wiseman also found that the successful people in the study stayed focused on the benefits they would gain from making the change, they told other people about their aspirations and their goals were concrete, specific, time-bound and documented in writing.

Once each person has completed Next Steps they have their TLA Action Plan. This document will then form the template for the coming weeks and the focus of the TLA conversations so that the targets they identify come to fruition. Although each person will be held accountable for delivering and following through on the targets they identify they are not set in stone the minute they are recorded in the TLA Action Plan. If someone decides between the change launch and start of the TLA conversations that they want to change a target they can, but it's essential that a plan is completed for each person. A completed TLA Action Plan can be viewed in Appendix 1 and a blank form can also be downloaded from the website: **www.transferoflearning.com/resources.**

Once everyone has completed their TLA Action Plan they need to be recorded and distributed. How this is done and who receives the TLA Action Plans will depend on each situation and the confidentiality that has been agreed within the process. As a minimum they should be photocopied, ideally on the spot, and the originals returned to each individual.

Each person must also have confirmed a definite time and date for their first TLA follow-up conversation. Where possible, it's always best if the participant chooses their preferred time and date as this improves buy-in and ownership. This can be achieved through one-on-one discussion or you can simply make a variety of dates and times available on a calendar and each participant can choose their preferred slot. We will discuss this further in Chapter 13 where we discuss how to roll out in scalable projects.

The only documentation left to complete is the TLA Change Agreement.

The TLA Change Agreement

The final piece of preparation is the TLA Change Agreement, which each person involved in the change reads and signs.

Basically the agreement sets up the expectations of the change participant and the TLA facilitator. The agreement covers things like:

- how the conversations will take place;
- confidentiality;
- how many conversations the individual can expect;
- how long each conversation will last;
- the optimum environment for that conversation;
- how the session will be documented;
- what the participant can expect from the facilitator and vice versa;
- signatures from the individual and the TLA specialist.

This Change Agreement serves several purposes. The information covered in the agreement is typically discussed verbally with the group but documenting it means if anything is missed verbally or misremembered the employee can go back to the agreement to review it. It also clarifies and emphasizes what the individual is signing up to and therefore further demonstrates that they are going to be held accountable during the change process. Signing the document physically creates a deeper level of commitment.

The Change Agreement is a moral agreement regarding conduct, confidentiality and expectations for the TLA sessions. It's important that each individual knows that the conversation that takes place in the follow-up TLA sessions is confidential, which helps them to relax into the process and get the most out of it. Of course, the level of confidentiality varies depending on the initiative but even if the session actions are shared internally the detail of the sessions never are. The agreement also sets out how the sessions will take place, when they will take place and how long they will take, so people know what to expect from each conversation. In the same way that our friend was reassured by the detail provided by the nurse prior to her laser eye surgery, change participants are reassured by the detail of the Change Agreement prior to the TLA process.

The phasing of the TLA conversations will vary depending on the project. Typically the flow would be with the initial conversation being scheduled to occur within two weeks of the change briefing or change launch to maintain momentum. The second conversation will take place three to four weeks after the first, and the third three to four weeks after the second. And each TLA conversation will last 20 minutes.

Once the individual is told the details they can see that they will have ownership and control over the conversation because they will initiate the conversation to the TLA facilitator or coach. This is important so that the participant doesn't feel that the process is something that is done to them, but rather something they do and control. The Change Agreement also lays out the required environment for the conversation. These conversations are short, punchy and action orientated; they are not polite chats about the weather so both parties need to be focused on the conversation which means no mobile phones, no e-mail and no multitasking. The individual must ensure they are in a quiet place where they will be disturbed for the duration of the conversation. The agreement also clarifies responsibilities, meaning the individual making the change documents their own action points from each conversation – again putting them and keeping them in the driver's seat of change. And finally the agreement sets out the expectations and ground rules for the process so the participant and the facilitator are on the same page.

There is considerable evidence that when someone consciously commits to a process and signs up to a code of conduct they are much more likely to follow through on that personal commitment.

In one experiment, two social scientists solicited college students to volunteer for an education project to be carried out in local schools. Students were encouraged to volunteer by either filling out a form and actively volunteering, or not filling out a form that said they did not want to participate and therefore passively volunteering. Those that completed a form and actively volunteered kept their commitment 49 per cent of the time, whereas those who passively volunteered only kept their commitment 17 per cent of the time. Of all the people who turned up as scheduled to help with the education programme 74 per cent had actively volunteered (Goldstein, Martin and Cialdini, 2007).

Reading the Change Agreement and then committing to that agreement with a signature helps to hold everyone involved to a higher standard and emphasizes the seriousness of the process they are about to embark on.

At this early stage the TLA facilitator shouldn't worry too much about the level of commitment. People will only really buy in to the process and the conversations when they start to see the benefits. Quite often people don't get the relevance or impact of supporting change in this way until they start to make changes and see the results.

A sample TLA Change Agreement can be viewed in Appendix 2 and a blank version is available to download from the website: **http://transferoflearning.com/resources/**.

This preparation stage is crucial in setting the scene, ensuring that those expected to change appreciate the change process and are encouraged to get into the right frame of mind around the change. It also clarifies that what they are about to embark on may be quite different to previous change initiatives because ongoing follow-through in the TLA conversations is going to support them through the change and hold them accountable for the targets they have identified. Now it's time for the ACTION phase.

Summary of key points

- As the name would suggest the preparation stage of TLA is focused on what the people involved in the change need to know and expect from the change initiative and the follow-up TLA process.

- Often people can think that preparation before the change is basically a euphemism for 'revving up the troops'. It's not.

- It's always wise to reassure people about the nature of change and how change actually occurs for human beings. Behavioural change spirals through phases.

- Even when those involved in change feel that they are making progress there is almost always a lapse as the individual will stumble and retreat back to old behaviours. As a result change is not linear; it is not a step-by-step forward process. Instead it can feel more like the individual is taking two steps forward and three back.

- Unfortunately this non-linear progress can feel remarkably like failure.

- If this normal change process is fully explained to the people most affected at the start they know what to expect and are therefore less likely to be discouraged when those experiences arise.

- If we know what to expect and recognize the signs and symptoms of change as and when they arrive, rather than being upset or put off by them, then we are much more likely to follow through and experience the full benefit of change.

- Behavioural change is rarely an on/off phenomenon; it's a gradual process. More often than not lapses are the rule rather than the exception, and knowing that up front can make change much less daunting and much more likely to stick.

- The best way to create change is to get those involved to want to change for their own reasons by activating their intrinsic motivation.

- This is backed up and expanded upon by David Rock, who proposes the SCARF model to explain our behavioural reactions to change.

- Delving into the field of social science Rock suggests that much of our social behaviour is governed by the need to minimize threat and maximize reward and that several domains of social experience draw upon the same brain networks used for primary survival needs. Or as Rock puts it, 'social needs are treated in much the same way in the brain as the need for food and water [in the body]'.

- The SCARF model therefore summarizes the common factors that can activate a reward or threat response in social situations. SCARF is an acronym of these factors, namely: status, certainty, autonomy, relatedness and fairness.

- These five domains activate either the 'primary reward' or 'primary threat' circuitry (and associated networks) of the brain.

- Everyone experiences the same or similar feelings when trying to change behaviour and often just knowing that can make a massive difference to our willingness and ability to persevere and see the change through to successful implementation.

- Almost all change requires learning of some sort. Unfortunately by the time we are involved in company-sponsored change initiatives we are adults, and that can make change even more difficult.

- By the time we reach adulthood we have evolved through various developmental levels including the one that makes us acutely aware of what we look like. This developmental level kicks in during the teenage years and social conditioning and peer pressure become very important influencers of decision making.

- As a result by the time we are adults we will do just about anything to avoid situations where failure is even an option, and sadly learning new information so we can change behaviour is one of those situations.

- Stanford University psychologist Carol Dweck proposes that it is our mindset that determines our ability to handle failure and therefore our ability to change. Everything in life comes down to mindset and she believes that there are only two – fixed and growth.

- When an individual has a fixed mindset they believe that their skills, abilities and natural talent are down to a genetic quirk of fate. What they are capable of is essentially carved in stone at birth – determined by their genetic makeup and environment.

- When an individual has a growth mindset they do not believe that their relative attributes are carved in stone. Instead they believe that what we are born with is the starting line not the finish line and as such they can improve, enhance and add to those attributes with effort, practice and perseverance.

- We are all born with a growth mindset. Children are not fazed by learning and change; they are not threatened by it and embrace it without fear. But over time that changes as failure becomes something to avoid, and fear becomes distorted into cynicism as a way to avoid even trying.

- Understanding the process of change and knowing what to expect can help people relax into the change. Encourage those involved in change to experiment, admit when they don't know and foster a growth mindset.

- Once people understand change and know what to expect during the process it's time to create the TLA Action Plan and explain the transition between the launch of the change initiative and the individual follow-up conversations.

- It's worth pointing out that the TLA Action Plan is different to any action plan they have probably encountered because this one will actually be followed up on through a series of one-on-one conversations to help transition through the change.

- The TLA Action Plan reframes the weeks and months after the change and therefore helps to shift the momentum and energy away from a 'launch date' and onto the forthcoming action planning session.

- It is the source document which will ignite and steer the change process for each person affected by the change at an individual level.

- Allow 45–60 minutes for the TLA planning session. Typically this is held at the end of the launch or communication phase of the change, when people need to start doing things differently.

- There needs to be a clear distinction between the change initiative, change launch date or theory of the change, and the creation of the TLA Action Plan so that those expected to change their behaviour appreciate the change is not going to disappear or peter out but they are going to be held accountable for it.

- Each person must complete a TLA Action Plan which includes:

  - their **Target(s)**;

  - what **Success** looks like for them in relation to the change initiative;

  - **Calibration** – where they consider themselves right now in relation to their chosen target(s);

  - **Why** the target is important for them;

  - their chosen **Next Steps** to achieve the target.

- Once each person has completed their TLA Action Plan, it is recorded and distributed. It then forms the template for the coming weeks and the focus of the TLA conversations so that the targets they identify come to fruition.

- Each person must also have confirmed a definite time and date for their first TLA follow-up conversation. Where possible, it's always best if the participant chooses their preferred time and date as this improves buy-in and ownership.

- The final piece of preparation is the TLA Change Agreement which each person involved in the change must read and sign. It sets up the expectations of the change participant and the TLA facilitator.

References

Bregman, P (2012) I Don't Know, *TEDx* [online] http://tedxtalks.ted.com/video/
TEDxMillRiver-Peter-Bregman-I-D

Dweck, C (2007) *Mindset: The new psychology of success*, Ballantine Books,
New York

Gladwell, M (2005) *Blink: The power of thinking without thinking*, Little Brown
and Company, New York

Goldstein, N J, Martin, S J and Cialdini, R B (2007) *Yes! 50 secrets from the
science of persuasion*, Profile Books, London

Gordon, E (2000) *Integrative Neuroscience: Bringing together biological,
psychological and clinical models of the human brain*, Harwood Academic
Publishers, Singapore

Lieberman, M and Eisenberger, N (2008) The Pains and Pleasures of Social Life,
NeuroLeadership Journal, Edition 1

Prochaska, J O, Norcross, J and DiClemente, C (2007) *Changing for Good: A
revolutionary six-stage program for overcoming bad habits and moving your
life positively forward*, Harper Collins, New York

Rock, D (2008) SCARF: A brain-based model for collaborating with and
influencing others, *NeuroLeadership Journal* Edition 1 [online]
http://www.davidrock.net/files/NLJ_SCARFUS.pdf

Rock, D (2009) *Your Brain at Work: Strategies for overcoming distraction,
regaining focus, and working smarter all day long*, Harper Business, New York

Weber, E (2014) *Turning Learning into Action: A proven methodology for effective
transfer of learning*, Kogan Page, London

Wiseman, R (2009) *59 Seconds: Think a little change a lot*, Pan Macmillan,
London

ACTION
conversation

06

The next stage of the TLA process is action. This is where the follow-up conversations actually take place over a period of several weeks after the change initiative is launched and begins in earnest. This is the actual process that will move someone from their old behaviour to the new desired behaviour. This chapter explores in more detail how that is actually done. We will unpack the ACTION Conversation Model to demonstrate the dichotomy between structure and flexibility that makes TLA so potent, and separates it from traditional coaching conversations.

Essentially, the TLA specialist engages in a very tailored and specific coaching conversation where they ask questions in an effort to get the individual to take ownership for the changes they are being asked to make.

Each TLA follow-up conversation moves through the ACTION Conversation Model (Figure 6.1). This model unpacks the theory and provides a framework that then guides those conversations.

FIGURE 6.1   The TLA ACTION Conversation Model

The ACTION Conversation Model expresses the fluidity between structure and flexibility that we discussed in Chapter 4. It is this balance between structure and flexibility that creates the results and separates TLA from traditional coaching.

TLA vs traditional coaching

The most frequent response we hear on explaining TLA is, 'Oh right, so you are talking about coaching.' Whether embedded in learning and development or change initiatives most people in business – certainly those at a more senior level – have heard about coaching. Very often managers are trained in a coaching methodology so they can get the best out of their team. All three authors have met many managers who have been taught basic coaching techniques for that exact purpose. Of course knowing how to do something and then actually doing it are two very different things.

This jack-of-all-trades approach to coaching is often proposed as the solution to a wide and varied range of business issues. In fact it's the versatility of coaching skills that so often attracts businesses to acquiring these skills. Unfortunately it is the same versatility that is often traditional coaching's downfall.

The manager may learn a few coaching techniques in a half-day coaching course or during a module of a broader leadership training programme but the teaching environment rarely resembles the real work environment. So the enthusiastic manager tries out their new-found coaching skills with a staff member, only the staff member doesn't answer the question the way the training suggested they might. With the manager confused and unsure how to get the conversation back on track the discussion fizzles out and both go their separate ways feeling frustrated and decidedly underwhelmed by the 'coaching process'. Coaching is a conversation and as such it's very easy to assume 'everyone can do it'. Everyone can coach but it is not an automatic or easy skill to learn and it is certainly not something that can be perfected in a few hours.

Coaching as most people recognize the term is too fluid and flexible. As a result it works sometimes for some people and not for others, and the people involved don't really understand why. The basic coaching so often taught to managers therefore becomes the proverbial 'jack-of-all-trades' and master-of-none. It's very difficult to work out the actual skills we need to be a good coach when those skills are applicable to so many different scenarios and it is much easier to learn a skill when there are very definite parameters around what we are trying to achieve.

TLA is a very specific application of coaching which removes all the guesswork and creates a structure that identifies very definite parameters around effective behavioural change. By adding much-needed structure the TLA specialist puts the individual in charge of their own change process and then holds them accountable for the commitments to change that they made in the TLA Action Plan.

As a result TLA takes the flexibility of traditional coaching and adds structure to the coaching process to effectively facilitate behavioural change. This fine balance between flexibility and structure is what creates the results while also removing the ambiguity from the coaching process.

Traditional coaching is often too flexible, creative and free flowing. Being listened to in a coaching conversation can often feel incredibly nurturing and enjoyable but it doesn't necessarily translate into concrete results and it certainly doesn't guarantee behaviour change.

It can lead to behaviour change when it's done properly but the vast majority of coaching is not done properly because it's not done with a firm enough action focus. Although the model on which most coaching is built does include action, the execution of that model in real work situations rarely focuses on action.

Instead people get too carried away with the reflective part of the conversation and fail to convert that to tangible outcomes. Consequently the coaching conversation dissolves into a discussion and analysis of the individual's personal 'story' – part naval gazing, part psychiatrist's couch. There is no place for such diversions in TLA. The focus is firmly on action and what the individual needs to do before the next discussion around the targets they have already identified.

TLA is not a passive process; it is not something that can be done to someone without their consent or involvement. If we think about having a conversation with someone to help them move from A to B we need to think about what is going to work and what is not going to work. So we all know that it doesn't work to be told; we know that we need to encourage the individual to work it out for themselves. We all know that no one takes advice unless it's what they secretly thought anyway. We all know that we have to get the individual crystal clear about where they currently are and where they want to be so as to help them close the gap between the two. TLA, with its specific balance between structure and flexibility, takes someone from where they are to where they want to be in the context of change.

The tightness of the logistics also sets TLA apart from regular coaching. 'In-the-moment coaching' or 'coaching moments' has created a shift toward coaching and a coaching culture in many organizations. At least that's the plan. The reality, however, is that finding 'coaching moments' or engaging in 'in-the-moment coaching' is not easy. It requires a shift of mindset from the person doing the coaching and often requires them to change 'hat' from their traditional managerial role. Plus the accountability is often the missing piece of the puzzle, which means that even if a manager by some miracle manages to switch 'hats' and slip into coaching mode to coach an employee, they rarely follow through with accountability and check in to make sure the individual has actually actioned what was discussed. Accountability needs a certain level of structure that is difficult to manufacture in the moment or subsequent moments. Setting aside a structured time to focus on the change – even for a constructive 20-minute conversation – can pay huge dividends and this is at the heart of the TLA methodology. TLA facilitates a fast, deep and sustaining conversation which can in turn create sustained change. The methodology will demonstrate how the process can work at such speeds.

The ACTION Conversation Model

The ACTION Conversation Model is an acronym for the various stages that the conversation must pass through, from structure to flexibility and back to structure, in order to successfully facilitate behavioural change in the workplace.

- **A** – Accountability: Setting up the context of the process and the TLA facilitator/participant relationship.
- **C** – Calibration: Calibrating a score for where the individual is now, and the score for where they want to get to.
- **T** – Target: Where is the individual trying to get to? What's the target for the project?
- **I** – Information: Gather information about what is happening in the workplace.
- **O** – Options: What options does the individual have in this situation? What could they do?
- **N** – Next Steps: How is the individual going to commit to action and move toward the target? How do both parties follow this up?

The TLA conversation travels through a process of Structure – Flexibility – Structure (Figure 6.2). If we think of any accomplishment in life there is always a dance between structure and flexibility. Watching a play at the theatre we might be amazed at the performance, which may seem so spontaneous and creative and yet there was a great deal of structure and discipline required to pull it off. Watching a swimmer break a world record may appear like poetry in motion, but behind the scenes that athlete left nothing to chance, and no stone was left unturned in her quest for that record. Even when something looks effortless, natural and fluid, there is always structure behind the scenes that makes that creativity possible and the same is true for behavioural change.

FIGURE 6.2 The interplay of structure and flexibility within the ACTION model

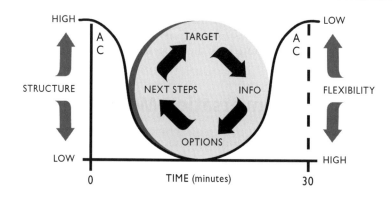

Structure – start

The initial structure is made up of accountability and calibration and it is these elements that give the TLA follow-up conversation a structure and context. Without this formality the conversation can easily degenerate into a chat about what might be possible or what would be nice rather than a committed conversation in the context of the change about action, accountability and outcome.

The reason TLA is so effective is because every conversation opens and closes with structure in the form of accountability and calibration.

Accountability

The accountability process begins with the scene-setting part of preparation when individuals are told about the TLA process, complete the TLA Action Plan, and sign the Change Agreement. Then, at the opening of the first TLA conversation and each subsequent conversation the participants are reminded of their responsibilities to the process and how they are ultimately accountable for their own success.

Of course, accountability is a two-way street. The facilitator of the TLA follow-up conversations is also accountable to the individual. It is imperative that the facilitator manages the conversation from the start and manages the individual's expectations about what is about to occur. This exchange of information acts to reassure the individual about what to expect, especially in the first conversation, and it also reminds the individual that there is a process being followed to maximize results.

At the start of the first conversation in the series the TLA facilitator needs to cover the following set points:

1 Provide positive reinforcement if the conversation started on time.

2 Check in with the individual. 'How was your morning/afternoon so far?'

3 Use 'You'll remember...' to remind the individual what was covered at the end of the training or set-up process for the change.

4 Tell the individual how long the conversation will last.

5 Reiterate that the conversation is confidential.

6 Remind the individual that they are encouraged to give feedback at the end of the process.

7 Remind the individual about the best use of time for both parties.

8 Ask their permission to manage the conversation.

9 Ask for ownership from them.

10 Remind them that they need to take their own notes and have their TLA Action Plan handy.

11 Ask questions of the participant to establish the context for the conversation.

12 Ask, 'Are there are any questions before we start?'

13 Close out this opening section by adding, 'Great! Let's start with your action plan; which goal would you like us to start with today?'

We'll cover who is best suited to roll out TLA in Chapter 13 but the level of confidentiality in the conversation will depend on whether the TLA is being facilitated by an internal specialist or change agent within the business or an external specialist.

Here is an example of the structured start of the conversation at a first session.

Hi Julie – thanks for being punctual and calling through on time. It certainly helps to make my day run smoothly so I really appreciate it. [1]

So tell me – how have you been since the change initiative was announced? [2]

Well, Julie, you'll remember from the briefing that today's conversation is about supporting you through the change so you can make the transition as quickly and effectively as possible and we'll be using your TLA Action Plan as a base for our work. [3]

Our conversation today will last around 20 minutes. Just to remind you that everything we cover is confidential and the only feedback that goes to your company is what you choose to relay at the end of the TLA process via your feedback form. [4,5,6]

Obviously 20 minutes can fly by in no time so can I just confirm with you that if I feel we either need to go into a little bit more detail or take a bigger picture view I'm OK to flag that with you so we can stay on track and make the best use of your time. Equally if you think we are covering material that you just don't think is relevant then be sure to let me know so we can shift focus for maximum results. [7, 8]

Just to be clear, TLA is a discussion-based process where we have a conversation – we get clear on where you are now, where you want to get to and then we work together to assist you in moving forward to bridge the gap between the two. It's not about me telling you what to do because you are the expert in your life, including your job, but we may brainstorm ideas and share experiences to help you come up with next steps that work for you. [9]

One final bit of admin, Julie – we'll be using your TLA Action Plan as a base but you might want to take some notes during the conversation. Have you got a pen, paper and your TLA Plan handy? If you need me to slow down or recap so you can jot down the things that are important to you then just let me know. [10]

OK – one of the things that helps me to stand in your shoes is to have a bit of understanding about you. If you could tell me a little bit about your role, how long you've been with your company and how many people you have on your team that would be great. So do you want to tell me a little bit about yourself? [11]

Excellent – that helps put your TLA Action Plan in context. Thank you. Now the admin is all done. Before we start, Julie, do you have any questions about me or the TLA follow-up process? [12]

Let's begin...
I've got your TLA Action Plan in front of me here and you've highlighted three areas you want to work on to help deliver the change project for your

company. We'll take these one at a time so which one would you like us to start on today? [13]

The outline above is for the first TLA conversation following the start of the change initiative. Each subsequent call has a similar level of structure at the start of the conversation albeit with a little less emphasis on scene-setting and a little more emphasis on accountability for the agreed actions carried over from the previous conversation. This level of accountability is essential to the success of the TLA process.

At the start of the second and third TLA conversations the facilitator needs to:

1 welcome the participant;

2 set the scene for today's conversation;

3 check on progress;

4 identify what 'gap' or what aspect of the change initiative the participant wants to address in today's conversation.

This reminds the participant of the process, how it works, and allows them to get excited about what they have achieved so far or disappointed if they haven't gained any traction – either way the emotion will spur them forward. The facilitator might say:

Morning, Julie, how has your day been so far? Are you ready to get stuck into this today? [1]

Ideally today we can talk through the specific actions that you generated last time and you can update me on how you are progressing with those. Then we will go back to your original TLA Action Plan and review where that leaves us and then we can decide what we want to use our time for today. Is that OK with you? [2]

So last time's actions were… Do you want to give me an update? [3]

If achieved: *That's an outstanding effort – well done – it sounds like you've made some good progress.*

If not achieved: *Taking a moment to think about that – is that something that is still important to you?* (It's important that the TLA facilitator verifies what they are being told but we'll cover more on how to handle what happens if people haven't followed through on their commitments in Chapter 12.)

OK, great, so what would you like to focus on today? [4]

Calibration

Remember, calibration is about gaining an early benchmark on the individual's current ability around the required change versus where they would like to be. Calibration therefore acts as the bridge between the structured part of the conversation and the flexible part of the conversation. A skilled facilitator will use calibration repeatedly during the TLA process.

At the change briefing or when the participant created their TLA Action Plan they will have scored their current ability against each of their chosen targets. At the start of each subsequent TLA conversation the participant will be asked to calibrate their new score. Once a target for the conversation or sessions is established calibration can be used to ascertain a start point so that progress or otherwise can be assessed in the next conversation. This might include asking the participant questions such as:

- *You noted that you were at a 3 around that change when it was first started – where do you think you are now?*
- *What are you doing differently to achieve this change?*
- *What is the maximum score you think you can get to on this within three months?*

Before starting to work on a particular target, the TLA facilitator needs to check in with the individual to calibrate their own position so as to establish where they consider they have moved to since the change process began or since the previous conversation.

Imagine company A decides that they need to implement a new sales process to capitalize on the changing way their customers are purchasing. This will usually involve a number of changes, from the way orders are processed to the script used by telephone sales executives. When the change is announced and explained to those involved, and they are asked about their current ability to use the new script they are likely to say '0' or '1' on a scale of 1 (low ability) to 10 (high). The TLA facilitator has no way of knowing if that number is accurate or not but it doesn't matter. What matters is that the participant has assigned a starting point or their position 'A' and identified a target point or position 'B' that they are going to achieve using the TLA conversations. At the start of the first conversation, which is typically two to three weeks following the start of the change process, the participant will then be asked to calibrate their ability to use the customer service process. At this stage they may indicate an improvement from '0' to '4'. The facilitator can then ask the participant what number they want to get their script skill up to in a three-month period.

The facilitator's job on that initial TLA conversation and all subsequent conversations is to work out the difference between their current calibrated score and their destination score and help that individual to identify how they can make positive progress. In effect the facilitator is helping to close an arbitrary but still real gap that the person has assigned to their current and future skill level in that area. What makes calibration so useful is there is no right or wrong answer, but a benchmark is laid down that can then guide the conversations toward behavioural change.

When asked to calibrate a score for anything we will automatically provide a number even if we don't really know why we have chosen that particular number. Gut response and thin slicing can help to explain this. Nobel Prize winner Daniel Kahneman also explains why this is the case and talks about the two systems of the brain which he calls System 1 and System 2. According to Kahneman, 'System 1 operates automatically and quickly, with little or no effort and no sense of voluntary control,' whereas 'System 2 allocates attention to the effortful mental activities that demand it, including complex computations.'

It is System 1 that is providing the number when someone is asked to calibrate a current skill level. Or, as Kahneman writes: 'Whether you state them or not, you often have answers to questions that you do not completely understand, relying on evidence that you can neither explain nor defend' (2012).

Just think about this for a moment. If you were to ask your friend to calibrate the current health of their marriage on a scale of 1–10 they would give you a number in a few moments. That single digit will tell you and your friend more about the health of their relationship than three hours of discussion. And that's the beauty of calibration. It allows an individual to immediately put a stake in the ground and get a remarkably clear indication of where they are and how far away they are from their own ideal without needing the whole story.

Calibration is also very quick and removes or at least limits emotional justifications and excuses so that both parties can get on with the job at hand – assisting behavioural change.

Flexibility – middle

The middle of the ACTION Conversation Model is the flexibility of the traditional coaching conversation (Figure 6.3). In the model I refer to these parts as:

- T – Target.
- I – Information.
- O – Options.
- N – Next Steps.

FIGURE 6.3   Detailed breakdown of the flexibility within the TLA Conversation

TARGET → INFORMATION

IDENTIFY THE GAP WE ARE CLOSING

- ✔ Where would you like to start the action plan to help you implement the change?
- ✔ Where are you now with the calibration?
- ✔ Where do you want to get to on a scale of 0 to 10?
- ✔ If we were taking it up to the next level of a 7 – what would the difference be?
- ✔ Imagine you are a world leader in this field *using a new software* – what would best practice and a 10 look like?
- ✔ What do you think they would be doing differently to what you are doing now to make this even smoother?

GATHER INFORMATION AND GET DETAILS OF THE GAP AND OWNERSHIP

- ✔ What is relevant to you in this situation as you begin the change?
- ✔ Which parts of this are working well?
- ✔ Which parts of this have worked well in the past?
- ✔ How have you checked out if that's true?
- ✔ What other factors are relevant?
- ✔ In the past, was it the idea that was wrong or the implementation?
- ✔ What's the bottom line of the situation?
- ✔ What's not easy about the situation?
- ✔ What's the most challenging part of what you're trying to do?
- ✔ Tell me more about that?

NEXT STEPS ← OPTIONS

WHAT ARE YOU GOING TO COMMIT TO DOING? HOW WILL WE FOLLOW THIS UP?

- ✔ Given all the ideas we have discussed which one feels best to you?
- ✔ What will you do and by when?
- ✔ What are you taking away from our conversation today?
- ✔ What are you going to do differently before we next speak to help the change agenda move forward?
- ✔ What is/are the next steps?
- ✔ Precisely when will you do them?
- ✔ How are you going to know if you are successful?
- ✔ What might get in the way?
- ✔ Can you foresee any challenges?
- ✔ How are you going to ensure you follow through?
- ✔ What support do you need to implement the change?
- ✔ How will we know if you have been successful?
- ✔ How can you measure it?

WHAT OPTIONS DO YOU HAVE IN THIS SITUATION? WHAT **COULD** YOU DO?

- ✔ What are the alternatives?
- ✔ What are the first three ideas that come to mind for you?
- ✔ What are the possible ways to move forward, not what you will do, but what you could do?
- ✔ How could you move forward on this?
- ✔ What could you do differently to get a better result?
- ✔ Who might be able to help?
- ✔ What are the benefits and pitfalls of doing this?
- ✔ Which of these do you like the most?
- ✔ Of these, which are of interest to you?
- ✔ What other angles can you think of?
- ✔ What is just one more possibility?
- ✔ If you were advising a friend in your situation, what would you say to them?
- ✔ What other options are there?

Essentially this part of the conversation is looking at the target, so the individual can identify the gap they are seeking to close during the course of the TLA follow-up process. We will explore this gap in more detail in Chapter 12.

Although this four-part process is extremely useful we believe its effectiveness can be transformed when the flexibility is wrapped up with structure at the start and finish of the TLA conversation. Everyone is busy and often change just adds more pressure on top of an already frantic schedule so the purpose of these conversations is to support the individual through the change as quickly and efficiently as possible. This is why the conversations are delivered in 20 or 30-minute blocks. There is no time or space for meandering and navel gazing in a TLA conversation; instead it is a very deliberate and action-focused discussion. And that can be very different from a traditional coaching conversation.

Appendix 3 contains a worked example of the flexible section of the ACTION conversation. This illustrates the flow through the different stages of the TION process and how important it is for the facilitator to find out which action point(s) the participant considers most difficult so they can really add value and ensure the participant experiences the biggest possible early wins.

Due to the inherent flexibility in this part of the conversation it's impractical to provide several transcripts of possible conversations in the book but audio samples of TLA conversations are available at **http://transferoflearning.com/resources/**.

Structure – end

Each TLA follow-up conversation needs to close out with structure again. This helps to reiterate accountability and sets the targets for the next session while also recalibrating current skill levels around the required change. The individual must leave the conversation knowing when the next conversation will take place and what they have agreed to work on before that next conversation.

Accountability

Part of the TLA facilitator's role is effectively bringing the conversation to a close in the allocated time. It's important that the calls stay accountable to the process and agreed parameters – that means making sure the conversation doesn't run over time. This also helps to build trust and credibility in the process, and means the facilitator must honour the structure and move the conversation along when necessary. Part of the skill of TLA is to ask a lot of open questions to encourage the person to talk, but when it is within 2–3 minutes of the end of the conversation the TLA facilitator should switch to closed questions to bring the conversation to a natural close.

So rather than asking, 'What else do we need to go through today so you can make additional progress with your change?' the facilitator might ask, 'Is there anything else we need to go through today that will enable you to progress with your change?' Most people will say 'No' to the latter question which gives them ownership of the process and lets them feel as though they are winding up rather than feeling they've run out of time or been cut off.

If the person is a real talker, the facilitator can inform the person when there are 20 minutes to go. So they might say, 'Julie, we're two-thirds of the way through the conversation today and I just want to make sure we make good use of our time – what do we need to cover in the remaining time?'

What that does is signal to the individual that there is only a set time left. The TLA facilitator can't shy away from imposing the necessary structure. It's their job to make sure that the conversation stays on track and finishes on time.

It is also wise for the facilitator to get into the habit of using calibration to gauge commitment to what has been discussed in the conversation. Asking the person to rate their confidence level regarding what has been discussed allows the facilitator to establish how confident the individual feels about their ability to follow through on the action steps they identified. The facilitator might ask, for example, 'On a scale of 1–10, 1 being not confident at all and 10 being completely confident, how confident are you that you will follow through on the actions you've committed to today?' If the participant says '7' then the facilitator can ask them what needs to happen to get that confidence level up to an 8 or a 9 – which they will invariably know. If they answer '2' then obviously there is a problem and it needs to be addressed before the end of the conversation.

At the end of the conversation the facilitator needs to:

1 Recap on what has been covered.

2 Ensure that both the TLA facilitiator and individual being coached are clear on what the next steps and actions are.

3 Get commitment to those actions (usually before the conversation has finished).

4 Assess their likelihood of follow-through by asking the individual to calibrate their confidence level in achieving those next steps.

5 Set the time for the next conversation (for some programmes this will be prearranged).

6 Leave the client feeling clear and excited about the next steps.

7 Have clear notes that can be used to guide the next session.

Example of the structured end of the conversation:

So, Julie, that's us finished – can you confirm what you are taking away from our conversation today? [1]

And what are the actions you are going to take? What specifically are you going to do differently as a result of our conversation today? [2, 3]

When we next speak we will review how you've gone with your actions and then start moving forward with your next target. Is that OK?

All that is left now is to arrange when we are next going to speak. Let's look at diaries. [4]

Good stuff – so you will call me on [insert telephone number] at [time] on [date] – is that locked away in your diary? [5]

Excellent. You've made great progress and have a clear plan for your next steps – congratulations! Have a good couple of weeks, Julie, and good luck with your new action – have fun. [6]

Bye.

As always the TLA facilitator must take control of the process and finish in a professional way. Plus it's very important to leave the individual feeling inspired and positive about the changes they have made and what's possible in their future.

Documentation and distribution

During the TLA conversations the individual will take their own notes about what they discuss and decide to action. This helps them to take ownership of the changes they are committing to and making.

That said, the facilitator also has to be taking notes, especially around what the individual commits to for the next session. If a client misses out an action, either accidentally or deliberately, the facilitator is then able to remind them about that missed item, which also confirms that both parties are fully engaged in the process. The facilitator might want to check in during the conversation to make sure their client is jotting down notes as the conversation progresses as this is really important for their ownership of the process. So if the individual states a task or action he is going to progress before the next conversation the facilitator might say, 'That's a great idea, have you jotted that down because we'll be checking in against that point next time and I need you to be ready with your feedback.'

The facilitator must always finish the notes with a bullet point list of the three or four points that the individual has committed to action. Ideally these should be recorded in the client's own words, as this will be more meaningful to the individual.

Involving the manager and keeping him or her in the loop on actions and progress can enhance accountability and act as additional incentive for the individual to follow through. It is also extremely important to keep the manager of the participants engaged in the process in order to create a healthy change climate. If the manager is able to see that they are being kept informed of progress without being responsible for that progress they are much more likely to support the TLA process and create the right environment for the participant to make the behavioural change needed. A manager who feels sidelined or ignored can negatively impact the change climate, making real-world behavioural change almost impossible.

Whether the facilitator uses an online reporting system or not, they must make a note of the three or four action points arising from each conversation, have the client confirm them and e-mail those agreements to the client immediately after the conversation. It is these action points that form the basis of the second and subsequent conversations and it is impossible to encourage accountability without them.

The ACTION Conversation Model allows the facilitator and the person being supported through change to know exactly where they are in the TLA conversation. It acts as a road map through the change. The person being coached feels supported and confident that there is a process while still having the flexibility to explore what they choose to action. It also puts them in the driver's seat and allows them to regain control and certainty through the change process. The final stage of change is evaluation, which is thoroughly unpacked in the next part of the book as part of the alignment model, so you know how to evaluate change effectively.

Summary of key points

- The next stage of the TLA process is action. This is where the follow-up conversations actually take place over a period of several weeks after the change initiative is launched and begins in earnest.

- This is the actual process that will move someone from their old behaviour to the new desired behaviour.

- Essentially, the TLA specialist engages in a very tailored and specific coaching conversation where they ask questions in an effort to get the individual to take ownership for the changes they are being asked to make.

- Each TLA follow-up conversation moves through the ACTION Conversation Model. This model unpacks the theory and provides a framework that then guides those conversations.

- The ACTION Conversation Model expresses the fluidity between structure and flexibility and it is this balance between the two that creates the results and separates TLA from traditional coaching.

- TLA takes the flexibility of traditional coaching but removes all the guesswork and creates a structure that identifies very definite parameters around effective behavioural change.

- The ACTION Conversation Model is an acronym for the various stages that the conversation must pass through, from structure to flexibility and back to structure, namely, Accountability, Calibration, Targets, Information, Options and Next Steps.

- The initial structure is made up of Accountability and Calibration and it is these elements that give the TLA follow-up conversation a structure and context.

- The reason TLA is so effective is because every conversation opens and closes with structure in the form of Accountability and Calibration.

- The accountability process begins in the scene-setting part of preparation when individuals are told about the TLA process, complete the TLA Action Plan, and sign the Change Agreement. It then continues at the opening of the first TLA conversation and in each subsequent conversation the participant is reminded of their responsibilities to the process and how they are ultimately accountable for their own success.

- Calibration is about gaining an early benchmark on the individual's current ability around the required change versus where they would like to be. Calibration therefore acts as the bridge between the structured part of the conversation and the flexible part of the conversation. A skilled facilitator will use calibration repeatedly during the TLA process.

- The middle of the ACTION Conversation Model is the flexibility of the traditional coaching conversation. Essentially this part of the conversation is looking at the target, so the individual can identify the gap they are seeking to close during the course of the TLA follow-up process.

- Each TLA follow-up conversation needs to close out with structure again. This helps to reiterate accountability and sets the targets for the next session while also recalibrating current skill levels around the required change. The individual must leave the conversation knowing when the next conversation will take place and what they have agreed to work on before that next conversation.

- During the TLA conversations the individual will take their own notes about what they discuss and decide to action. This helps them to take ownership of the changes they are committing to and making. That said, the facilitator also has to be taking notes, especially around what the individual commits to for the next session.

Reference

Kahneman, D (2012) *Thinking, Fast and Slow*, Penguin, New York

PART THREE
Evaluation

Evaluation planning

07

Change initiatives require a significant investment – not only in direct time and resources but in managing the frequent disruption change can bring to the workplace. It is therefore essential that we evaluate the success of change to ensure the investment pays off and we learn from the experience. This chapter introduces the ROI Methodology, which has become the most applied and documented approach to evaluating training and development programmes and can be equally applied to change initiatives. Partnering the ROI Methodology for evaluation and the TLA methodology for creating change creates a powerful combination for change initiatives.

The evaluation process includes ten steps, captured in four phases. Each phase will be unpacked in this and the following three chapters. The first phase is evaluation planning where objectives are developed and plans are made for an evaluation project. The second phase is data collection (Chapter 8). This includes data collection during the programme and after implementation. Phase three is data analysis (Chapter 9). During this phase, improvement in business impact data is isolated to the initiative, and then, when necessary, these data are converted to monetary benefits, compared to the programme costs, and an ROI is calculated. Intangible benefits are identified in this phase as well. The final phase of the process is reporting the results (Chapter 10). After all there is no point starting a change initiative unless you plan to see it through and report the outcome to those involved.

The ROI Methodology

Evaluation is an important part of the change process. The key to successful evaluation is to integrate it so that it is an inherent part of the change process. Evaluation should be seamless so that all the necessary data can be developed to the degree of comprehension necessary, or allowed, given available resources. The ROI Methodology consists of five critical elements that must come together for sustainable integration:

- evaluation framework;
- process model;
- standards;
- case application and practice;
- implementation.

Evaluation framework

The first element is the evaluation framework. This framework represents a data-categorization scheme that organizes evaluation results in a logical order. Chapter 2 introduced the framework and described its use in aligning change initiatives. As you may remember, the five-level framework represents a chain of impact that describes results from multiple perspectives or levels.

The data from these levels give a complete view of programme success. Each level of evaluation represents different measures as shown in the chain of impact in Table 2.1. It is this framework that ensures all necessary data are captured and developed to inform decisions from all stakeholders.

Process model

The next element is the process model. The process model provides a step-by-step approach that keeps the process manageable so users can address one issue at a time.

The process model also gives evaluators a systematic approach and supports consistent evaluation replication. It is important that change initiatives are all evaluated in the same way otherwise it's impossible to measure comparable success. Application of the model provides consistency from one evaluation project to another. Figure 2.3 introduced the model. As shown, the ten steps in the process are completed in four phases: evaluation planning, data collection, data analysis, and reporting.

Operating standards

Operating standards and philosophy represent the third element of the evaluation approach. This element ensures consistent decision making around the application of the model. Standards ensure consistent, reliable practice.

Twelve standards, or guiding principles, support the process. These twelve guiding principles, shown in Table 7.1, serve as a decision-making tool,

TABLE 7.1   Twelve guiding principles

Guiding Principles	
	1 When conducting a higher-level evaluation, collect data at lower levels.
	2 When planning a higher-level evaluation, the previous level of evaluation is not required to be comprehensive.
	3 When collecting and analysing data, use only the most credible sources.
	4 When analysing data, select the most conservative alternatives for calculations.
	5 Use at least one method to isolate the effects of the programme or project.
	6 If no improvement data is available for a population or from a specific source, assume that no improvement has occurred.
	7 Adjust estimates of improvements for the potential error of the estimates.
	8 Avoid use of extreme data items and unsupported claims when calculating ROI calculations.
	9 Use only the first year of annual benefits in the ROI analysis of short-term solutions.
	10 Fully load all costs of the solution, project, or programme when analysing ROI.
	11 Intangible measures are defined as measures that are purposely not converted to monetary values.
	12 Communicate the results of the ROI Methodology to all key stakeholders.

influencing decisions on the best method for collecting data; the best sources and timing for data collection; and the most appropriate approach for isolating the effects of the programme, converting data to money, costs, and the stakeholders to whom the results are reported. Operating standards are an important part of the evaluation process because they ensure that practitioners make decisions using consistent guidelines, allowing multiple programmes to be evaluated and those results compared.

Case application and practice

The fourth element represents the actual application of the ROI Methodology.

Case applications and practice offer a deeper understanding of the comprehensive evaluation process. They also provide evidence of programme and evaluation success, which furthers the integration of the change evaluation process in organizations.

Implementation

Implementation is the final element of an evaluation process. This is probably the most important piece because it is through implementation and integration that evaluation can be conducted consistently. This piece of the evaluation puzzle allows changes to be made as a result of evaluation data and allows organizations to reap a return on their change investment.

An important issue to remember is that evaluation is not an add-on approach. It is an integral part of any change initiative and should always be assumed as part of that practice from the very beginning. Environmental issues and events will influence evaluation implementation, and they must be addressed early to ensure that the process is successful. Specific actions that can facilitate successful implementation include:

- developing a policy statement concerning results;
- developing procedures and guidelines for different elements and techniques of the evaluation process;
- developing strategies to improve management commitment and support for evaluation;
- developing mechanisms to provide technical support for data collection, data analysis, and reporting;
- developing specific techniques to change or improve organizational culture to place more attention on results;
- using criteria for deciding which initiatives should be evaluated to which levels.

The evaluation process can fail or succeed based on the success of these and other implementation issues. For this reason, it is important to keep evaluation front of mind when planning any change initiative.

Purpose and objectives

Evaluation planning begins with a clear purpose for the evaluation. There are many purposes for evaluating change initiatives. In some cases, the purpose is to take a pulse of the participants' perception. Another purpose might be to determine if those involved in the change process are gaining the requisite knowledge, skill, or information. Yet another is to understand the extent to which the programme is driving change in the organization. Change can refer to change of the individual's performance on the job as well as change in critical business measures. When this is the purpose of the evaluation, follow-up data are important. This follow-up data will include measures at Level 3, Application, as well as measures at Level 4, Business Impact.

Another reason for evaluating programmes is to demonstrate the value the change initiative is bringing to the organization. This value may be defined in terms of changed performance on the job, improvement in key business measures, and ROI.

In addition to clarifying the purpose of the evaluation, objectives developed during the alignment process (Chapter 2) are used to guide the planning process. Objectives are set for each level in the evaluation framework. The levels of objectives are shown in Table 7.2.

TABLE 7.2 Levels of objectives

Level of objectives	Focus of objectives
Level 1 Reaction and planned action	Defines a specific level of reaction to the project or programme as it is revealed and communicated to stakeholders.
Level 2 Learning	Defines specific skills and knowledge needed to implement the project.
Level 3 Application	Defines key issues for successful use of skills and application and implementation of the project.
Level 4 Business impact	Defines the specific business measures that will change or improve as a result of the project.
Level 5 ROI	Defines the specific return on investment from the implementation of the project, comparing project costs to monetary benefits.

As described in Chapter 2, objectives are the output of the needs assessment. They are the core of the alignment process. Typical areas for reaction objectives include measures of usefulness, relevance, importance, necessity, appropriateness, amount of new information, and overall satisfaction. Learning objectives may reflect actual skill-building goals or they may reflect gains in understanding a policy or an approach. Awareness of the need for change is another form of learning.

Application objectives describe how things should be in terms of performance, action, or changes in behaviour. They emphasize what should occur on the job as a result of implementing the change process. Business impact objectives represent key business measures that should be improved as change occurs. They emphasize the importance of achieving bottom-line results that key clients expect.

The fifth level of objectives is the acceptable return on investment (ROI). This objective defines the expected payoff from the programme by comparing the input resources (the cost of the programme) to the monetary benefits of the change initiative. Table 7.3 presents the levels of objectives for the Southeast Corridor Bank change initiative described in Chapter 2.

TABLE 7.3   Southeast Corridor Bank

Reaction	On a scale of 1–5 (1 disagree; 5 agree), participants rate the following 4.0 out of 5 regarding the skill-based pay programme.

- I am motivated to develop knowledge and skills that will help me take on additional responsibilities.
- I perceive the skill-based pay programme as a challenge.
- I intend to take on the challenges presented by the skill-based pay programme in order to progress in the company.
- I view the skill-based pay programme as a rewarding opportunity.

On a scale of 1–5 (1 disagree; 5 agree), participants rate the following 4.0 out of 5 regarding training programmes targeting knowledge and skills relevant to job progression.

- The programme is relevant to the job that I am pursuing.
- The programme should be useful to me as I progress toward advancement in the company.
- I intend to apply the knowledge and skills learned in the programme, even though I have not yet been promoted.

TABLE 7.3   *Continued*

Learning	On a scale of 1–5 (1 disagree; 5 agree), participants rate the following 4.0 out of 5.
	• I understand why the skill-based pay programme is being implemented.
	• I understand what is required of me to be successful with the programme.
	• I understand how promotion decisions are made.
	• I understand the timing of various aspects of the programme.
	For each training programme attended that targets job progressions, participants will:
	• Acquire knowledge/skills as measured by that programme.
	• Demonstrate abilities with skill pertinent to promotional level as measured by supervisor assessment.
Application	• 100% participation in programme.
	• Increase in number of requests for training (45 per month baseline).
	• Review meetings with managers regarding developmental plan taking place.
	• Increase in actual promotions (139 per year baseline).
Business impact	• Reduce branch employee turnover (baseline: 71%; 336 per year).
	• Reduce branch staffing levels (baseline: average 480 total).
	• Customer satisfaction.
	• Job satisfaction.
	• Deposits.
	• Loan volume.
	• New accounts.
	• Transaction volume.
	• Cross-selling.
ROI	• 25% based on first year actual plus second year forecast.

Objectives define the measures to be taken during the evaluation process. If well developed, they can also lead the evaluator toward the appropriate technique and timing for data collection. The more specifically the objectives of the change initiative are laid out and clarified the easier the evaluation. Using an objectives map like that shown in Table 7.4 can help change agents and evaluators develop specific, measurable, achievable, relevant, time-bound objectives.

As shown, the process begins with identifying the broad objectives for the change initiative. From there specific measures are developed. These measures indicate how the evaluator will know the objective is being met. Next is the attribute of the measure. Is it a Likert-type response choice, a quantitative measure, or an open-ended comment? The next step is to define the baseline data. Baseline data are important because they represent the starting point. Any time a change initiative is put into place, it is done so in order to 'change' a current state. Baseline data represent that current state. Targets, in the next column, represent the minimum acceptable improvement the initiative should achieve. A target is not a forecast. A forecast of improvement represents what the potential for improvement is; a target represents the minimum acceptable performance. Targets also include the timing at which the improvement will occur. The last column is the SMART objective.

Working through this objectives map takes time. But, given that objectives serve as the blueprint for building the change initiative and aligning it with the business need, the more detail developed at this stage, the stronger the foundation for change. Additionally, the more specific the objective, the easier it will be to measure what matters in the way that is most effective.

TABLE 7.4   Objectives map

Broad objectives	Measures	Attributes	Baseline	Targets	SMART Objectives
Reduce employee turnover	Annual turnover rate of frontline employees	Metric: voluntary separations/ average number of employees × 100	71% (336 employees)	Reduce by 10% (33 employees) within one year	Reduce turnover of frontline employees by 10% within one year of initiative

Objectives are the first element of the data collection plan. The data collection plan is the first of three plans developed for the evaluation of a major change initiative.

Evaluation plans

During the planning phase, three planning documents are completed:

- data collection plan;
- ROI analysis plan;
- project plan.

The ROI analysis plan and project plan are developed when a comprehensive evaluation calls for higher levels of evaluation and the scope of the project is quite large.

Data collection plan

The data collection plan provides a place to list the major elements and issues regarding the collection of data for the four levels of evaluation, and gives a place for the objectives.

The data collection plan addresses five critical issues:

- objectives of the initiative;
- data collection method/instrument;
- data sources;
- timing of data collection;
- responsibility for data collection.

Broad objectives are appropriate for the initial planning, but specific measures of success that are defined during the planning process will make the instrument's data collection design efficient. For example, Table 7.5 shows a broad objective and a more specific measure. The specific measures tell the evaluator what measures to take as well as the target for improvement.

The data collection plan is an important part of the evaluation strategy and should be completed prior to moving forward with the change initiative. If the initiative is under way, the plan is completed before pursuing the evaluation. The plan provides a direction as to what type of data will be

TABLE 7.5 Broad objective and specific measure

Broad objective	Measure
Reduce employee turnover	Annual turnover rate of frontline employees of bank branches (10% reduction)

collected, how they will be collected, when they will be collected, and who will collect them. Table 7.6 is a sample template of a data collection plan. Chapter 8 describes each of the components in this planning tool in more detail.

ROI analysis plan

Table 7.7 shows a template for the second planning document, the ROI analysis plan.

This planning tool helps ensure that when the higher levels of evaluation are being conducted, all parties understand the approach that is to be taken in order to analyse the data.

Looking at Table 7.7 in the first column, Level 3 Application or Level 4 Business Impact measures are listed. Level 4 measures are used in the ROI analysis. In the second column, the method used to isolate the effects of the change initiative is listed next to each data item. In most cases the method will be the same for each data item, but there could be variations.

The third column includes the method of converting data to monetary values. Completion of this column is necessary when conducting ROI analysis. Converting data to money can be carried out in several ways, including the use of standard values, historical costs, and expert input. The fourth column outlines the categories of costs that will be captured for the initiative. Instructions about how certain costs should be prorated would be noted here. Normally, the cost categories will be consistent for every initiative and programme. However, a specific cost that is unique to the programme being evaluated would also be noted. The fifth column outlines the intangible benefits expected from this programme. This list is generated from discussions about the programme with sponsors and subject matter experts. Chapter 9 provides more information on the elements of the ROI analysis plan.

TABLE 7.6 Data collection plan template

DATA COLLECTION PLAN

Programme: _____ Responsibility: _____ Date: _____

Level	Programme objective(s)	Measures	Data collection method/instruments	Data sources	Timing	Responsibilities
1	REACTION/PLANNED ACTION					
2	LEARNING					
3	APPLICATION					
4	BUSINESS IMPACT					
5	ROI					

Comments:

TABLE 7.7 ROI analysis plan template

Programme: _____ Responsibility: _____ Date: _____

Roi Analysis Plan

Data items (usually Level 4)	Methods for isolating the effects of the programme/ process	Methods of converting data to monetary values	Cost categories	Intangible benefits	Communication targets for final report	Other influences/ issues during application	Comments

The sixth column outlines communication targets. Although many groups should receive the information, four target groups are always recommended:

1 senior management;

2 change participants' supervisors;

3 participants who are involved in the change initiative;

4 change managers, facilitators of the change, programme managers.

All four of these groups need to know the results of the evaluation, including the ROI analysis. Other issues or events that might influence the implementation of the programme would be highlighted in the seventh column. Typical items include the capability of participants, the degree of access to data sources, and unique data analysis issues.

Project plan

Treating comprehensive evaluation as a project is important because project scope can creep causing delays and confusion. A good project plan will keep scope in check and keep progress on track. Typical Level 1 Reaction or Level 2 Learning evaluations are simple enough that detailed project planning is not necessary. However, large change initiatives that involve data collection at multiple time frames from multiple sources can be daunting projects. When this is the case, a complete project plan may be helpful. Key components of a project plan may include (Project Management Institute, 2013):

- scope of the project;
- deliverables from the project;
- activities/tasks to complete the deliverables;
- time to complete each activity/task;
- cost of each activity/task;
- schedule toward completion;
- responsibility.

Of course adding the TLA phasing or behavioural change reinforcement process into the project plan can also be beneficial. There are a number of project plan templates available online. Table 7.8 is one example of a project plan template.

When combined, the data collection plan, ROI analysis plan, and project plan provide the detailed information needed to develop a comprehensive evaluation of a change initiative.

TABLE 7.8 Project plan template

Project title: _____ Target completion date: _____

Project scope: _____

Deliverables	Time to complete	Est. cost to complete		Timeline													Responsibility
				J	F	M	A	M	J	J	A	S	O	N	D	
Deliverable 1																
Task 1.1	_____ hrs	$ _____														_____
Task 1.2	_____ hrs	$ _____														_____
Task 1.3	_____ hrs	$ _____														_____
Task 1.4	_____ hrs	$ _____														_____
Estimated cost of deliverable 1		**$** _____														
Deliverable 2																
Task 2.1	_____ hrs	$ _____														_____
Task 2.2	_____ hrs	$ _____														_____
Task 2.3	_____ hrs	$ _____														_____
Task 2.4	_____ hrs	$ _____														_____
Estimated cost of deliverable 2		**$** _____														
Deliverable 3																
Task 3.1	_____ hrs	$ _____														_____
Task 3.2	_____ hrs	$ _____														_____
Task 3.3	_____ hrs	$ _____														_____
Estimated cost of deliverable 3		**$** _____														
Estimate cost of time on project		**$** _____														

Other resource requirements (printing, technology, etc):

Planning the evaluation is important. Although it does take time and effort, it has many advantages. It provides a road map to complete the evaluation process. Agreeing up front with the client, whether internal or external, on how the evaluation will take place will avoid frustration during the process. Presenting the planning documents to the project team will communicate expectations of programme success and the process by which success will be measured. This step reinforces that the evaluation is a process-improvement tool, rather than an individual performance evaluation. Communicating the evaluation plan to those people involved in the change initiative will reaffirm the importance of the change process. It will also prepare participants to provide appropriate data at the appropriate time. This not only helps ensure that credible data are received, but will also help to create response rates during post-implementation follow-up.

The next chapter will introduce the key issues in terms of collecting data when evaluating change initiatives.

Summary of key points

- Change initiatives require a significant investment. It is therefore essential that we evaluate the success of change to ensure the investment pays off and we learn from the experience.

- The evaluation process includes ten steps, captured in four phases:
  - evaluation planning (Chapter 7);
  - data collection (Chapter 8);
  - data analysis (Chapter 9);
  - reporting results (Chapter 10).

- The key to successful evaluation is to integrate it so that it is an inherent part of the change process.

- Evaluation should be seamless so that all the necessary data can be developed to the degree of comprehension necessary, or allowed, given available resources.

- The ROI Methodology consists of five critical elements that must come together for sustainable integration:
  - evaluation framework;
  - process model;
  - standards;
  - case application and practice;
  - implementation.

- Evaluation planning begins with a clear purpose for the evaluation.
- In addition to clarifying the purpose of the evaluation, objectives developed during the alignment process are used to guide the planning process.
- Objectives are the first element of the data collection plan. The data collection plan is the first of three plans developed for the evaluation of a major change initiative.
- During the planning phase, three planning documents are completed:
  - the data collection plan;
  - ROI analysis plan;
  - project plan.
- The data collection plan provides a place to list the major elements and issues regarding the collection of data for the four levels of evaluation and gives a place for the objectives.
  The data collection plan addresses five critical issues:
  - objectives of the initiative;
  - data collection method/instrument;
  - data sources;
  - timing of data collection;
  - responsibility for data collection.
- The data collection plan is an important part of the evaluation strategy and should be completed prior to moving forward with the change initiative.
- The ROI analysis plan helps ensure that when the higher levels of evaluation are being conducted, all parties understand the approach that is to be taken in order to analyse the data.
- Treating comprehensive evaluations as a project is important because project scope can creep causing delays and confusion. A good project plan will keep scope in check and keep progress on track.
  Key components of a project plan may include:
  - scope of the project;
  - deliverables from the project;
  - activities/tasks to complete the deliverables;
  - time to complete each activity/task;
  - cost of each activity/task;

 – schedule toward completion;

 – responsibility.

- When combined, the data collection plan, ROI analysis plan, and project plan provide the detailed information needed to develop a comprehensive evaluation of a change initiative.

- Planning the evaluation is important. Although it does take time and effort it has many advantages.

Reference

Project Management Institute (2013) *A Guide to the Project Management Body of Knowledge (PMBOK® Guide)* 5th edition, Project Management Institute

Data collection

08

The strength of any evaluation process depends almost entirely on the quality and availability of the data to be evaluated. This chapter describes key issues in collecting data when evaluating change initiatives. These issues include choosing the right methods, sources of data, and timing of data collection.

Unsurprisingly, data collection is the cornerstone of measurement and evaluation. Reaction and learning data serve as useful indicators regarding the potential use of knowledge, skills and insights. These early indicators of success are important because they give insight into a change initiative's effectiveness in enabling change, as well as the opportunity that exists for successful implementation. Application data describe the extent to which change is occurring through implementation of activities and changes in behaviour. Impact data describe the extent to which business measures are improving as a result of the change. This improvement is the basis for calculating the ROI in the change process.

Data collection occurs at multiple time frames, depending on the purpose and objectives of the initiative. Considerations such as value of information, customer focus, frequency of use, and difficulty of the data collection process are important factors when planning data collection. For example, reaction data offer the least valuable information in terms of the impact the information will have on client decision making. Participants, facilitators, coaches and other consumers involved in a change initiative appreciate reaction and learning data, but clients, or those funding the project, often have a greater appreciation for application, impact, and ROI data. Understandably evaluation occurs more frequently at the reaction and learning levels, and its use decreases at the application, impact, and ROI levels, but for change initiatives the true value of the project will only be seen from Level 3 Application upwards.

While the characteristics of evaluation at each level differ, the one thing that is common among all of them is that each level provides an important input into describing success or an opportunity to improve a change initiative. As described in Chapter 2, a clear purpose and measurable objectives can lead to the appropriate evaluation approach, including the data collection technique. The best approach to data collection also depends on factors such as cost, usefulness, time requirements, amount of disruption and other practical matters.

Methods and instruments for data collection

Table 8.1 lists different methods for collecting data at the reaction, learning, application, and impact levels. Regardless of the method or technique, instruments should be:

- valid;
- reliable;
- simple;
- economical;
- easy to administer;
- easy to analyse.

Below is a description of some common methods used to capture data at the different levels of evaluation.

Surveys and questionnaires

Surveys and questionnaires are the most common data collection method. They come in all types, ranging from short reaction forms to detailed, multi-paged instruments addressing issues important to all five levels of evaluation.

The fundamental difference between a survey and a questionnaire is in the type of questions and the purpose of the instruments. Surveys attempt to measure changes in attitude toward a process, policy, procedure, the organization, and even people. They typically use dichotomous/binary questions and Likert-type scales. Likert scales are when the person completing the survey has to indicate on a scale from 1 to 5 whether they strongly disagree with the statement (1), disagree (2), neither agree nor disagree (3), agree (4) or strongly agree (5).

Questionnaires represent a more comprehensive instrument that measures what participants think about a programme, what they plan to do with what they learn, how they are applying what they learned or how their

TABLE 8.1   Methods of collecting data for each level

Method	Types of data			
	1	2	3	4
Surveys	✓	✓	✓	
Questionnaires	✓	✓	✓	✓
Observation		✓	✓	
Interviews	✓	✓	✓	
Focus groups	✓	✓	✓	
Tests/quizzes		✓		
Demonstrations		✓		
Simulations		✓		
Follow-up meetings	✓	✓		
Action planning/ improvement plans			✓	✓
Performance contracting			✓	✓
Performance monitoring				✓

behaviours are changing, and the impact their change in performance has on business measures. Questionnaires may include similar types of questions as those found in attitude surveys, but they will also include numerical scales, rank ordered questions, checklists, and multiple-choice and open-ended questions.

Table 8.2 presents sample questions that could appear on a questionnaire. Questionnaires provide deeper insight into the opinions and perceptions of respondents than a simple attitude survey. They are also useful in collecting data describing the alignment between a change initiative and improvement in business measures along with the monetary benefits of a programme.

TABLE 8.2 Sample questions on a questionnaire

Agreement/disagreement

	Strongly agree				Strongly disagree
	5	4	3	2	1
1 The initiative is relevant to my work.	○	○	○	○	○
2 The initiative is important to my success.	○	○	○	○	○
3 The initiative is a worthwhile investment for my organization.	○	○	○	○	○

Opened-ended lists

Please indicate specific actions you will undertake as a result of this initiative (please be specific).

1 _____

2 _____

3 _____

4 _____

Open-ended essay

Please describe how you plan to apply what you learned in the programme.

_____

_____

_____

_____

Rank order questions

Please rank the top 1–3 barriers to your changing your processes (check only up to 3).

☐ opportunity to use the skills

☐ management support

☐ support from colleagues and peers

☐ sufficient knowledge and understanding

☐ confidence to apply knowledge/skills

☐ systems and processes within organization will support application of knowledge/skills

☐ other _____

Open-ended numerical

As a result of the actions you have taken, please estimate the amount of money you have saved your organization (ie reduced redundancies, improved quality, reduced turnover, etc) over a period of one year: $ _____

How confident are you in your estimate? (0% = No confidence; 100% Certainty)

_____%

While technically the two instruments are different, the words 'survey' and 'questionnaire' are used interchangeably. Both are self-administered instruments, and both present challenges in terms of design, distribution and analysis. One of the biggest challenges is asking the right questions. Any given follow-up questionnaire (Level 3 and Level 4) for example, could include the following issues:

- progress with objectives;
- action plan implementation;
- relevance/importance;
- perception of value;
- use of materials;
- knowledge/skill enhancement;
- skills use;
- changes with work actions;
- linkage with output measures;
- other benefits;
- barriers;
- enablers;
- management support;
- other solutions;
- recommendations for other audiences/participants;
- suggestions for improvements;
- other comments.

Additionally, if knowing impact and ROI is important, additional content can be included such as:

- improvement/accomplishments;
- defined measure;
- provide the change;
- unit value;
- basis;
- total impact;
- list other factors;
- improvement linked with programme;
- confidence estimate.

Another challenge is asking the questions the right way. Questions should be written in such a way that people can and will answer them. When creating survey questions ensure each question only focuses on a single issue, keep the question brief and to the point, write the question clearly so respondents know how to answer the question, and ask questions so respondents will answer objectively rather than biasing the question with leading terms.

With regard to the response choices, one scale does not necessarily fit all questions. A consideration when developing the response choices is how much variance the scale requires to capture an appropriate measure. Another consideration is discrimination between response choices. A three-point scale may be useful for some question items, but something to consider is whether or not enough variance exists to give respondents opportunity to respond accurately. Labelling responses is also important. If the question asks about effectiveness, the response choice descriptors should represent effectiveness versus something else, like agreement. Finally, symmetry is a consideration when developing survey question response choices. Consider whether or not there is a balance between the choices, and if they reflect a continuum that demonstrates the direction of response choices, eg lowest to highest, best to worst, etc.

Many books exist to help design and administer surveys and questionnaires as well as analyse the data. One book, *Survey Basics* (Phillips, Phillips and Aaron, 2013) describes the fundamentals of writing survey questions.

Interviews and focus groups

Interviews and focus groups are useful data collection methods. Interviews are helpful when it is important to probe for detail about an issue. They can help the evaluator gain clarity on the link between the initiative under way and its outcomes.

A disadvantage of the interview process is that it is time consuming. A one-hour interview involving an interviewee and the interviewer equals two hours of time. Interviewing a large number of people can therefore be expensive. For example, 36 people were interviewed within a four-week time frame for a change initiative in a large organization. Considering there were two interviewers (one scribe and one interviewer), 36 interviewees, and the interviews lasted 90 minutes each, the total time requirement was 9,720 minutes. Converting minutes to hours equals 162 hours of interview time. That was a lot of time and cost for data collection. Considering the scope of the project, it was justifiable and necessary to capture the data. But this is not always the case. So, while powerful, interviews are expensive and should be used selectively.

Focus groups are helpful when trying to obtain in-depth feedback, but particularly so when it is also important for the group to hear from others. A focus group involves a small group discussion facilitated by a person with experience in the focus group process. It is important that the facilitator keeps on track, otherwise the group can derail the process. Having a strong facilitator and a very structured process is therefore very important. Change initiatives can cause fear and anxiety, so a focus group could present participants an opportunity to express their anxiety. This should not be its intent. Focus groups, in the context of evaluation, are intended to capture meaningful information about the change initiative.

Observations and demonstrations

Observation and demonstration are useful techniques because they allow data capture in real time. By watching participants at a learning stage of a change initiative, and taking note of their actions and behaviour, you can quickly tell if they are ready to apply what they need to know to make the change successful, back on the job. Of course, to observe if the change is applied back on the job the observation actually needs to happen within the person's day-to-day role.

At either stage, a useful tool for this process is the observation checklist. It can help measure success with knowledge, skill, and information acquisition or application through observation. A checklist allows the observer to check off whether or not the individual is following a procedure. Checklists with yes/no response choices are useful when there is either a right or wrong way to perform a skill. But most of the time, performance success is based on a gradient. Sharon Shrock and Bill Coscarelli offer an observation tool (or performance test) they refer to as a behaviourally anchored numerical scale (2000). This scale requires observers to rank the behaviour of participants using a five-point scale that is anchored in descriptions of good and poor behaviours.

A classic example of collecting data through observation and demonstration, usually for Level 3 Application data, is the use of participant observers or mystery shoppers. Mystery shoppers go into a store and pose as customers, observing the way salespeople perform. After the shopping experience, they write up an after-action report, describing their experience and rating the salesperson on behaviours identified by the client organization. Another example of this type of data monitoring is with call centre representatives. In this process, observers listen to conversations between the call centre representative and the customer, rating them on a series of behaviours.

Another form of observation is customer surveys. Through the customer survey process, the customer rates a sales representative or service provider on performance. Unlike an ex post facto, self-administered questionnaire where the respondents reflect on what they remember happening in the past, this form of observation takes place in real time, capturing data in the moment. As an example, in some retail stores, at the point of checkout, a system is in place that asks customers whether or not the cashier greeted them as they walked up to the checkout line. By simply answering yes or no, the customer has been placed in the role of observer, providing a rating of the performance of the cashier.

Even if the observation is conducted in the workplace there is a fine line between observation at Level 2 Learning and observation at Level 3 Application. That line is drawn at the point where observation influences performance. For example, if a supervisor brings a checklist and asks a staff member to perform five tasks, checking off each task from the checklist, that observation is likely to influence performance because the staff member knows they are being assessed and will probably lift their performance accordingly. On the other hand, when the observer is unknown or invisible to the person being observed, the data are usable to assess Level 3 Application. They answer the question: when no one is watching is the individual applying the learning required to execute the change initiative and truly changing their behaviour? The benefit of observation is that data are collected in real time, hopefully from an objective observer. To enhance this objectivity, protocols, checklists and other tools are provided to the observer to enhance the reliability of their observation. The downside of observation, however, lies in the fact that multiple observers can see different things – hence the need for protocols and checklists.

Tests and quizzes

Tests and quizzes are typical instruments used in evaluating Level 2 Learning. Tests are validated instruments that meet specific requirements of validity and reliability and are useful for determining whether individuals have successfully acquired certain knowledge or information and can retrieve it when asked. Quizzes are less formal and typically represent an exercise in recall as refreshers of learning or change content. Often quizzes are used to summarize key points and are often precursors to an actual test.

There is a variety of different types of test. The work of Schrock and Coscarelli, along with others, provides in-depth detail on the mechanics of good test design. Testing is, however, not frequently used when measuring learning that occurs during major change initiatives, so we have not gone into it in great detail here. This is not to say that testing and quizzes are not appropriate tools to measure learning; it only means that for most major change initiatives other forms of data collection are more appropriate and useful.

Simulations

Another technique for gathering data is job simulation.

Simulation involves the construction and application of a procedure, process, behaviour, or task that simulates or models the behaviour change or performance improvement the initiative was designed to facilitate. The simulation is designed to represent, as closely as possible, the actual performance required in the real-world setting in which it should occur. Simulations may be used during the change initiative, at the end or as part of the follow-up evaluation. There is a variety of types of simulations including:

- electrical/technical simulations;
- case studies;
- role-plays;
- assessment centre method.

Electrical/technical simulations

Electrical and technical simulations use a combination of electronics and mechanical devices to simulate the real-life situations. Programmes to develop operational and diagnostic skills are candidates for this type of simulation.

An expensive example of this type is a simulator for a nuclear plant operator, or the simulator used for boat operators leading large boats and ships through the Panama Canal. Other, less expensive types of simulators have been developed to simulate equipment operation.

Case studies

A popular approach to simulation is a case study. A case study represents a detailed description of a problem and usually contains a list of several questions posed to the participant. The participant is asked to analyse the case and determine the best course of action. The problem should reflect the conditions in the real-world setting and the content of the change initiative. There is a variety of types of case studies that can help determine the depth of a person's knowledge and their experience. These include exercises, situational case studies, complex case studies, decision case studies, critical incident case studies, and action maze case studies. Readers of case studies must be able to determine conclusions from the text, discern the irrelevant from the relevant portions of the case, infer missing information, and integrate the different parts of the case to form a conclusion (Ellect, 2007). Case studies may be useful in preparing people for a change initiative or reviewing suitability for a change role.

Role-plays

Role-plays require participants to practise a newly learned skill or behaviour. Other participants observe and score the participant on his or her performance. The participant under assessment is assigned a role and given specific instructions, which sometimes include an ultimate course of action. The role and instructions are intended to simulate the real-world setting to the greatest extent possible. Given that such events are often in a learning environment and not in the real world this is typically a Level 2 measure.

Assessment centre method

A final type of simulation is a formal procedure called the Assessment Centre Method (Byham, 2004). Assessment centres are not actually a location or building. The term refers to a procedure for evaluating the performance of individuals. In a typical assessment centre the individuals being assessed participate in a variety of exercises that enable them to demonstrate a particular skill, knowledge or ability, usually called job dimensions. These dimensions are often important to individual on-the-job success for which the change initiative was developed.

Action plans

Action plans are an excellent tool to collect both Level 3 Application and Level 4 Impact data. Action plans can be built into the launch of a change initiative so that they are a seamless part of the process, rather than an add-on activity. Indeed, this is exactly what happens with the creation of the TLA Action Plan.

Using action plans, participants identify specific actions they plan to take as a result of the change initiative. When using action plans for Level 4 data collection, participants identify specific measures before the initiative and target their actions toward improving their predefined measures. Table 8.3 is an example of an action plan completed for the coaching portion of a corporate change initiative. As shown in the action plan, Caroline Dobson has identified the specific measure that she wants to improve and set the objective for improvement in that measure. On the left-hand side of the action plan, she has listed the specific actions that she plans to take to improve the measure. She completes items A, B, and C prior to leaving the briefing on the change initiative. These items represent the specific measure of interest, the monetary value of that measure, and how she came to that value. She completes items E, F and G during the six months of transition following the change initiative launch. These items describe the improvement in the measure due to the programme.

Each individual in the coaching experience completed an action plan similar to that completed by Caroline Dobson. The output of the process is a table such as that shown in Table 8.4. Caroline Dobson's results are listed at Executive# 11. Using input from the executives, the results show the improvement in business measures important to each executive that occur due to the programme and the monetary value for that improvement. Results from each executive are summed up in order to calculate the total monetary benefit of the programme.

The key to successful implementation of action plans lies in the following steps:

Prior to the intervention

- Communicate the action plan requirement early.
- Have participants identify at least one impact measure to improve as a result of the change initiative.

During the intervention

- Describe the action planning process at the beginning of the change programme/project.
- Teach the action planning process.
- Allow time to develop the plan.
- Have the facilitator support the creation of the action plan.
- Require participants to assign a monetary value for each improvement.
- If time permits, ask participants to present their action plans to the group.
- Explain the follow-up process.

TABLE 8.3 Completed action plan

Name: Caroline Dobson   Coach: Pamela Mills   Follow-up date: 1 Sept.

Objective: Improve retention for staff   Evaluation period: January to July

Improvement
measure: Voluntary turnover

Current
performance: 28% Annual

Target
performance: 15% Annual

Action steps		Analysis
1 Meet with team to discuss reasons for turnover – using problem-solving skills.	31 Jan	**A** What is the unit of measure? _One voluntary turnover._
2 Review exit interview data with HR – look for trends and patterns.	15 Feb	**B** What is the value (cost) of one unit? _Salary x 1.3._
3 Counsel with 'at-risk' employees to correct problems and explore opportunities for improvement.	Mar	**C** How did you arrive at this value? _Standard Value._
4 Develop individual development plan for high-potential employees.	5 Mar	**D** How much did the measure change during the evaluation period? _11% (annual %) (4 turnovers annually)._
5 Provide recognition to employees with long tenure.	Routinely	**E** What other factors could have contributed to this improvement? _Growth opportunities, changes in job market._
6 Schedule appreciation dinner for entire team.	31 May	**F** What percent of this change was actually caused by this programme? _75%_
7 Encourage team leaders to delegate more responsibilities.	31 May	**G** What level of confidence do you place on the above information? (100% = Certainty and 0% = No Confidence) _90%_
8 Follow up with each discussion and discuss improvement or lack of improvement and plan other action.	Routinely	
9 Monitor improvement and provide recognition when appropriate.	11 May	

Intangible benefits: _Less stress on team, greater job satisfaction_

Comments: _Great coach – he kept me on track with this issue._

TABLE 8.4 Actual data reported

ACTUAL DATA REPORTED – BUSINESS IMPACT FROM COACHING

Exec #	Measurement area	Total annual value	Basis	Method for converting data	Contribution factor	Confidence estimate	Adjusted value
1	Revenue growth	$ 11,500	Profit margin	Standard value	33%	70%	$ 2,656
2	Retention	175,000	3 turnovers	Standard value	40%	70%	49,000
3	Retention	190,000	2 turnovers	Standard value	60%	80%	91,200
4	Direct cost savings	75,000	From cost statements	Participant estimate	100%	100%	75,000
5	Direct cost savings	21,000	Contract services	Standard value	75%	70%	11,025
6	Direct cost savings	65,000	Staffing costs	Standard value	70%	60%	27,300
7	Retention	150,000	2 turnovers	Standard value	50%	50%	37,500
8	Cost savings	70,000	Security	Standard value	60%	90%	37,800
9	Direct cost savings	9,443	Supply costs	N/A	70%	90%	5,949
10	Efficiency	39,000	Information technology costs	Participant estimate	70%	80%	21,840
11	Retention	215,000	4 turnovers	Standard value	75%	90%	145,125
12	Productivity	13,590	Overtime	Standard value	75%	80%	8,154

TABLE 8.4 *Continued*

ACTUAL DATA REPORTED – BUSINESS IMPACT FROM COACHING

Exec #	Measurement area	Total annual value	Basis	Method for converting data	Contribution factor	Confidence estimate	Adjusted value
13	Retention	73,000	1 turnover	Standard value	50%	80%	29,200
14	Retention	120,000	2 annual turnovers	Standard value	60%	75%	54,000
15	Retention	182,000	4 turnovers	Standard value	40%	85%	61,880
16	Cost savings	25,900	Travel	Standard value	30%	90%	6,993
17	Cost savings	12,320	Administrative support	Standard value	75%	90%	8,316
18	Direct cost savings	18,950	Labour savings	Participant estimate	55%	60%	6,253
19	Revenue growth	103,100	Profit margin	Participant estimate	75%	90%	69,592
20	Revenue	19,500	Profit	Standard value	85%	75%	12,431
21	Revenue	21,230	Profit %	Standard value	80%	70%	18,889
22	Revenue growth	105,780	Profit margin	Standard value	70%	50%	37,023
	TOTAL $1,716,313						**TOTAL** $817,126

After the intervention at a predetermined time

- Ask participants to report improvement in the impact measure.
- Ask participants to isolate the effects of the programme.
- Ask participants to provide a level of confidence for estimates.
- Collect action plans, summarize the data, and calculate the ROI.

This data collection approach is not suitable for every initiative nor for every audience. But when a process represents a cross-functional group of participants whose business needs vary and the participants are familiar with those measures, action planning can be a powerful tool resulting in credible output.

Performance contracts

A performance contract is similar to an action plan. Performance contracts are used to document agreements between multiple parties around what they will do in order to achieve a specific outcome. Organizations use performance contracts with their external contractors on a routine basis. Performance contracts can also be used within the organization as people become involved in programmes, projects, and initiatives.

A performance contract specifically states the impact measure or measures that need to improve. Parties charged with implementation agree to their role, the actions they will take, and dates by which they will take those actions. Those involved in the process tend to be the participants most heavily involved in the initiative, the supervisor, and sometimes the facilitator or project leader.

The supervisor, participant, and any other party involved in the process mutually select the actions to be performed or improved prior to the beginning of the programme. The process of selecting the area for improvement is similar to the process that is used in the action planning process.

Follow-up meetings

In some situations, an initiative may include a series of follow-up sessions. Each follow-up session is an opportunity to collect data regarding the use of knowledge and skills acquired from the initial or previous follow-up session. For example, in a large non-governmental organization, a change initiative included three, in-person sessions over the period of one year, along with e-based modules that served as the basis for the upcoming in-person session. At each follow-up session, the facilitator asked participants to provide information on success with implementation including the barriers and enablers. Programme follow-up sessions are an ideal way to build evaluation into the initiative and capture meaningful data without incurring additional costs.

Performance monitoring

Performance data are available in every organization and often serve as the primary reason for the change initiative. Monitoring performance data enables management to measure performance in terms of output, quality, cost, time, and customer satisfaction. Measures such as sales, safety violations, rejects, inventory turnover, customer satisfaction and employee engagement, among many others, are found in performance records. Examples of performance records include:

- sales records;
- safety records;
- quality records;
- scorecards;
- operating reports;
- production records;
- inventory records;
- timekeeping records;
- technology that may capture data on a routine basis.

While there is no one best way to collect data, monitoring performance records can prove to be the simplest, most cost-effective and most credible approach.

Sources of data

A variety of sources of data exists. The most important consideration in selecting the source of data is credibility. Credibility is defined by how much a source knows about the measure being taken and the reliability of the method used to collect the data. Sometimes it may be important to go to multiple sources, but you must always weigh the benefits against the costs of doing so. There is a variety of sources of data including:

- participants;
- participants' manager;
- direct reports;
- peer group;
- internal customers;
- facilitators or change leaders;
- sponsors/clients;
- external experts;
- performance records.

Participants

Participants – people who are participating in and driving the change – are likely the most credible source of any level of data, particularly reaction, learning, and application data. Given they are the audience that engages, or should engage, with the change, it goes without saying that they have the best perspective of the relevance and importance of initiatives. Participants are also the key source when it comes to learning. Their ability to perform a task, take action, or change their behaviour is evident through the various techniques presented earlier. In terms of Level 3 Application data, participants know the most about what they do every day with what they learn. The challenge is to find an effective, efficient, and consistent way to capture these data. Occasionally, when collecting application data, another perspective enhances the credibility and reliability of results; however, participant input should not be discounted when capturing Level 3 data.

Participants' managers

Another source of data is the immediate supervisor, manager, or team leader of the participant. This audience often has a vested interest in evaluation, since they have a stake in the process due to the involvement (or lack of involvement) of their employees. In many situations, they observe the participants as they attempt to apply the information, knowledge, and skills acquired through the change initiative. Consequently, they can report on success as well as difficulties and problems associated with the process and can assess the relevance of the content and capability of the employee as a result of the process.

Direct reports

Direct reports are an excellent source of data, particularly when the participants' behaviours affect their work. For example, if leadership development is part of the change process, it is often the direct report who feels the change in the leadership behaviour. The challenge with this data source, however, is the potential bias that can occur if they fear providing negative data will impact their jobs.

As with any data collection approach, the individual must feel comfortable providing the information. This is when confidentiality and/or anonymity become important. Assuring the direct report that their data will be held in confidence and that the assessment is around the process and not the individual providing the data will often alleviate any fear of repercussion if negative input is provided.

Peer groups

Peers of change participants can provide good input into the extent to which a participant is using knowledge, skill, and information and therefore actually changing their behaviour. This is especially true when that performance affects the peer's work. Peers are good sources of input when collecting data through a process known as 360-degree feedback. Often peers are not in a position to provide comprehensive, objective data; however, if they engage closely with that participant, they can provide valuable insights into behavioural change and performance on the job. With regard to Level 4 Impact data, a peer may or may not be the best source.

Internal customers

The individuals who serve as internal customers of the change initiative are another source of data when the initiative directly affects them. In these situations, internal customers provide reactions to perceived changes linked to the process. They report on how the process has influenced or will influence their work or the service they receive. Because of the subjective nature of this process and the lack of opportunity to fully evaluate the application of skills of the participants, this source of data may be limited.

Facilitators and change leaders

In some situations, the facilitator or change leader may provide input on the success of the initiative. The input from this source is usually based on observations as the process is being implemented. However, data from this source have limited use because of the vested interest facilitators have in the programme's success. While their input may lack objectivity, particularly when collecting Level 1 Reaction and Level 2 Learning data, it is sometimes an important consideration.

Sponsors/clients

The sponsor or client group, usually a member of the senior management team, is an important source of reaction data. Whether an individual or a group, the sponsor's perception is critical to programme success. Sponsors can provide input on all types of issues and are usually available and willing to offer feedback.

External experts

Occasionally, external experts can provide insights that we cannot obtain from participants, their supervisors, peer groups, or direct reports.

External experts are those people who are observing behaviours from a distance. They may capture these data through conversations or engagement in the workplace. An expert may also be someone who is working closely with the participant on a project, providing coaching and support as the project is completed. Typically, experts have a set of standards they follow to assess performance and can provide insight often missed when the supervisor or direct reports are unfamiliar with a process or project.

Performance records

As mentioned earlier in the discussion on performance monitoring, performance records are an excellent source of data, particularly at Level 4, Impact. Performance records often already house the information that we need, making it accessible and inexpensive. Performance records come from the systems already in place and for all practical purposes are perceived as a credible source of data providing credible information.

Timing of data collection

A complete picture of success (or otherwise) is achieved by collecting data at multiple time frames. Staged assessment also allows amendments to be made to improve the change process in situ if outcomes are not being met. As described earlier, reaction and learning data are early indicators of programme success. These data provide information necessary to make immediate adjustments to the change initiative. They also determine actions needed to further support changes in behaviours and actions. This is why reaction and learning data are collected during the initial implementation of a change initiative.

Application data describe how people are using what they know on a routine basis, the barriers that prevent them from using that knowledge, and the enablers that support them in using it. Therefore, application data are collected post implementation. Improvement in business measures or Level 4 Impact data result as a consequence of the application of what people know. Therefore, these data are also collected post implementation. As mentioned in Chapters 2 and 7, objectives will lead toward the right timing for data collection. Other timing considerations are:

- availability of data;
- ideal time for behaviour change;
- ideal time for impact;
- convenience of data collection;
- constraints on data collection.

Availability of data

The evaluation approach described in this book includes a set of standards that ensure consistent and reliable implementation of the process. One such guideline is 'no data, no improvement'.

Data availability is critical in the evaluation process. During the planning process, it is therefore important to identify the time in which the data will become available and collect the data at that point. If the data are non-existent, a system must be put in place to create the data to make them available for tracking and accessing at the time needed. At a minimum, use an available proxy. Proxy measures are good alternatives when the actual data are unavailable or too costly to collect.

Ideal time for behaviour change

Level 3, Application, measures the extent to which people are applying what they know is required for the change programme and how their behaviour is changing. The time at which routine application occurs depends on what the process is offering in terms of knowledge, skill and information and how supportive the environment is of the change. Many of the case studies published on the ROI Methodology describe data collection occurring at approximately three months after the change or learning programme. This three-month time frame represents the typical time after which behavioural change should have occurred. But it is not intended to suggest that all Level 3 data collection occurs at the three-month mark. In fact, in many cases a measure of behaviour change should take place much sooner.

Ideal time for impact

Just like behaviour change, the ideal time for impact depends on a variety of issues. One issue is the type of data. For some data immediate impact will occur, allowing for data capture at any point in time.

Other measures take time to respond to behaviour change. For example, if the change initiative involves a new purchasing process, the purchasing agents may be applying what they learn on a routine basis soon after the programme. But because of the nature of contracting, the reduction in cost may not occur until six months later because it takes that long for the contracts to close. Many times impact data are captured at the same time as the application data. This again depends on the nature of the measure, but it is also driven by the desires of stakeholders.

Convenience of data collection

Another consideration when deciding on the best timing for data collection is convenience. How easily accessible are the data?

Convenience depends on many of the issues just covered including availability of data, ideal time for behaviour change, and ideal time for impact. But it also considers convenience from the perspective of those who are providing the data. The data collection process should be easy for everyone. If it is not convenient, the likelihood of obtaining the necessary information from the appropriate number of people is always going to be diminished.

Constraints on data collection

Constraints are the final consideration when deciding when to collect data. Constraints are those roadblocks to the ideal time frame. For example, working with a large accounting firm, we (Phillips and Phillips) had the opportunity to conduct an evaluation of a tax fundamentals course. Our ideal time frame for collecting the information was at multiple, three-month intervals occurring over the period of one year. Unfortunately, one collection interval occurred the second week in April. In the United States, this is the peak tax season so we had to adjust the timing to work around this unavoidable constraint while still delivering our plan.

Timing for data collection is important. Collecting data at the right time, from the right people, using the right approach leads to the most credible and reliable data possible.

Accurate, timely data collection from a broad range of sources pertinent to the change initiative is essential for successful evaluation. The next chapter describes issues with data analysis including how to calculate the ROI of change initiatives.

Summary of key points

- Data collection is the cornerstone of measurement and evaluation.
- Reaction and learning data serve as useful early indicators regarding the potential use of knowledge and skills.
- Application data describe the extent to which change is occurring through implementation of activities and changes in behaviour.
- Impact data describe the extent to which business measures are improving as a result of the change. This improvement is the basis for calculating the ROI in the change process.
- Data collection occurs at multiple time frames, depending on the purpose and objectives of the initiative.
- While the characteristics of evaluation at each level differ, the one thing that is common among all of them is that each level provides an important input into describing success or an opportunity to improve a change initiative.
- A clear purpose for the change initiative and measurable objectives can lead to the appropriate evaluation approach, including the data collection technique.
- The best approach to data collection will depend on factors such as cost, utility, time requirements, amount of disruption and other practical matters.
- Regardless of the method or technique, instruments should be:
  - valid;
  - reliable;

- simple;
- economical;
- easy to administer;
- easy to analyse.

● Common methods used to capture data include:
  - surveys and questionnaires;
  - interviews and focus groups;
  - observations and demonstrations;
  - tests and quizzes;
  - simulations;
  - action plans;
  - performance contracts;
  - follow-up meetings;
  - performance monitoring.

● A variety of sources of data exists. The most important consideration in selecting the source of data is credibility.

● There is a variety of sources of data including:
  - participants;
  - participants' manager;
  - direct reports;
  - peer group;
  - internal customers;
  - facilitators or change leaders;
  - sponsors/clients;
  - external experts;
  - performance records.

● A complete picture of success (or otherwise) is achieved by collecting data at multiple time frames.

● Staged assessment also allows amendments to be made to improve the change process in situ if outcomes are not being met.

● Other timing considerations are:
  - availability of data;
  - ideal time for behaviour change;

- ideal time for impact;
- convenience of data collection;
- constraints on data collection.

References

Byham, W C (2004) The assessment center method and methodology: new applications and technologies, *DDI* [online] http://www.ddiworld.com/DDI/media/monographs/AssessmentCenterMethods_mg_ddi.pdf?ext=.pdf [accessed November 2015]

Ellect, W (2007) *The Case Study Handbook: How to read, discuss, and write persuasively about cases*, Harvard Business Press, Boston

Phillips, P P, Phillips, J J and Aaron, B C (2013) *Survey Basics*, ASTD Press

Shrock, S and Coscarelli, W (2000) *Criterion-Referenced Test Development* (2nd edition) International Society of Performance Improvement, Silver Spring, MD

Data analysis

09

Although careful and thorough data collection is crucial for reliable and accurate evaluation, it is the analysis of that data that demonstrates whether the change initiative was successful or not. This chapter explores key issues important to the analysis of evaluation data. Through these processes, results of the change initiative become evident.

It is through analysis, the next stage of evaluation, that the results of change become evident. Analysis begins by isolating the impact of the change initiative. By taking this crucial step, the change agent can connect improvement in business measures to the initiative while accounting for other factors that may have influenced improvement. Completion of this step leads to a credible report of the initiative's impact. To calculate ROI on the change initiative, impact data are converted to money and compared to the cost. This process tells a compelling story about the benefits of change. ROI combined with intangible benefits provides potent evidence for the effectiveness of change.

There are effectively five critical steps, each explained below:

1 isolating the impact of change;
2 converting data to monetary value;
3 tabulating fully loaded costs;
4 calculating ROI;
5 defining intangible benefits.

Isolating the impact of change

Isolating the effects of the programme on improvement in business measures allows change agents to give credit where credit is due and offer an explanation as to how much improvement is due to their specific initiative. While some might argue that there is no need to include this step, others argue that without it, there is no way to answer the question, 'How do you know the investment in the change initiative caused the results?' There is a variety of ways to isolate the effects of a programme on improvement in business measures. Each one has benefits; each one has challenges and opportunities. Below are the most commonly used approaches.

Control group arrangement

The gold standard technique to isolate the effects of an initiative is control group arrangement. While there are many types of control group designs (classified as experimental and quasi-experimental designs) there are two basic designs. The first is the classic design, which includes two groups: pre- and post-implementation measures are taken from each group. The second is post-programme only design. In this case, there are also two groups but measures are only taken post implementation.

Classic experimental design

The classic experimental design involves random selection of participants where half are randomly assigned to the experimental group and half to the control group. Pre-programme data are compared to post-programme data for each group. Because participants are randomly selected from a specific population, and randomly assigned to either of two groups, the assumption is that the only influence not accounted for is the initiative. This design answers the question, 'What is the difference in the change in performance between the two groups?' Figure 9.1 depicts this arrangement.

FIGURE 9.1 Classic control group arrangements

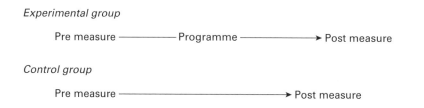

Post-programme only design

Another control design is called post-programme only design. Post-programme only design answers the question, 'What is the difference between the two groups?' Figure 9.2 depicts this arrangement.

FIGURE 9.2   Post-programme only design

Experimental group

Programme ———————————————————→ Post measure

Control group

—————————————————→ Post measure

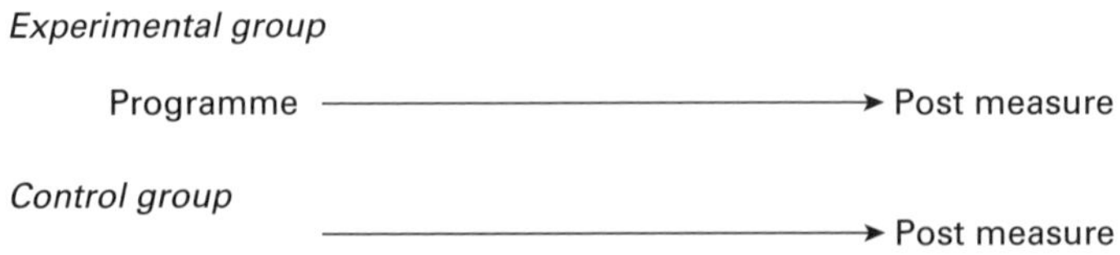

Using this design, participants of each group are randomly drawn and the observation of performance is conducted on a post-programme basis. Unfortunately, it is not always feasible to randomly select participants. One alternative to random selection is to purposely identify the factors by which the groups should be matched – such as performance – in the measure of interest. While this lack of randomization does not account for all other unidentified factors, it does provide an opportunity to use a quasi-experimental design to help isolate the impact of the initiative under way.

The critical issue in using either the classic design or the post-programme only design is in matching the groups so that, as much as possible, the only difference between the groups is the change intervention. The more homogeneous the population from which to draw, the easier it is to identify like participants and assign them to the control and experimental groups.

There are, however, times when neither of these control group arrangements is feasible. If that is the case, consider the following techniques.

Trend line analysis

Another technique for isolating the effects of the change programme is trend line analysis. Trend line analysis requires tracking existing data over a period of time and seeking to determine whether a trend exists and to what extent. A trend means that the data are stable, improving, getting worse, or stagnating – depicted by a flat line. If the data are stable, using Excel or some other tool, project how the trend would perform if all things remained constant. Implement the initiative at a point of time, and then track the measure post programme. The difference between the project performance and the actual performance in the measure is therefore most likely due to the programme.

Figure 9.3 shows trend data for reject rate. In January, the reject rate for this particular organization was 20 per cent. From January to June, the actual reject rate goes down, resulting in a six-month average of 18.5 per cent using the data. The organization forecasts that if the trend continues for the next six months, the reject rate would fall to an average of 14.5 per cent.

FIGURE 9.3   Trend line analysis

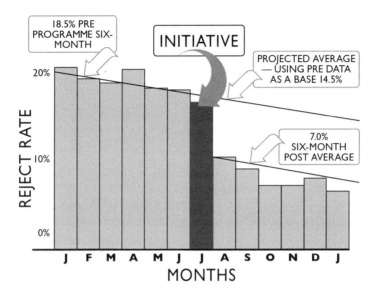

An initiative is implemented in July, and the reject rate is tracked for the next six months. The average post-programme performance is 7 per cent.

By comparing the projected reject rate of 14.5 per cent to the actual post-programme reject rate of 7 per cent, it can be deduced that the difference of 7.5 per cent is due to the change initiative. There are four important considerations to ensure that trend line analysis is an effective tool in isolating the impact of a change initiative:

1 the data exist;

2 the data are stable;

3 the trend is likely to continue;

4 no other major influence occurs during the evaluation period that could also impact the outcome.

Forecasting techniques

A third technique used to isolate the effects of a change initiative is based on regression analysis. Regression analysis compares the movement in independent and dependent variables (measures). The correlation between the two measures indicates that there is a relationship between those two measures; as one moves, so moves the other at a certain level of statistical significance. As many will argue, just because a correlation exists does not mean causation exists. If the correlation is strong enough, an evaluator can be relatively confident that there is some cause-and-effect relationship. But it is important to note that the relationship must be meaningful. Strong correlations exist between many variables, yet the relationships may have little meaning.

Demonstrating relationships between variables via correlation analysis has long been discounted as a proper approach for showing causal relationships. However, Dr Joris Mooij and his team at the University of Amsterdam in the Netherlands have begun to explore ways to determine cause and effect using observational data (Mooij et al, 2014). The basis of their approach assumes that the relationship between X and Y is not symmetrical. They say that in any set of measurements there will always be noise from various causes. The assumption is that the pattern of the noise in the cause will be different to the pattern of the noise in the effect. They use their additive noise model to work out which of the variables is the cause and which is the effect, and report that this model is up to 80 per cent accurate in correctly determining cause and effect.

Estimations

While, from a research standpoint, the previous techniques are the most credible for isolating the effects of an initiative they are not always the most feasible. When this is the case, the use of estimates may be an appropriate alternative.

The estimation process begins with the improvement in the measure. From there, the most credible sources of data provide input into what caused the improvement. Each factor is assigned a weight in the form of percentages. The total value is 100 per cent, indicating that all factors have been accounted for. The value is then adjusted for estimate error by providing their level of confidence in the estimate. The result is an adjusted level of improvement in the measure.

Table 9.1 presents data from one bank branch. The average number of credit cards increases 175 per month. Sources of data reported the factors that contributed to this improvement. These factors were all part of a change process occurring at the bank. The table shows the estimated contribution and the confidence level for the estimates. To calculate the improvement in credit card accounts due to new incentives, for example, the evaluator multiplied 175 new credit cards by an estimate of 41 per cent. The output was then multiplied by 87 per cent. The improvement due to the programme was: $175 \times .41 \times .87 = 62.42$. This explains that 62 new credit cards are due to incentive systems that had been put into place.

TABLE 9.1   Estimation process

Monthly increase in credit card accounts: 175

Contributing factors	Average impact on results	Average confidence level
Sales training programme	32%	83%
Incentive systems	41%	87%
Goal setting/ management emphasis	14%	62%
Marketing	11%	75%
Other _____	2%	91%
	100%	

Converting data to monetary value

Economists have been placing monetary value on a variety of measures for centuries. From placing monetary value on park development and recreation centres to converting human life to money, the topic of converting measures to money has a long history. Money is the ultimate normalizer and it makes the intangible tangible. This helps to demonstrate the value of the change initiative in a way that resonates with stakeholders. Additionally, by converting measures to money, the improvement in business measures can be compared to the cost of the initiative – ultimately demonstrating the ROI.

Data conversion techniques

Measures represent either hard data or soft data. Hard data are measures of output, quality, cost, and time. They are 'hard' because the measures are objectively based and it is possible to count them. Plus they are relatively easy to convert to money. Soft data are 'soft' because they are measured along a continuum or scale of some sort rather than actually counted. Soft data may include measures such as customer satisfaction, job satisfaction, work habits, and innovation. These measures can also be converted to money with the right technique. The main data conversion techniques for converting measures to money are:

- standard values;
- historical costs;
- expert input;
- databases;
- linking soft measures to hard measures;
- estimations.

Each is explained in more detail below.

Standard values

A standard value is a value that the organization already accepts. Standard values include the monetary value of the output of productivity or profit on sales. A standard value may be the value placed on a quality measure, such as a reject rate.

The value of time is a standard value, based on salary and benefits of a person's time. Standard values are often available for measures categorized as hard data.

Historical costs

Value of some measures is determined by historical costs. Historical costs are costs for which there is a receipt or record. For example, an initiative may influence reduction in expense account violations occurring in the organization. Taking the average amount of the historical expense account violations would be the basis for converting one violation to many.

Another example is reduction in litigation costs. If an initiative reduces the number of grievances that result in actual litigation, the historical cost of litigation serves as the basis for monetary value. The use of historical costs is a classic approach to converting measures to money.

Expert input

If historical costs are not available, internal or external experts can provide input into the monetary value. An expert is a person who knows the measure, and can easily identify the value of that measure. For example, the head of market research is probably an expert in valuing customer satisfaction. The challenge is to seek out an expert that is widely perceived as such in the organization, otherwise the expert input may be refuted.

Along with your internal experts, there is a variety of external experts available to help convert measures to money. The topic of ROI in non-capital investments has grown exponentially over the past 20 years. Researchers and practitioners are converting all types of measures to money. While there is a variety of experts available to help with this process, care must be taken to verify expert status and ensure the experts are not simply self-proclaimed!

Databases

A variety of databases is available to help us identify monetary values for measures. A good starting point is the use of search engines, such as Google, Yahoo, Bing and others. While using these search engines can result in unusable information, it can conversely provide information that is very valuable. The key is verification. Make sure you vet the information and identify credible sources. Ideally you should be able to find the same data from various credible sources.

Another source that can be used alongside search engines is online book-sellers, such as Amazon.com, Barnes and Noble, and others. Books that represent content associated with the measures of interest may have online references leading to specific articles that can provide the needed information.

Databases such as NexisLexis and EBSCOhost are excellent sources for identifying monetary values of measures. Subscriptions to these databases are available for corporations, universities and public libraries. EBSCOhost, for example, is the world's largest repository of peer-review journals, and offers access to universities and public libraries worldwide. By tapping into these databases, monetary values can be identified for all measures across countless disciplines.

Linking soft measures to hard data

Many measures of improvement seek to quantify soft data. These measures are typically more difficult to convert to money. Sometimes it is feasible to link these softer measures to money by linking them with other measures. Table 9.2 demonstrates some of the most common linkages between soft measures and those measures more easily converted to money.

Using these statistical approaches can develop models that can not only define value for certain measures, but also provide predictive indicators of what an organization is likely to achieve. The model that serves as the basis for many of the more recent models is Sears's Employee–Customer–Profit Chain (Rucci, Kirn and Quinn, 1998).

Estimations

Ideally, converting data to money will employ one of the above techniques. If conversion is not critical then estimation may also be an appropriate approach. The estimation process to convert measures to money is similar to

TABLE 9.2   Common linkages between measures

Job satisfaction	vs	Turnover
Job satisfaction	vs	Absenteeism
Job satisfaction	vs	Customer satisfaction
Organization commitment	vs	Productivity
Engagement	vs	Productivity
Customer satisfaction	vs	Revenue
Conflicts	vs	Productivity

that used when estimating the connection between improvement in a measure and the initiative under investigation.

Credible sources provide input into the monetary value of improvement in a measure. The estimate is then adjusted for error by asking for the sources' levels of confidence in their estimates. This technique is not ideal, but can be useful if no other technique is possible.

Steps to calculate annual monetary value

Understanding the annual monetary value of a change initiative provides a complete look at the value of initiatives. This value also serves as the numerator of the ROI calculation.

There are essentially five steps for converting change improvements or measures into annual monetary value. They are:

1 define the unit of measure;

2 convert the measure to money;

3 determine the change in performance;

4 annualize the change in performance;

5 determine the annual monetary value for the change in performance.

The first step is to define the unit of measure. This reflects one unit of the business measures targeted for improvement. For example, if the intent is to increase sales to new customers, a unit of measure is one new customer sale.

If the intent is to reduce grievances, a unit of measure is one grievance. Identifying these measures occurs when developing objectives for the initiative.

The second step is to place a value on the measure using the techniques previously described. The value of a sale is the profit on the sale. Or the value of a grievance must be based on the time to deal with the grievance, or on the input of a labour relations expert. As an example, in a healthcare organization the head of labour relationships (the expert) determined the cost of a grievance as $6,500 per grievance.

The third step is to determine the change in performance in the measure. Change in performance is the output of analysing Level 4 data, after isolating the effects of the initiative. For example, six months after the programme, grievances in the above example decreased on average by 10 per month. After isolating the effects of the initiative, the improvement was only seven per month. A reduction of seven per month was the change in performance due to the initiative.

The fourth step is to annualize the change in performance. In the example above, the average monthly reduction in grievances was multiplied by 12, resulting in an annual value of the improvement of 84.

The fifth and final step is to multiply the annual improvement by the value of the unit of measure to calculate the annual monetary benefits of the initiative. In this case, if one grievance is valued at $6,500 and the annual improvement is 84, the annual monetary value is $546,000. For stakeholders this shows that the initiative contributed to a cost saving of $546,000 over the course of one year.

These five steps lead to the annual monetary value of implementing a change initiative. When multiple measures are influential these five steps are taken and the annual monetary value for each measure is totalled to capture the complete benefit of implementing change.

Tabulating fully loaded costs

Investments in change include all of the resources necessary to implement the initiative. This goes beyond accounting for budgeted resources for a change initiative. The investment requires accounting for the fully loaded costs – meaning all costs associated with planning, implementing and evaluating a change initiative. Broadly speaking, these investments in change initiatives include items such as:

- needs assessment;
- development;

- design;
- delivery;
- implementation;
- evaluation;
- overhead.

These categories of cost represent the full cycle of implementation. Each component includes a variety of cost considerations, making up the full investment of an initiative. Defining which specific costs to include is a critical and sometimes daunting task. It involves making decisions in collaboration with management, sometimes the chief financial officer (CFO), or the CFO's representatives. Programme costs represent the investment the organization is making in change.

Costs may sometimes be prorated over the number of people involved in an initiative over the lifetime of that initiative. Other costs are expensed, meaning the direct costs are included as part of the evaluation. Table 9.3 summarizes the cost categories that represent the full investment in a change initiative. Additionally, the table reflects the cost categories that are typically prorated versus those that are expensed.

Calculating ROI

Return on investment (ROI) is a comparison between the monetary benefits and the costs of the change initiative. There are many measures of return on investment. Given the type of investments made in executing change in an organization, the three most appropriate measures are:

- benefit–cost ratio (BCR);
- ROI as a percentage;
- payback period.

Benefit–cost ratio

Benefit–cost ratio (BCR) is the output of cost–benefit analysis, a theory that is grounded in welfare economics and public finance. It was initially used as a feasibility metric to help project managers make decisions about investing in projects such as bridges, dams, and other large initiatives. BCR represents gross benefits compared to cost. To calculate the benefit–cost ratio, simply follow this equation:

$$BCR = \frac{\text{Change initiative benefits}}{\text{Change initiative costs}}$$

For example, with benefits of $750,000 and costs of $425,000, the BCR would be 1.76 or 1.76:1.

$$BCR = \frac{\$750,000}{\$425,000} = 1.76$$

The principal advantage of this approach is that it avoids traditional financial measures, so there is no confusion when comparing investments in change initiatives to other company investments. For example, investments in plants, equipment and subsidiaries are not usually evaluated with the benefit–cost ratio. The ROI for change initiatives is a unique type of investment.

TABLE 9.3   Cost categories

Cost item	Prorated	Expensed
Needs assessment	✓	
Design and development	✓	
Acquisition	✓	
Delivery		✓
• Salaries/benefits – facilitators		✓
• Salaries/benefits – coordination		✓
• Programme materials and fees		✓
• Travel/lodging/meals		✓
• Facilities		✓
• Salaries/benefits – participants		✓
• Contact time		✓
• Travel time		✓
• Preparation time		✓
Evaluation		✓
Overhead/training and development	✓	

ROI as a percentage

The most appropriate formula to evaluate a change initiative is the ROI percentage. This ratio compares net change initiative benefits to change initiative costs multiplied 100 times. Net initiative benefits are the benefits minus the initiative costs. For example, a BCR of 2.45 is the same as an ROI of 145 per cent. Below is a calculation showing the difference between the BCR and the ROI.

$$\text{BCR} = \frac{\$750,000}{\$425,000} = 1.76$$

$$\text{ROI} = \frac{\$750,000 - \$425,000}{\$425,000} \times 100 = 76\%$$

The ROI formula is essentially the same as ROI for other types of investments. For example, when a firm builds a new plant, the ROI is annual earnings divided by investment. The annual earnings are comparable to net benefits (annual benefits minus costs), and the investment is comparable to initiative cost which represents the investment in a change initiative.

Payback period

The payback period is the common method for evaluating capital expenditures. It presents the annual savings produced by an investment compared to the original investment. The measurement is usually in terms of years and months. For example, if a project generates a cost saving and this cost saving is constant each year, the payback period is calculated by dividing the total original investment (needs assessment, development cost, implementation, evaluation, etc) by the amount of the expected annual or actual savings. Below is an illustration of this calculation.

$$\text{Payback period} = \frac{\text{Programme cost}}{\text{Programme benefits}} = \frac{\$425,000}{\$750,000}$$

$$= .567 \times 12 = 6.8 \text{ months}$$

The payback period is simple to use, but has limitations. For example it ignores the time value of money. Its use is not as widespread as benefit–cost ratio and the ROI, but it does provide insight into how long it will take to recoup the investment in change.

Defining intangible benefits

Intangible benefits are benefits of a change initiative not converted to monetary value. These measures may include measures of customer satisfaction, job satisfaction, teamwork, loyalty, and initiative. While each of these can lead to monetary value, sometimes reporting them as intangible can be as provocative as reporting the ROI. Whether or not these measures need to be converted to money will depend on the answers to four questions:

1 Is there a standard value?

If there is a standard value, convert the measure to money. Standard values exist throughout the organization. If it is standard, the organization has already bought into the value of that measure. If there is not a standard value, answer the next question.

2 Is there a technique to convert it to money?

If there is not a standard value, consider the techniques described in this chapter. Determine if one of these techniques is a viable approach. First, consider historical costs to determine if there is a receipt or record for that particular measure. If there is not, consider the availability of experts within or outside the organization who can provide you a monetary value for that measure. If there is no expert, consider databases to determine the availability of research describing monetary value of measures. If no database is available, consider the feasibility of linking the improvement in the measure to a measure that is more easily converted to money. As a last resort, consider using estimates from a credible source. If none of these options work, report the improvement in that measure as an intangible benefit. If, however, you can use one of the above techniques, then answer the next question.

3 Can the chosen technique be used, given the existing cost constraints?

This question gets to the issue of spending too much time and money converting a measure to money. If implementing a particular technique is going to cost more than the information is worth, report the improvement in that measure as an intangible benefit. However, if the chosen technique is feasible, answer the following question.

4 Will executives believe the values being reported?

Consider the response to this question carefully. Executives may view the value credible even if the project team questions it. However, if they will not view the value as credible, you may be better off reporting the improvement as an intangible benefit. It is important that executives and other stakeholders perceive the data as credible.

Intangible measures can be captured from different sources and at different times throughout the implementation cycle. They can be uncovered early in the process, during the needs assessment, and planned for collection as part of the overall data collection strategy.

Intangible benefits are critical to reporting the success of an initiative, which we will unpack in the next chapter. They may not carry the weight of measures expressed in monetary terms, especially for some stakeholders, but they are nevertheless an important part of the overall evaluation. Intangible measures should be identified, explored, examined, and monitored for changes linked to change initiatives. Collectively, they add a unique dimension to the evaluation report since most, if not all, change initiatives involve intangible benefits. After all, behavioural change, so often the ultimate objective in change initiatives, usually involves significant intangible benefits.

Summary of key points

- Although careful and thorough data collection is crucial for reliable and accurate evaluation it is the analysis of that data that demonstrates whether the change initiative was successful or not.

- Analysis begins by isolating the impact of the change initiative. By taking this crucial step, the change agent can connect improvement in business measures to the initiative while accounting for other factors that may have influenced improvement.

- Completion of this step leads to a credible report of the initiative's impact.

- To calculate ROI on the change initiative, impact data are converted to money and compared to the cost. This process tells a compelling story about the benefits of change.

- ROI combined with intangible benefits provides potent evidence for the effectiveness of change.

- Effectively, data analysis consists of five critical steps:
  1 isolating the impact of change;
  2 converting data to monetary value;
  3 tabulating fully loaded costs;
  4 calculating ROI;
  5 defining intangible benefits.

- There is a variety of ways to isolate the impact of change including:
  - control group arrangement;
  - trend line analysis;
  - forecasting techniques;
  - estimations.
- Economists have been placing monetary value on a variety of measures for centuries. Money is the ultimate normalizer and it makes the intangible tangible. This helps to demonstrate the value of the change initiative in a way that resonates with stakeholders.
- The main data conversion techniques to convert measures to money are:
  - standard values;
  - historical costs;
  - expert input;
  - databases;
  - linking soft measures to hard measures;
  - estimations.
- There are essentially five steps for converting change improvements or measures into annual monetary value. They are:
  1 define the unit of measure;
  2 convert the measure to money;
  3 determine the change in performance;
  4 annualize the change in performance;
  5 determine the annual monetary value for the change in performance.
- When determining the investment in a change initiative it is important to consider the fully loaded costs.
- Return on investment (ROI) is a comparison between the monetary benefits and the costs of the change initiative.
- The three most appropriate measures of ROI are:
  - benefit–cost ratio;
  - ROI as a percentage;
  - payback period.

- Intangible benefits may include measures of customer satisfaction, job satisfaction, teamwork, loyalty, and initiative. While each of these can lead to monetary value, sometimes reporting them as intangible can be as provocative as reporting the ROI.

- Whether to convert intangible benefits to a monetary value will depend on the answers to four questions:

  1 Is there a standard value?

  2 Is there a technique to convert it to money?

  3 Can the chosen technique be used, given the existing cost constraints?

  4 Will executives believe the values being reported?

References

Rucci, A J, Kirn, S P and Quinn, R T (1998) The Employee–Customer–Profit Chain at Sears, *Harvard Business Review* Jan–Feb, pp 84–97

Mooij J M, Peters, J, Janzing, D, Zscheischler, J and Schölkopf, B (2014) Distinguishing cause from effect using observational data: methods and benchmarks, *Journal of Machine Learning Research*

Reporting results

10

Reporting results is the final phase of the evaluation process and the focus of this chapter. It is through this reporting process that evidence of the effectiveness of the change initiative is communicated to the stakeholders. All too often evaluation is conducted only to have the results languish on a shelf, or distributed to a very small senior team. This lack of transparency and communication can amplify change fatigue for stakeholders – especially those lower down in the business. When those affected by the change are not given feedback on the results they may be unclear of the company-wide impact of the change initiative. This lack of discussion and sharing of results can diminish trust levels and lead to reluctance to embrace future change.

Through a variety of reporting formats, change agents can describe the success of initiatives as well as opportunities for improvement. This chapter provides a brief look at the different approaches to reporting results and offers tips to ensure the communication strategy is effective.

The most common forms of result communication are:

- detailed evaluation reports;
- meetings;
- routine publications;
- routine feedback on progress;
- the communication plan.

Detailed evaluation reports

The presentation of results depends on the level of information required by the target audience. This depends on the decisions the audience will make regarding the initiative. Brief summaries of project results with appropriate charts may be sufficient for some communication efforts. In other situations, particularly those involving major projects requiring extensive funding, presenting a detailed evaluation report may be more appropriate.

A complete and comprehensive report is usually necessary for programmes evaluated to impact or ROI. This report can then be used as the basis for more streamlined information aimed at specific audiences and using various media. Table 10.1 is a report outline used to convey results in an effective manner. It has all the necessary ingredients to communicate outcomes in the best possible way.

TABLE 10.1   Complete communication report outline

- **General information**
  - Background:
    - What were the needs that precipitated the programme?
    - Why was this programme selected?
  - Objectives of study:
    - What are the goals and targets for this programme?
    - What are the intended results?
- **Methodology for impact study**
  - Levels of evaluation:
    - Describe the evaluation framework to set the stage for showing the results.
    - Briefly describe the process that was used.
  - Collecting data:
    - What methods were selected to collect data and why?
    - When were data collected?
  - Isolating the effects of the programme:
    - What method was used to isolate the effects of the intervention and why?
  - Converting data to monetary values:
    - What methods were used to convert data to money?
  - Data analysis:
    - How were data analysed?
    - What methods were used?
  - Costs:
    - Itemize the costs of the intervention.

TABLE 10.1 *Continued*

- **Results**
  - General information
  - Response profile:
    - Include demographics of the population that responded or participated in the evaluation.
    - If a questionnaire was used, what was the return rate and the anticipated return rate?
  - Reaction and planned action:
    - Data sources
    - Data summary
    - Key issues
  - Learning:
    - Data sources
    - Data summary
    - Key issues
  - Application:
    - Data sources
    - Data summary
    - Key issues
  - Impact:
    - Data sources
    - Data summary
    - Key issues
  - ROI
  - Intangible measures
  - Barriers and enablers:
    - This section of the report can be a powerful mechanism to lead into conclusions and recommendations. What obstacles were experienced that kept the organization from experiencing the kind of results they wanted? If there were barriers noted, then this should turn into some action items for the organization.
- **Conclusions**
  - Summarize key findings from the data.
- **Recommendations**
  - Based on the conclusions, what type of action needs to take place?
  - What are stakeholders willing to do?

While the impact study report is an effective, professional way to report ROI data, there are several caveats. Since this report documents the success of an initiative involving other individuals, credit for the success must go completely to those involved – it was the performance of individuals embedding the change initiative that generated the success.

The report should include a clear explanation of the implementation and evaluation approach. This explanation includes any assumption in the analysis. Final results should be presented in a logical order, following the chain of impact. The reader should be able to easily see how the values were developed and how specific steps were followed to make the process more conservative, credible, and accurate. Detailed statistical analyses should be placed in an appendix. The report should include conclusions, recommendations, and next steps.

Meetings

Under the right conditions, meetings are a fertile ground for the communication of programme results. All organizations hold a variety of meetings, and some may provide the proper context to convey programme results.

Staff meetings are held to review progress, discuss current problems, and distribute information. These meetings are an excellent forum for discussing the results achieved by implementing a change initiative.

Routine meetings

Regular meetings with management groups are a common practice. Typically, discussions will focus on items that might be of help to work units. The discussion of a programme and its results can be integrated into the regular meeting format.

Organizations may also initiate the use of periodic meetings for all key stakeholders, where a project leader reviews progress and discusses next steps. A few highlights from interim programme results can be helpful to maintain interest and momentum as well as build commitment and support for the programme.

Senior management meetings

Perhaps one of the most challenging approaches to communicating results is presenting an impact study to the senior management team. This group also serves as the client for a change project. The challenge is convincing this sometimes-sceptical group that exceptional results have been achieved (assuming they have) in a reasonable time frame, addressing the salient points, and making sure the managers understand the process.

Two potential reactions can create problems. First, if the results are extremely positive, convincing managers to accept the data may be difficult. On the other extreme, if the data are negative, ensuring that managers do not overreact to the results is equally important. Below are tips to help ensure that this process is planned and executed properly.

Establish the purpose of the meeting

It's vital that you always seek to establish the purpose of the meetings ahead of time so as to:

- create awareness and understanding of the evaluation process;
- build support for the evaluation process;
- communicate results of the change initiative;
- drive improvement from results;
- cultivate effective use of the evaluation process.

Follow ground rules

Useful and productive meetings are made easier if you institute and follow a set of ground rules. These ground rules may include:

- hold off on distributing the study until the end of the meeting;
- be precise and to the point;
- avoid jargon and unfamiliar terms;
- spend less time on the lower levels of evaluation data;
- present the data with a strategy in mind.

Follow a consistent presentation sequence

When using meetings to communicate with stakeholders about the results of the change initiative it's always best to follow a consistent presentation sequence:

- describe the programme and explain why it is being evaluated;
- present the methodology process;
- present the reaction, learning, and application data;

- list the barriers and enablers to success;
- address the business impact;
- present the costs and ROI (when applicable);
- show the intangibles;
- review the credibility of the data;
- summarize the conclusions;
- present the recommendations.

Routine publications

To reach a wide audience, internal, routine publications may be used to communicate with stakeholders regarding the results of a change initiative. Whether a newsletter, e-zine or other routine publication these types of communication usually reach all employees or stakeholders. The content can have a significant impact if communicated appropriately. The scope should be limited to general-interest articles, announcements, and interviews.

Results communicated through these types of media must be important enough to generate general interest. For example, a story with the headline 'Change Matters: Results Show Positive Impact Due to Initiative' will catch the attention of many readers because they probably know about the initiative and can appreciate the relevance of the results. Reports on the accomplishments of a small group of organization members may not generate interest if the audience cannot relate to the accomplishments.

For many initiatives, results are not achieved until weeks or even months after the implementation. This is especially true for behavioural change that may only fully emerge after TLA or some other change methodology has been implemented. Reinforcement is needed from many sources. Communicating results to a general audience may lead to motivation to proceed with an initiative or expand its reach.

Stories about those involved in the process and the results they have achieved can help create a favourable image of the change. Employees see that the organization is investing resources to improve performance and prepare for the future. This type of story provides information about a programme that may otherwise be unknown, and sometimes creates a desire for others to participate. Public recognition of participants who deliver exceptional performance can enhance confidence and drive them to excel.

Routine feedback on progress

A primary reason for collecting reaction and learning data is to provide feedback so that adjustments can be made throughout the implementation of a change initiative. For most programmes, data are routinely collected and quickly communicated to a variety of groups. A feedback action plan designed to provide information to several audiences using a variety of media may be an option. These feedback sessions highlight actions that need to be taken. This process becomes complex and must be managed in a very proactive manner.

The following steps are recommended for providing routine feedback on progress and managing the overall process. Many of the steps and concepts are based on the recommendations of Peter Block in his landmark book *Flawless Consulting* (2011) whether you work with internal or external customers.

- **Communicate quickly**. Whether the news is good or bad, it should be passed on to individuals involved in the change initiative as soon as possible. The recommended time for providing feedback is usually a matter of days and certainly no longer than a week or two after the results become known.

- **Simplify the data**. Condense the data into an easily understandable, concise presentation. You may want to consider using a one-page infographic. However, it is not always appropriate to simplify the data when the situation calls for more detailed explanations and analysis.

- **Examine the role of the learning and development team and the client in the feedback process**. The learning and development team can wear many hats in the process. On the other hand, sometimes the client plays roles that the team is used to filling. These respective functions must be examined in terms of reactions to the data and the recommended actions.

- **Use negative data in a constructive way**. Some of the data will show that things are not going so well, and the fault may rest with the project leader or the client. In this case, the story basically changes from 'let's look at the success we've achieved', to 'now we know which areas to change'.

- **Use positive data in a cautious way**. Positive data can be misleading, and if they are communicated too enthusiastically they may create expectations that exceed what finally materializes. Positive data should be presented in a guarded way, allowing the response to be fully in the hands of the stakeholders.

- **Choose the language of the meeting and the communication carefully.** The language used should be descriptive, focused, specific, short, and simple. Language that is too judgemental, full of jargon, stereotypical, lengthy, or complex should be avoided.

- **Ask the client for reactions to the data**. After all, the client is the number one customer, and it is most important that the client be pleased with the project.

- **Ask the client for recommendations**. The client may have some good suggestions for what needs to be changed to keep a project on track, or to put it back on track should it derail.

- **Use support and confrontation carefully**. These two actions are not mutually exclusive. At times, support and confrontation are both needed for a particular group. The client may need support and yet be confronted for lack of improvement or sponsorship. The project team may be confronted regarding the problem areas that have developed, but may need support too.

- **Act on the data**. The different alternatives and possibilities should be weighed carefully to arrive at necessary adjustments.

- **Secure agreement from all key stakeholders**. It is essential to ensure that everyone is willing to make suggested changes.

- **Keep the feedback process short**. We discourage allowing the process to become bogged down in long, drawn-out meetings or lengthy documents. If this occurs, stakeholders will avoid the process. It's imperative that they are willing participants.

Following these steps will help move the project forward and generate useful feedback, often ensuring that adjustments are supported and can be executed.

The communication plan

Any activity must be carefully planned to achieve maximum results. This is a critical part of communicating the results of any initiative. The actual planning of the communication is important to ensure that each audience receives the proper information at the right time and that necessary actions are taken. Several issues are important in planning the communication of results:

- What will be communicated?
- When will the data be communicated?
- How will the information be communicated?
- Where will the information be communicated?
- Who will communicate the information?
- Who is the target audience?
- What are the specific actions required or desired?

The communication plan is usually developed at the launch of a change initiative along with the evaluation plan. This plan details how specific information is developed and communicated to various groups and the expected actions. In addition, this plan details how the overall results will be communicated, the time frame for communication, and the appropriate groups to receive the information.

A word of caution

Communication can quite easily go astray or miss the mark if not considered seriously and planned for appropriately. To maximize results and minimize the opportunity for error:

- **Be transparent with results**. The least desired action is not communicating anything. Communicating results is almost as important as producing results. Achieving results without communicating is a wasted activity and can actively diminish morale. By not sharing the findings from an initiative, the organization may miss out on a key opportunity to make adjustments and bring about the change that is desired.

- **Bear in mind political ramifications**. Communication can be delicate. Because the results of an initiative may be perceived as a 'political threat' within an organization, it is important to consider the ramifications of pleasing one group but upsetting another. If certain individuals do not receive the information, or if it is delivered inconsistently between groups, problems can quickly surface. The information must not only be understood, but issues relating to fairness, quality, and political correctness make it crucial that the communication be constructed and delivered effectively to all key individuals.

- **Make action-orientated recommendations**. Recommendations are probably one of the most critical issues and yet this part of the report or presentation is often a last-minute thought. In some cases, recommendations are skipped altogether. Recommendations are the main conduit to change. The best recommendations include specific action-oriented steps that come from the conclusions of the evaluation study and are then discussed with key stakeholders for buy-in and ownership. Collaboration with stakeholders on what actions to take based on results is essential.

- **Respect audience opinion**. Opinions are difficult to change; a mere presentation of results may not influence those opinions in the least. However, the presentation of facts alone may strengthen the opinions held by those who already support the programme and provides them with a defence in discussions with others. A project team with a high level of credibility and respect may have a relatively easy time communicating results. Low credibility can create problems when one is trying to be persuasive.

Guidelines for reporting results

Communicating results effectively should be a systematic process with specific rules and steps. Of course, many of the guidelines set out for routine feedback during the change process also apply when you report results and final outcomes. Project results should be communicated as soon as they are known or as soon as feasibly possible. Timing of the results is a critical factor in the success of the change initiative. Not sharing the results in a timely fashion can lead to a missed opportunity for well-timed improvement.

While timing is important, it is also important to customize the presentation to the audience. The message can be specifically tailored to the interests, needs, and expectations of the group. The length, content, detail, and perspective will vary with the audience. This is not to suggest that the story be altered but rather the message should be targeted to what each stakeholder audience wants to know.

The most important target audience is the client, and this often involves senior management because they need information to approve or validate funding. The entire management group may also need to be informed about project results in a general way. Management's support for, and involvement in, any change process is important to the success of the effort. The department's credibility is another key issue. Communicating project results to management can help establish this credibility.

The importance of communicating with the immediate manager of staff involved in change is probably obvious. In some cases, these managers need to support and allow employees to be involved in change programmes. An adequate return on investment improves their commitment to change while enhancing the team's credibility with their manager.

Employees involved in the change process also need feedback on the overall success of their efforts. This target audience is often overlooked under the assumption that participants do not need to know about the overall success of the programme.

Naturally, those affected by the change initiative should receive information about results, and depending on the team's reporting relationships, perhaps include HR too. For small teams, the individual conducting the evaluation may be the same person who coordinated the change effort. For larger departments the evaluation may be a separate function. In either case, the team needs detailed information on the programme's effectiveness so that adjustments can be made if the project is repeated.

Modes of communication matter

One medium of communication may be more effective than others, depending on the audience. Face-to-face meetings may be better with some groups than special reports. A brief summary dashboard to senior management will likely be more effective than a detailed evaluation report.

The selection of an appropriate medium will help improve the effectiveness of the process. Table 10.2 illustrates options for communicating results.

Neutrality is central

While it can be a challenge, it is important that the evaluator remains neutral at all times. The results should speak for themselves. Some target audiences may look for biased information and opinions, especially when the project team is also the evaluation team. Boastfulness will sometimes turn off the audience and the content of the communication will be lost. Observable, believable facts carry more weight than extreme claims.

Testimonials about results, when solicited from individuals who are generally respected in the organization, can have a strong impact on the effectiveness of the message. They often balance what may be considered potentially biased results.

TABLE 10.2   Options for communicating results

Detailed reports	Brief reports	Electronic reporting	Mass publications
Impact study	Executive summary	Website	Announcements
Case study (internal)	Slide overview	E-mail	Bulletins
Case study (external)	One-page summary	Blog	Newsletters
Major articles	Brochure	Video	Brief articles

Consistency pays off

Reporting results should be consistent with organization practices. A special communication at an unusual time may create more work than it is worth. When a particular group, such as senior management, regularly receives communication, the information should continue even if the results are undesirable. If selected results are omitted, it might leave the impression that only good results are reported.

Communication drives results

Information is collected at different points during the process, and providing feedback to all stakeholders enables them to take action and make adjustments if needed. Thus, the quality and timeliness of communication are critical to making improvements.

In the end, that is the purpose of the evaluation. Even after the evaluation is completed, communication is necessary to make sure the target audience fully understands the results achieved, and how the results may be enhanced in future. Communication is key to making important adjustments at all phases of the project.

Reporting results may be the final phase of the evaluation process but it is not the final step in ensuring the change initiative has ongoing impact. Those expected to change must be supported to do so over time and, as we've pointed out, this is greatly facilitated by TLA.

So far we've explored the theory of TLA; in Part Four we will unpack TLA in practice to ensure that behavioural change is supported in the workplace so the results really do shine.

Summary of key points

- Reporting results is the final phase of the evaluation process.
- It is through this reporting process that evidence of the effectiveness of the change initiative is communicated to the stakeholders.
- All too often evaluation is conducted only to have the results languish on a shelf, or distributed to a very small senior team. This lack of transparency and communication can amplify change fatigue for stakeholders – especially those lower down in the business.
- Through a variety of reporting formats, change agents can describe the success of initiatives as well as opportunities for improvement.
- The most common forms of result communication are:
  - detailed evaluation reports;
  - meetings;
  - routine publications;
  - routine feedback on progress;
  - the communication plan.
- The presentation of results depends on the level of information required by the target audience. Brief summaries of project results with appropriate charts may be sufficient for some communication efforts. In other situations, particularly those involving major projects requiring extensive funding, presenting a detailed evaluation report may be more appropriate.
- Under the right conditions, meetings are a fertile ground for the communication of programme results.
- To reach a wide audience, internal, routine publications such as a newsletter or e-zine may be used to communicate with stakeholders regarding the results of a change initiative.
- A primary reason for collecting reaction and learning data is to provide routine feedback on progress so that adjustments can be made throughout the implementation of a change initiative.

- The actual planning of the communication is important to ensure that each audience receives the proper information at the right time and that necessary actions are taken.
- Communication can quite easily go astray or miss the mark if not considered seriously and planned for appropriately. To avoid problems:
  - be transparent with results;
  - bear in mind political ramifications;
  - make action-orientated recommendations;
  - respect audience opinion.
- Communicating results effectively should be a systematic process with specific rules and steps. Project results should be communicated as soon as they are known or as soon as feasibly possible.

Reference

Block, P (2011) *Flawless Consulting: A guide to getting your expertise used*, 3rd edition, Pfeiffer, San Francisco

PART FOUR
TLA in practice

Making TLA work
Skill set

11

TLA is a deceptively simple process. You may have read the TLA process and theory section and thought, 'Hey, that sounds pretty simple!' It is simple but it's not necessarily easy. The following two chapters therefore explore how to make TLA work in practice, looking in this chapter at the skill set needed to facilitate behavioural change and in the next at how to guide the conversation.

Executing TLA successfully requires specific skills.

There are three critical skills required for successful TLA delivery. Like most skills in life, they come with time and experience and successful TLA facilitators use them all the time. They are:

1 asking power questions;
2 being listening;
3 using intuition effectively.

Asking power questions

The crux of coaching in all its forms is that when we are communicating and interacting with another person, asking questions to allow the individual to arrive at the best answer is always going to be more successful than simply telling that individual what to do. Even if the other person is receptive to our opinion or advice they will often soon forget the words of wisdom if they were not something they came up with themselves, or had a hand in coming up with. Asking questions is therefore a great tool for soliciting involvement and engagement in the challenge at hand. Properly pitched questions allow the individual to explore the situation and their own thinking. An individual is always much more likely to action and maintain a change they had a hand in identifying than one handed down to them from someone else.

Obviously most change initiatives are rolled out to facilitate behavioural change – people are required to do something differently. That may range from using a new IT system to a new sales process to a new order system. But there is often a reasonable degree of latitude in how each person makes that change. An individual could for example decide to use a certain part of the IT system first, or they could adopt the new sales process but tweak a few things here and there to suit their personality or method of working. Asking questions allows the individual to take ownership of the change and, within reason, tailor that change to suit them and their own change timeline. This also allows for the fact that each person knows their own role and their own behaviours best – they will know better than anyone else what needs to happen, in a practical way, to make the change successful.

Questions are an essential tool in the TLA facilitator's kitbag. But like most tools, some types of questions are more useful than others. One of the primary distinctions is between a closed and an open question. The easiest way to remember the difference is to match them to what they do to the conversation. Closed questions tend to close down the conversation because they can be answered with 'Yes', 'No' or another one-word response. We can see how challenging this is on TV chat shows when the person being interviewed is being difficult. The interviewer will ask a series of questions and the celebrity will answer using single-word responses. It's usually pretty uncomfortable to watch and even more uncomfortable to experience because there is no flow in the conversation. The most common closed questions begin with 'Is it...?', 'Are they...?', 'Do you...?', 'Have you...?' All of which will usually lead to a 'Yes', 'No' or single-word response.

Closed questions can also allow the facilitator to manipulate the agenda through what US coach Michael Stratford calls a 'queggestion'. A queggestion is a suggestion disguised as a question for the purpose of nudging someone into a conclusion that the coach has already arrived at. If the TLA facilitator asks the person expected to change, 'Would it be worthwhile setting up a process to ensure that happens weekly?' or 'Do you need to report back to your manager on that regularly?' they have already decided the best way to address the individual's challenge without genuinely engaging the individual and allowing them to find their own solution. This approach effectively mani-pulates the discussion and plants the favoured solution in the head of the person making the change without due process. Plus the facilitator is driving their agenda, or the solutions they think are best, rather than holding a neutral space for the dialogue to unfold. Queggestions have no place in TLA.

In addition, closed questions can be used as a 'get out of jail free' card. They are often easier to ask and answer and therefore allow both parties off the hook. If the TLA facilitator asks, 'Is it this…?' or 'Is it that…?' the question allows the person to dismiss it and shut down the line of enquiry without a great deal of thought. If on the other hand the facilitator asks, 'What are the top three things…?' there is no convenient escape hatch built into that question, and the individual's brain is automatically directed to think about and find the three things. Plus the answers they come up with are entirely their own and are not influenced or swayed by the facilitator's opinion or assumptions. 'What are the top three things…?' is an example of an open question and it's significantly more powerful.

Open questions open the conversation up and allow the conversation to flow naturally. Good open questions usually start with 'What' and 'Why' and will usually prompt a longer, more considered response. Open questions encourage the individual to engage with the question and think about their own situation.

This encouragement to think and engage means that certain open questions – especially those starting with 'Why' – can be quite confronting. As children, typically if someone asked us, 'Why did you do that?' we knew we were in trouble! The 'Why' at the start of a question can be a trigger for people as it often feels judgemental and blunt if not tempered in some way. The best way to soften the delivery is to frame it up in advance to help take the sting out of the question. The facilitator may for example ask, 'I'd love to understand where you are coming from; can you explain more about why you did that?' or 'I'm just curious as to why that is?' That is far less threatening and therefore far more likely to get a useful response than 'Why did you do that?' or 'Why is that?'

Technically, 'How', 'When' and 'Where' are also precursors to open questions but they tend to illicit a shorter, less considered answer or simple data download of a date, time or location. 'What' and 'Why' are the most useful and potent because the client can answer anything, which often opens the conversation up and allows for real progress. Besides, each person being coached knows their situation far better than the facilitator so they are absolutely the best person to source the best way forward for them.

The TLA process focuses on the use of power questions which are a form of open question. The power question ensures that the facilitator doesn't arrive with an agenda or pollute the discussion with assumption. Power questions also prevent the facilitator from asking 'queggestions' or wasting too much time exploring issues that are not relevant.

The best power questions are the ones where the TLA facilitator has no idea how the individual will answer, because it explores their way of thinking, not the facilitator's. Often in response to a power question the individual will pause for a moment and say, 'Wow, that's a really good question,' as they are forced to think deeply about the answer.

Power questions are particularly useful in the TLA process because:

- They open up the conversation and allow the individual to express themselves and take ownership of the conversation.
- They work to the individual's agenda, not what the facilitator believes the agenda should be.
- They probe the individual so they can experience insights that allow them to make the necessary changes quicker.
- They show the individual that the facilitator is interested in their situation and wants to listen.
- They build the individual's confidence that they are the expert. If the facilitator allows the individual to engage with what they already know they will always be far more receptive to addressing what they don't know.
- They create curiosity for the participant to explore for themselves.

TABLE 11.1 Examples of power questions

Power questions	Result
Tell me more about that...	Opens up the conversation, allows the individual to feel comfortable and build confidence by getting them talking.
What do you think/feel when you say that?	Encourages them to reflect on what they think and feel about that statement, event or situation.
What does that mean to you?	Allows the individual to go into greater detail which may offer up personal insights.
What's the bottom line of the situation?	Encourages the individual to get to the heart of the matter and think about the outcome and all its ramifications.
What's your intuition telling you here?	Encourages the individual to view the change from a different angle which could spark off additional insights.

TABLE 11.1 *Continued*

Power questions	Result
What's important about that?	Gets the individual to home in on key issues.
What makes you say that?	This encourages the individual to elaborate, which can help both parties get a clearer picture of the situation.
What specifically...?	When someone is asked for specifics they must go to a different place in the brain to retrieve a memory or experience. This journey can help to illuminate the issue.
What are three things...?	Asking for a number of things stops the individual from worrying about what they do or don't know and instead focus on the three things they do definitely know. It's a tangible goal that gives the question a context which in turn makes it much easier to answer and always delivers a more insightful and useful answer.
What could you do differently to contribute to this change and get a better result for the business?	This question encourages the individual to consider different solutions without negating the previous solutions. It asks them what they could do differently, not what they could do better to improve the result.
What's important about that to you?	This question encourages the individual to articulate his or her priorities from the change initiative.
Irrespective of whether you will do it or not what could you do right now?	This helps open the mind up to possible solutions that the individual may never have considered. The pressure is taken off the answer by reassuring the individual that they will not necessarily have to implement any of the suggestions.
What if X was your biggest strength?	If someone describes something as their 'Achilles heel' or biggest weakness, flip the issue and encourage the individual to imagine for a moment what life would be like if their 'Achilles heel' was actually their 'crowning glory' or biggest strength. Getting them to describe what life would be like can be really illuminating and inspiring for the person involved. It also allows them to see a path through the change.

Being listening

When preparing this manuscript our publisher pushed back quite hard on this phrase. Their point was that it was bizarre terminology so they were keen for us to change it to something simpler or more common. If however we had changed the heading to 'Being a good listener' for example, you would have assumed you'd heard this material a thousand times and skipped forward. Being listening is not the same thing as being a good listener.

For those involved in negotiations or conflict resolution or who have attended communication skills training or any form of coaching training, you will probably already know about 'active listening'. Just to say, up front – 'being listening' is also not 'active listening'.

Human beings are actually not very good at listening. For most, listening is 'waiting to speak'. So when two people are in conversation one is talking and the other is figuring out what they are going to say next – that is not listening. As a result when two people talk to each other they are often not listening to what is actually being said. Active listening came about to try and improve that situation so that we heard the words and engaged with their meaning – really listened to the other person. Obviously listening is a key skill of the TLA facilitator during the follow-up conversations. It's useful to repeat what the person has said in their own words so that the person seeking to make behavioural change feels listened to and validated. This in turn helps the person relax into the process and offer up more information and insight.

The problem with active listening, however, is there is now a pretty significant gap between how it was intended to be used and how it is actually used in practice. If used properly then active listening will improve your listening skills but it's often simply hijacked and used to look like someone is listening when really they are not. It's very easy to fudge active listening with a few well-timed comments and pat phrases. The TLA facilitator could make encouraging noises and add the occasional, 'Yes, I hear what you are saying,' but that's not active listening and it will certainly not deliver the results necessary for TLA. When done correctly active listening has several benefits. It forces the facilitator to genuinely engage with the conversation and it also helps to prevent misunderstandings. But TLA requires a more applied approach to listening, called 'being listening'.

Whereas active listening implies a conversation with one person on either 'side' and a level of activity or attention, being listening is about being in the conversation with the individual. This means being completely still and doing nothing apart from staying present to the individual in the change process and listening. The facilitator who is being listening is simply present in the moment and 'holds the space' for them to open up and really communicate.

Being listening is particularly useful in the TLA process because:

1 It goes way beyond active listening.

2 It creates a non-verbal, non-visual connection with the individual.

3 It is a practical way of ensuring the facilitator delivers no opinion and no judgement.

4 It is a practical way for the facilitator to get out of their head and their ideas into their body where they can just be a listener with no agenda.

5 It creates a distinction between doing listening as an activity and being listening as a state of mind.

Exercise to get into the 'being listening' state

As part of the TLA training programmes those involved are initially asked to have a brief conversation as they normally would. Then we ask everyone to do the following breathing exercise, which was developed by HeartMath, and then to have a new conversation. Several things are noticeable after the breathing exercise. First the level of sound in the room is greatly reduced, people are gentler and calmer and the being listening process creates a level of coherence and closeness that was not present in the first coaching conversations. The conversation is no longer about talking to each other but rather being with each other. Everyone who has ever done this exercise agrees that being listening has a completely different feel.

- Take a couple of deep breaths and sit comfortably.

- Imagine that you are now going to breathe through your heart (some people like to place their hand on their chest so they can feel the rise and fall of their chest rather than the diaphragm).

- Take five breaths breathing in and out for five counts, with each breath focusing more on your heart.

- As you breathe through your heart, feel your heart expanding and contracting and imagine it growing in size each time it expands.

- Now you are breathing through your heart take your mind to a time where you felt real appreciation or gratitude for someone or something. It could be when you were observing a wonderful view from nature, when you were with loved ones or when you felt very peaceful and grateful for your life.

- Sit and relive these feelings of appreciation and gratitude as you breathe through your heart.

This simple technique allows the facilitator to manage their state. As for the environment each TLA conversation should be conducted away from distractions – no checking e-mail or looking at your smartphone. Instead, the TLA facilitator must place himself or herself into 'the TLA cocoon' where there is only the facilitator, their pen and paper, a clock and the person being coached toward behavioural change. Being listening is about finding coherence with the individual being coached and being in the flow of the TLA conversation. And this is only possible if the facilitator manages their environment and frame of mind.

Using intuition effectively

In simple terms, intuition is that thought, idea or insight that springs to mind when an individual says something during the conversation. Trusting that 'flash of genius' is part of the science of coaching but deciding what is intuition and what is just a knee-jerk personal reaction to what's been said is the art.

Often those trained in traditional coaching will be encouraged to go with their instincts and raise issues that they feel the person is skirting around or avoiding. In coaching as in life, it's always much easier to see other people's challenges, shortcomings or blind spots than it is to see our own. With this fact in mind, the coach is therefore encouraged to raise the things the other person may be unable to see, or want to see clearly. When the TLA facilitator is seeking to support someone through behavioural change this can be a huge mistake.

The process of change in any form is often challenging enough. Remember from David Rock's work that change can often trigger the primary threat circuitry in the brain, making those involved with change naturally resistant to it. If the TLA facilitator jumps into the conversation by offering up their intuitive insights into what they consider to be the individual's 'issues', they could easily be wrong, which is likely to alienate the already uncomfortable individual still further. Often in these situations what we think is intuition is actually our own buttons being pressed. Perhaps the facilitator gets an insight that the individual being coached through the change process is dragging their heels because the change means that they will move office and lose connection with a colleague they are close to. This may very well be an issue but that particular 'intuition' is actually a reaction to the fact that the facilitator has just heard that their best friend is moving overseas. The conversation triggered a personal memory and emotion for the facilitator that they then projected onto the individual.

Plus, even if the person is concerned about the loss of connection with their work colleague it may not be the most pressing issue or the most pertinent to the success of the change. How the facilitator shares the insights that they receive is often more important than the insight itself. Besides, the last thing the facilitator wants is to be wrong and put the individual off side. To avoid this scenario the facilitator should always reframe the insight by saying, 'I may be really off base here but are you uncomfortable in this situation because you feel a loss of connection to X?' That way the individual has the opportunity to consider that intuition and elaborate on it further, making it their own and gaining value from it, or dismiss it if it doesn't really 'land' for them.

No one likes being told what to do or how they can make the required changes faster or more effectively. TLA is a collaborative process that supports people going through change to find their own way from the old way to the new. The very best TLA facilitators ask the individual power questions so that when answered the individual will arrive at their own solutions and have their own personal 'a-ha moment'.

Of course, there are times, especially as the facilitator gets more experienced guiding people through change, where their intuition will alert them to something that may need to be addressed for maximum benefit to the individual. In order to use intuition effectively the TLA facilitator should always:

- follow the individual, whilst using...
- the ABC intuition rules.

Follow the individual

The TLA facilitator needs to 'follow the individual' and what they want to discuss rather than following their own set agenda. Obviously there is a process to follow but once the TLA follow-up conversation has started the individual can often appear to wander off topic or focus their attention on something other than what they had set out in their TLA Action Plan or agreed with the facilitator at the end of the previous conversation.

In this situation it's always better to follow the individual because whether the issue is relevant or not, it is on the individual's radar so the facilitator needs to have the courage to honour that and support them in where they want to go. In an effort to get back to the programme the facilitator could insist the individual return to their stated targets and objectives but this can easily backfire and push the individual back into resistance. By following the individual wherever they want or feel they need to go they are likely to be much more engaged, and once the issue has been addressed to return to the previous targets.

Of course, care is needed to ensure the conversation doesn't become circular and the individual isn't simply trying to stall and delay the change. During the change process the individual may feel overwhelmed by what needs to happen and the changes they are being asked to make. As a result they may raise issue after issue that they feel needs to be tackled rather than focusing in on one at a time so they can gain confidence and move forward. It can also feel as though there is no way these 20-minute conversations will be enough to address all the issues. This is common and for some people it's just how their minds work, jumping quickly from one issue to another. The problem is it raises too many issues to cover in a single session.

In this type of situation the facilitator's top priority is to help the participant think in a constructive way and break the issues down into discernible challenges. By helping the individual to separate the issues it gives them an opportunity to choose what issue to explore first, what is the most pressing, so they can drive the conversation rather than the facilitator making the decision or running the session to their agenda. This allows the TLA facilitator to follow the individual down a path of their choosing, whilst ensuring it's a worthwhile path to follow!

How to combat a circular conversation

1 The facilitator needs to summarize and repeat back to the individual the different issues or solutions they have raised.

2 Having listed the issues the facilitator then gives the individual the choice as to which issue or avenue he or she would like to explore to 'make the best use of your time and move us forward'.

3 Once the issues have been separated out and listed the facilitator can then refer back to the list later on in the session to help keep the individual focused on important issues for that session.

4 Often when the individual is able to separate the issues from each other they become less daunting and the individual can see a path through. Often there may only end up being two or three issues.

5 Typically with this kind of session the facilitator will need to split the issues or avenues of discussion more than once in the session.

The facilitator might hear the individual say something like, 'I am obviously keen to make the changes and use the new IT system but I just don't have time to do anything properly. I'm under so much pressure.'

The facilitator might say, 'I understand. There is obviously a lot going on. So where shall we focus our attention: 1. The IT system, 2. Not having time to do anything properly or 3. Being under pressure? Which is most important for us to make some headway on today?'

More often than not the person expected to make the change will inform the facilitator that all the issues are connected, to which the facilitator might reply, 'Absolutely, I can see that they are. In order to help you move forward let's put a stake in the ground against one of those three areas, though, as an indication of where we might start. Which are you most concerned about?'

Once the individual has identified the priority from the list, then the facilitator can continue with the TLA conversation and stay on track. If the facilitator then needs to separate the issues again later on in the session they can use a summary of the path they have taken as a guide. So the facilitator might say, 'So we started looking at your first action from your TLA Plan to help move the change initiative forward but as we have talked it became clear that the real challenge underneath this was your time management, not having time to do anything properly, being under pressure and feeling as though this made the changes with the IT system impossible. We then decided that the best path to take was to consider the pressure you are under and this has resulted in us considering the implications on your health and on your work. If we wanted to make some additional progress on one of these areas, which is most important to you – the implications on your health or the implications on your work?'

Often when we are faced with change, especially when we are already under pressure, the scale of what's ahead can seem overwhelming and insurmountable. In these situations the facilitator needs to remind the individual that often little shifts can make a huge difference, so the facilitator might say, 'Remember, Julie, often when we make a small move in one area it can have an impact across the board so don't worry that we only have time to look at one area today. Just be reassured we are making progress. Rome wasn't built in a day.'

Learning how to follow the individual ensures that the person being supported to change feels acknowledged and listened to. Plus if they feel able to deal with and address whatever is on their immediate radar they will be much more willing to get back on topic once it's handled.

Ironically the balance between structure and flexibility that is the hallmark of the TLA process means that individuals feel very liberated by it, even though there is a strict structure that lies beneath it.

The ABC intuition rules

As we mentioned earlier the biggest challenge with intuition is that it's a double-edged sword. On one hand it can massively fast-track progress by bringing a new perspective and some fresh insight to the person experiencing the change. But on the other it can alienate, especially when the facilitator is merely projecting their own thoughts and feelings onto the individual.

The best way to ensure you stay on the right side of intuition is to incorporate three simple rules for using intuition wisely and effectively. Easy to remember, these are the ABC rules and they stand for:

Aware;

Brave;

Call it as it is.

Aware

The TLA facilitator needs to be aware that they may be confusing their own personal reactions and assumptions arising from the conversation with intuition. The individual may just be pressing the facilitator's buttons or straying into topics the facilitator has strong opinions about. Staying engaged and consciously aware helps the facilitator to differentiate between the two so they can genuinely tap into their intuition. Remember:

- The facilitator's intuition could be spot on or it could be completely off the mark, but if the facilitator raises their insights respectfully it won't matter if they are wrong.

- It's always up to the individual to choose whether they want to explore what the facilitator has raised or not. The facilitator's job is to respectfully challenge the person when appropriate and not get attached to whether or not they take their insights on board.

- Whilst the individual being supported through change may be frustrating at times they are always doing the best they can with the resources they have and the facilitator needs to respect that.

Brave

It is part of the facilitator's role to challenge the individual and challenge the status quo. Sometimes that means the facilitator has to be brave. Specifically:

- Brave enough to go 'off piste' or follow a path outside what is expected or on the TLA Plan to give the individual the best results.

- Brave enough to sit in silence having no idea where the session is going or whether the individual will come to a resolution in the session – the facilitator needs to be brave enough to trust the process.

- Brave enough to completely throw the agenda over to the individual regardless of whether the facilitator feels they can handle what emerges or not.

Call it as it is

Change is never that easy for most people; it isn't something that comes naturally to us so there is almost always going to be resistance along the way. So the facilitator needs to be willing to call it as it is. Facing an issue directly and respectfully calling it out will almost always defuse the issue. Think about if someone upsets you or irritates you – if neither you nor the other person acknowledges the shift in energy that negativity can quickly take on a life of its own. But if the other person says, 'Hey, sorry, I get the impression I've just upset you, is that right?' a great deal of the simmering emotion is dissolved.

With that in mind, remember:

- If the person being supported through change sounds bored, resentful or disengaged it's always better for the facilitator to raise it with them immediately. It may not always change anything but calling the situation as it is gives the facilitator the very best opportunity to address the issues and get back into a positive conversation.

- The facilitator must call the individual to account when they are saying one thing and meaning or doing another. Without this intervention by the facilitator the conversation will quickly descend into a meaningless loop and waste everyone's time.

- The facilitator needs to call it as it is when the individual clearly doesn't want to be having the conversation or when they are openly or covertly hostile. Raising the issue will almost always defuse the situation and may help to get the conversation back on track. Unless the facilitator calls the individual on their behaviour or attitude nothing is going to shift.

TABLE 11.2   Examples of using intuition effectively

Situation in TLA conversation	What to ask to use intuition effectively
The individual is saying one thing but intuition is telling the facilitator that there is more to it.	*Reading between the lines, I get the sense that something else is on your mind – is this what you want to work on this session?*
The individual is telling the facilitator about lots of concerns but not highlighting one above another.	*What is the biggest concern or challenge you are facing right now?*
The individual sounds bored and disengaged.	*I'm hearing that you're not really inspired by this...*
The individual sounds fed up and resistant.	*You're sounding really fed up and not interested... what's going on for you at the moment?*
Towards the beginning of a session if the facilitator senses that the participant is not yet engaged in the session.	*What would you like to get out of our time today?*
The individual is telling the facilitator something but the facilitator has a sense there is something else going on and potentially already has an idea of what that might be.	*I'm getting a sense that x might be an underlying issue here – would you agree at all?*
Intuition is telling the facilitator there is more to the issue than the individual is telling them about.	*I think we're only looking at the surface – do you mind if I ask a couple of questions to take us below the surface?*
Intuition is telling the facilitator to ask a question that could potentially be difficult or challenging to the client.	*I know this sounds strange but I've got a question that's niggling in my mind – do you mind if I ask you...*
The facilitator has something that they want to say to the individual that could be perceived as being direct.	*I'm not going to beat around the bush – I know you would rather I am straightforward.*

TABLE 11.2   *Continued*

Situation in TLA conversation	What to ask to use intuition effectively
The TLA participant is completely disengaged with the action plan.	*Let's rip up the action plan.*
The individual says something that initiates the facilitator's intuition.	*I have no idea whether this is relevant but...*
The individual doesn't seem engaged in what the facilitator is working on.	*What would you really like to work on right now?*
The TLA participant needs more help than the facilitator can offer; they might be suggesting signs of depression or hopelessness or the facilitator may feel out of their depth.	Hold the space for the individual whilst directing them to counselling.

The skill set required to support people involved with change through the process so they can unfreeze their own behaviour, try out the new behaviour and then refreeze the new behaviour into habit is not something that happens overnight. By focusing on these three skills, you will be able to fast-track your progress. In the next chapter we will explore how to keep the conversations on track so that the person in the change makes the required adjustments.

Summary of key points

- Executing TLA successfully requires specific skills.
- There are three critical skills required for successful TLA delivery. Like most skills in life, they come with time and experience and successful TLA facilitators use them all the time.
- The skills are asking power questions, being listening and using intuition effectively.
- Properly pitched questions allow the individual to explore the situation and their own thinking. An individual is always much more likely to action and maintain a change they had a hand in identifying than one handed down to them from someone else.

- Asking questions allows the individual to take ownership of the change and, within reason, tailor that change to suit them and their own change timeline.

- This also allows for the fact that each person knows their own role and their own behaviours best – they will know better than anyone else what needs to happen to make the change successful.

- Questions are an essential tool in the TLA facilitator's kitbag. But like most tools, some types of questions are more useful than others. One of the primary distinctions is between a closed and an open question.

- The easiest way to remember the difference is to match them to what they do to the conversation. Closed questions tend to close down the conversation because they can be answered by 'Yes', 'No' or another one-word response. Open questions open the conversation up and allow the conversation to flow naturally. Good open questions usually start with 'What' and 'Why' and will usually prompt a longer, more considered response.

- The TLA process focuses on the use of power questions which are a form of open question. The power question ensures that the facilitator doesn't arrive with an agenda or pollute the discussion with assumption.

- Being listening is not the same thing as being a good listener.

- Being listening is also not active listening.

- Human beings are actually not very good at listening. For most, listening is 'waiting to speak'. So when two people are in conversation one is talking and the other is figuring out what they are going to say next – that is not listening.

- Active listening came about to try and improve that situation but there is now a pretty significant gap between how it was intended to be used and how it is actually used in practice. If used properly then active listening will improve your listening skills but it's often simply hijacked and used to look like someone is listening when really they are not. It's very easy to fudge active listening with a few well-timed comments and pat phrases.

- TLA requires a more applied approach to listening, called being listening.

- Whereas active listening implies a conversation with one person on either 'side' and a level of activity or attention, being listening is about being in the conversation with the individual.

- Being listening is about finding coherence with the individual being coached and being in the flow of the TLA conversation. And this is only possible if the facilitator manages their environment and frame of mind.

- In simple terms, intuition is that thought, idea or insight that springs to mind when an individual says something during the conversation. Trusting that 'flash of genius' is part of the science of coaching but deciding what is intuition and what is just a knee-jerk personal reaction to what's been said is the art.

- If the TLA facilitator jumps into the conversation by offering up their intuitive insights into what they consider to be the individual's 'issues' they could easily be wrong, which is likely to alienate the already uncomfortable individual still further and arrest progress. Often in these situations what we think is intuition is actually our own buttons being pressed.

- To avoid this scenario the facilitator should always reframe the insight by offering up any insight as an invitation. That way the individual has the opportunity to consider that intuition and elaborate on it further, making it their own and gaining value from it or dismiss it if it doesn't really 'land' for them.

- In order to use intuition effectively the TLA facilitator should always follow the individual, whilst using the ABC intuition rules (Aware, Brave, Call it as it is).

Making TLA work

Guiding the conversations

12

The skill set is just one part of making TLA work in reality. The other is how to guide the conversations toward behavioural change. This chapter explores those dynamics, the various ways the conversations may fail, and how to manage those situations.

What we need to appreciate is that a single conversation doesn't create change – it's the accountability that emerges from the series of conversations. What happens between the conversations is every bit as important as, if not more important than, what happens during the conversation. Personal accountability is created when the individual knows that in a matter of weeks another conversation is going to take place and they are going to have to account for their progress (or lack of progress) – then action and forward movement are much more likely.

And that doesn't mean that the facilitator is nagging the individual or cajoling them into change. In the course of our work we frequently find that people are trying to create change by utilizing various online methodologies. Essentially what they are trying to do with these online tools is to control the change by delivering more information via various change reminders. You can't remind someone into changing – if you are unsure of how accurate that is, try reminding your partner that they said they were going to join the local gym and lose a few pounds. It won't end well.

Many are still seeking compliance to a change by sending additional information or reminders in an effort to push it through but this approach does not create sustained behavioural change. Everything we already know about human beings (and neuroscience confirms it) tells us it won't work, and yet some persist – probably in the absence of any real workable alternative. Reminding participants about the change initiative through some funky online platform with video footage, PowerPoint decks or even an innovative app won't help with the behavioural change. It may be easy and it's certainly easier to manage but it still doesn't facilitate behavioural change.

TLA focuses on creativity rather than compliance, curiosity rather than control and context rather than content. Creativity, curiosity and context further facilitate and drive self-accountability and are a much more powerful way to approach change than compliance, control and content.

Even when the TLA facilitator understands the process through the ACTION Conversation Model, appreciates the crucial interplay between structure and flexibility, and has a level of proficiency in the TLA skills that will guide every TLA conversation, it can sometimes take a few minutes to find the groove in the process. The most common obstacle to finding that groove is when the individual isn't genuinely 'in the gap' or owning the gap.

Helping identify and get in the 'gap'

As we have said throughout the book, the whole point of any change initiative is for something to change. That's obvious and it almost always requires behavioural change. So there is the old behaviour or way of doing things, which is comfortable and known, and there is the new way of doing things, which is uncomfortable and unknown – and right now there is a 'gap' between the two. The TLA process is designed to bridge that gap but unless the TLA facilitator can encourage the individual to identify that gap and own it, then progress can be slow. It's absolutely vital that the individual being supported toward behavioural change identifies something they can change in their own working life or environment that will assist in that change process. They must then acknowledge that their calibration on that skill, ability or change is currently lower than they wish it to be, and be encouraged to commit to bridging the gap between where they are now and where they want to be.

Human beings are not always that straightforward; they can be contrary and difficult, and that's why change that doesn't address human nature is usually destined to fail. But TLA provides a framework for managing that complexity and the TLA facilitator needs to know how to deal with the complexity while nudging the person gently, or not so gently, into the gap.

One of the reasons coaching in the traditional sense of the word can produce brilliant results for one person and be a waste of time for another is the lack of appreciation around this 'gap'. Coaching that is successful identifies the issue the individual is seeking to resolve at the start of the conversation and focuses the person's attention and action on that shortfall. Whereas the coaching that fails to deliver tends to meander without the necessary focus on what the person wants or needs to address, never mind what they can actually do about it. And yet without this initial identification and ownership of the issue no real progress can be made.

The individual involved in the change will have identified approximately three things they want to address and these will be documented in the TLA Action Plan. At the start of every follow-up conversation the facilitator therefore needs to have the individual choose which issue they want to focus on for the next 20 minutes. The facilitator will then have the person reaffirm their calibration regarding that issue. In other words they must state where they think they are in that moment against that target or issue on a scale of 1–10. As mentioned earlier calibration is often used throughout the TLA process and acts as the transition from structure into flexibility. It allows the individual to put a stake in the ground about what they want to address and their current ability against that target – therefore identifying and getting into the gap they are seeking to bridge.

Calibration is a quick and effective way to identify and quantify the gap between current reality and where the person involved in the change wants to be. The individual already knows what their key change issues are and they also instinctively know how good or otherwise they are regarding those issues, so it's very easy for them to assign a personal score to their current ability in that area. Plus they also have a fairly good idea of how much they could improve and how they could go about making those improvements. If for example the individual wants to use the new order system then that is the goal. In that moment the person in the change initiative knows that they have the basic understanding of how to use the system from the training programme, but they have yet to use it in the workplace because it's just easier to use the old system for the time being. They therefore score their current ability against using the new order system as four. They know that the old way of making orders will not be possible in a month so they need to embrace the new system, so they want to shift that score to an eight. The gap is therefore the difference in skill level between four and eight, and the individual has ownership of that because they identified the goal and the gap regarding their own skill level. The process would then move on to identify what specifically needs to be done to close that gap. And the individual usually has a pretty good idea. So in this case for example the individual could identify certain types of orders that they could process on the new system because they are straightforward. This would give them confidence in the new system and allow them to make a start using it.

What if people refuse to 'get in the gap'?

Getting the individual into the gap is a straightforward process if the changes they identified on their TLA Plan are real and relevant. If the facilitator finds that the individual is not taking ownership of the gap then they need to uncover why before they progress with the conversation, otherwise nothing will change. The nuances here are more subtle and can be hard to pick up. If you try to proceed before really identifying and getting ownership of the gap the process will fall over and you'll be left wondering why the change hasn't happened. Although it makes for a harder conversation it is vital to get into the gap to create change.

Typically there are three things the individual will say when they have not identified or acknowledged a gap they wish to bridge.

- Scenario 1: Identify a gap and explain in detail why they can't fix it.
- Scenario 2: Identify a gap but won't be able to decide whether it's something they want to address or not.
- Scenario 3: Say they can't identify a gap.

Each of these responses requires a different approach and a different solution to get the individual to take ownership and move into an effective coaching conversation.

Solution for Scenario 1: OARBED

The most common problem during the TLA follow-up conversations is when the individual can identify a gap but spends all their time and energy telling the facilitator why they can't bridge that particular gap. The individual will almost certainly have thought about it before the TLA follow-up and will enthusiastically detail all the reasons why they have not been able to make any progress on their change targets between the change launch and this conversation, or between separate TLA conversations.

The best solution for solving this problem is to use a process one of us first learnt from John Matthews from the Institute of Executive Coaching known as the OARBED process (Figure 12.1).

FIGURE 12.1   The OARBED process

> **O** – OWNERSHIP
> **A** – ACCOUNTABILITY
> **R** – RESPONSILIBILITY
> _____
>
> **B** – BLAME
> **E** – EXCUSES
> **D** – DENIAL

The OARBED process is perfect for when the TLA facilitator hears the individual reeling off a variety of reasons why change is impossible for them right now.

How to use the OARBED process

1 Once the individual has finished explaining all the reasons why they can't bridge their identified gap, the TLA facilitator briefly summarizes the conversation and repeats back to the individual what they have heard so far. The facilitator might say for example, *'I'm hearing that there are several reasons that made it difficult for you to change your behaviour in line with your specified target. I'm going to take you through a short process that often helps in this situation so I can best support you to get the best result. Is that OK?'* This introduction to the process acts as a signpost for the individual and lets them know the facilitator is going to change approach and that they are seeking their permission to do so.

2 Assuming the facilitator gets the individual's permission they then ask the individual to get a clean sheet of paper and write the word OARBED vertically down the left hand side of the page, starting with O at the top and D at the bottom, and draw a line through the middle below the R and above the B.

3 The facilitator would also remind the individual that this step is crucial so they can move forward. The TLA facilitator might say, *'I often use this process to help people who feel they are stuck in a particular area and can't move forward. What usually happens is that the individual gets a new awareness that they are stuck "below the line" and that insight can create fresh opportunities for progress.'*

4 The facilitator then tells the individual that they are going to run through the situation using the OARBED process to see if most of the individual's reasons for not changing are 'above the line' or 'below the line'.

5 It's important that the facilitator reassures the individual that there is nothing wrong with being 'below the line' – it's the awareness that's really important. The facilitator may say, *'Before I explain the model I want to remind you that there is nothing wrong with being "below the line". This process simply allows us to get really clear about where we are right now so we can decide whether or not we want to do anything about it.'*

6 The facilitator then explains the model and might say, *'So looking at your sheet of paper. O stands for Ownership, A for Accountability and R for Responsibility. These are all "above the line" characteristics because they empower you to take control and take action. The characteristics "below the line" are B for Blame, E for Excuses and D for Denial. It's very hard to effect change when we are "below the line" because these are disempowering characteristics and leave us feeling helpless.'*

7 The TLA facilitator then reassures the individual again that although the 'below the line' elements can sound harsh they are intended to help those in the change process move into a more empowering position. The facilitator may say, *'I know these sound quite harsh but that's not their intention. This process is about encouraging you to think a little differently about your situation so that you can stop feeling helpless, take back control and make any changes you genuinely want to make. What you are considering is, of course, the reality of the situation but even though it's true it can still be helpful to investigate it. Would it be fair to say that... X could be described as an excuse? And remember this isn't about right or wrong. You may decide that you are actually quite angry and want to blame X person for a day or so, just as long as you also understand that you won't take control and change much from that position.'*

8 The facilitator must then encourage the individual to think of even a small part of the situation that they could move 'above the line'. The TLA facilitator might say, *'Looking at where you are now, what percentage of this situation is "below the line" for you and what percentage of the situation is "above the line"?'* This question uses

calibration again but is particularly useful in this situation to help the individual to take ownership. Even if the facilitator can get the individual to take a tiny percentage of ownership of the situation that's a start and can start to move the conversation forward because they recognize they do have control over a part of the change. So if the individual says, '*I'm 80 per cent "below the line" and 20 per cent "above the line"*,' then the facilitator can focus on the 20 per cent. This helps to relax the individual as it's not so confrontational. By taking the heat out of the situation the facilitator can really help to open up the discussion.

9 Again, the facilitator needs to reassure the individual that if they genuinely can't think of anything, however small, that they could influence then it's OK. If the individual suggests something, even if it's small, then use that as the gap and progress the conversation on that basis. If they can't think of anything or don't propose anything they could influence then the facilitator needs to move on. The facilitator may say, '*If you can't think of anything, even something that may feel really minor, that you could influence in this situation, then it's OK, it just means that this topic or situation is probably not the best use of our time so we'll need to move on to something else from your TLA Plan.*'

10 If the facilitator needs to move on, he or she must remind the individual to give the issue more thought so that it can be revisited in the next conversation. Ideally the facilitator should encourage the individual to think about one small thing they could influence in that situation. Once someone moves 'above the line' for a minor issue they are much more capable of moving 'above the line' for larger issues, and retake the power to change their situation and behaviour.

Other questions to help shift the individual 'above the line':

- 'What part of this situation do you think you could influence?'
- 'What part of this can you control?'
- 'What will the benefit be if you manage to influence it?'
- 'What's the truth in the situation here?'
- 'Who can help you to resolve this?'
- 'What resources do you have that could be useful right now?'
- 'What have you learnt in the past that can help shift the situation now?'

Example of the OARBED process in action

Say for example a sales team needed to embrace a new client relationship management system. The change initiative was given an inspiring name and the coffee mugs were distributed to remind the sales team to use the new process and keep the system up to date. Of course, reminding people to change doesn't facilitate behavioural change, so the business also invested in follow-up TLA conversations to ensure the sales force made the required changes in the workplace. The TLA facilitator's first conversation is with Liam, a key member of the sales team but someone who seems to suffer from inconsistent performance. In the conversation Liam admits that he's had a few instances where he hasn't kept the new system up to date since the change initiative kicked off. The facilitator asks him what he could have done differently to keep the system up to date. Liam then lists a whole host of reasons why he didn't keep it up to date and therefore doesn't really answer the question. Instead he says things such as 'The system wasn't working properly,' 'I didn't manage to prioritize the system because the invoicing was more important,' 'The prospect didn't give me clear information so I couldn't really update the system,' or 'I didn't have a chance to get to it yet but I am intending to.'

All the facilitator hears are reasons outside Liam's control. Unless the facilitator has a tool or technique to get past this bluster then it will be tempting to let Liam off the hook. All of Liam's reasons may be valid but it's still important not to let any of these get in the way of moving the change forward. Reality or not, the facilitator knows that if they let him off the hook then he is never going to own the issue and change his behaviour to embrace the new sales process, which should improve results. But if the facilitator suggests to him, 'Liam, perhaps you could have done X, Y or Z,' then he has zero ownership of the situation and probably won't action any of the facilitator's suggestions, so he will not make any changes.

The facilitator needs to find a way to get Liam to take ownership and see that there is a way forward, and the OARBED model is a great technique to help remind Liam that he has control over at least part of the situation. So instead of letting Liam off the hook the facilitator works through the process above, all the time assuring Liam that there is no right or wrong in this process – it's simply a way of seeing the situation more clearly so as to give him more options about what to do in the future.

When Liam writes OARBED on his sheet of paper and understands what each letter stands for he can more easily see whether his 'reasons' are 'above the line' or 'below the line'.

We have been taught that blame, excuses and denial are bad traits, but they don't have to be. Change requires that we are honest about where we are right now, and if we recognize that we are wasting time and resources in blame, excuses and denial then at least that's an honest appraisal of the situation. It may be that the individual acknowledges that and still decides that their excuses are valid, or they stubbornly hold on to them for the time being but at least the conversation isn't wasted discussing something that isn't going to change.

In most cases either in that session or a later session the individual will acknowledge the futility of 'below the line' behaviour and move 'above the line', take ownership of the situation, and move toward a different result. It's a technique that needs to be handled gently and with respect but unless the facilitator can move the individual 'above the line' then they will always be looking at other people to change, which is futile. The only thing that we can effectively change is our own behaviour. Trying to change other people or the environment is a waste of energy. And that's why getting the individual into the gap in the first place is so important. Unless they take ownership, accountability and responsibility for the change the change will not happen, or if it does it will not stick.

Blame, excuses and denial are pretty challenging and confrontational words so it's absolutely essential that the TLA facilitator frames the process properly from the start. If the facilitator just launches into the OARBED model, revealing what each letter stands for without explaining the purpose of the model and how it's designed to support them to get the results they want, then the individual may feel threatened and become defensive. When framed in the context of better understanding the individual's thinking it can feel much less threatening and help move the individual 'above the line' or allow both parties to park that issue and move on. Either is preferable to remaining 'below the line'.

When someone is 'below the line' they are uncoachable on that issue. Getting that individual to a point where they acknowledge that fact is essential. If the facilitator can't get someone 'above the line' then they need to change to an action that the individual is willing to make changes on or take them out of the TLA process. Unless the facilitator can identify a gap and get the individual to own that gap nothing will change and the process is a waste of time for both parties.

A simpler version of OARBED is to ask the individual to look at what is within their influence or what they can control but it's not as powerful as it doesn't call them to fully look at what is happening at the moment and may reduce the amount of traction the change achieves.

If you would like to listen to an audio recording of the OARBED process in action please visit **http://transferoflearning.com/resources**.

Solution for Scenario 2: Off the Fence

The next most common problem the TLA facilitator will encounter in the follow-up conversations is when the individual can identify a gap but can't decide if they actually want to change it or not. They may for example be able to identify the gap, assign a current score and an ideal score but they may also be unsure if they want to reach the new score.

This may seem counterintuitive but every change carries with it advantages and disadvantages. Even if a person can see what needs to be changed and agrees that it's their responsibility to make that change there may still be strong advantages to maintaining the status quo. As a result the person is sitting on the fence regarding the gap or perceived gap and the facilitator's job is to get them off that fence. Preferably the facilitator is aiming to get the individual off the fence onto the side of change where they identify the gap and want to make improvements. In some cases that won't be possible, in which case the facilitator needs to encourage the individual to get off the fence onto the side of the status quo. At least if the individual acknowledges that they don't actually want to change right now both parties can move on to another target from the TLA Action Plan that the individual does believe they can progress. It is always possible to come back to the first issue later when the individual has had experience of the TLA process working and feels more enthusiastic and confident about their ability to change.

Use the Off the Fence process to help an indecisive individual to identify a gap and agree to take action on that issue, or shelve the issue and move onto something they will change.

How to use Off the Fence

1 Once the individual has explained their dilemma, the TLA facilitator needs to briefly summarize the conversation and repeat back to the individual what they have heard so far. The facilitator might say, *'So what I'm hearing from you is that in some ways you want to... but at the same time you can see the benefits of the current situation. In a way you are having a conflicting conversation with yourself.'*

2 The facilitator needs to remind the individual how important it is to be clear about the advantages and disadvantages of each course of action so that they can decide if it really is something they want to pursue.

3 The facilitator can then explain to the individual that they are effectively running two arguments and that change won't be possible while they are running these two arguments.

4 The facilitator must then get the individual to look at and explore the two different arguments and articulate them to him/her. By getting the individual to explain their thinking and the pros and cons of each one they can get really clear on their own thought process around the alternatives.

5 Once unpacked in this way most participants will be able to see which alternative is best and choose which argument is the 'truth' or best action for them.

6 The facilitator then reassures the individual that there is nothing wrong with where they are right now but together they need to make a decision and move forward or they need to decide not to change and choose something else to tackle. The facilitator may say, '*There is no pressure here, there is no right or wrong answer. I'm not trying to make you change or going to try to convince you to change – it's none of my business!* * *If after we have been through the pros and cons of the situation you decide there is more benefit in not changing then we simply move on to a different issue. My job is to make sure you get the most out of these sessions and discussing a change that you're not 100 per cent committed to is not a good use of our time. It may be you need more time in contemplation and that's absolutely fine.*'

7 If the individual needs a little more coaxing then the facilitator can go through the respective pros and cons of the situation further. Focus on the upside if they decide to change and the upside if they don't while encouraging the individual to make a decision – either to make the change or maintain the status quo. If the individual decides to change then the facilitator should calibrate the outcome and move forward with the conversation. If they are unsure the facilitator needs to encourage them to think about the issue for the next conversation and move on to a different issue identified on the TLA Action Plan.

* You might be thinking here 'But it is the facilitator's business – they need to deliver the change for the organization by supporting the individual.' It's a fine line to reflect on but ultimately it's not the facilitator's job to move the individual from contemplation to action. The facilitator's job is to help them become aware of where they stand in relation to the pros and cons of change and let them decide what to do about it. If as a facilitator you try and move them prematurely to action, or to action where they are not bought in, it won't become sustained behavioural change.

Example of Off the Fence in action

Say part of the new sales process implemented by Company A involved a new objection-handling technique. Of all the parts of the new sales process, this was one of the changes that the sales executives liked least. As a result they were often reluctant to use it. Although they frequently included the objection-handling procedure on their TLA Action Plan, when it actually came to the follow-up conversations they sat on the fence. They could see the benefits of the new approach but were more comfortable with the traditional process for handling objections.

In this situation the facilitator needs to draw their attention to the fact they have either decided not to change or are in the middle of the change process. To keep them engaged in the conversation the choice has to be theirs.

To help in that decision-making process and nudging the individual off the fence, the facilitator explores why the individual thinks the new objection-handling technique is included in the sales process overhaul. So, the facilitator might say, *'Tell me, why do you think this objection-handling process is included in the new sales process as your company's recommended way of handing sales objections?'* The idea is to get the individual to get clearer and clearer about both sides of their own argument so they can get off the fence onto one side or another. Other questions that could help that process include:

- 'What's difficult about the process?'
- 'What could make it easier to use?'
- 'What might the benefits be of using this approach?'
- 'What's the benefit of maintaining the status quo?'
- 'What could the risks of using it be?'
- 'How could we minimize the risks?'

- 'What could it cost you not to change?'
- 'What are pros and cons of the change?'
- 'How would you feel if you made the decision one way or another?'
- 'Can you think of a time when you have been in a similar position and not known whether to make a change or not? How did you handle that?'

Having this kind of neutral exploratory discussion really helps the individual to gain clarity about what they feel about the new approach and can help to shift their perspective enough to allow them to identify the gap, get off the fence and hopefully commit to closing it. If not, at least the facilitator and individual can move to the next issue on the action plan.

If you would like to listen to an audio recording of the Off the Fence process in action please visit **http://transferoflearning.com/resources**.

Solution for Scenario 3: The Panel of Three process

The final problem that arises in TLA follow-up conversations is when the individual has either done everything they think they can on their action plan, they can't find something they want to work on or improve, or they appear to just want to bring the TLA to an end so they can tick the box that they've done it without necessarily adding a great deal of value. Equally, if they created the action plan just because they had to and not because they really wanted to be involved in the TLA process or contribute to the change, this is the time to address it and pick it up. The Panel of Three process is therefore useful when the person involved doesn't know where they can change or seems reluctant to change anything.

This can be really frustrating for the facilitator and the individual in the change process. Sometimes this confusion or reticence occurs because the person who is expected to change is disengaged or unhappy with the change initiative. In which case, as mentioned earlier, the facilitator needs to have an honest discussion about the individual's feelings and 'call them on it'. This direct, albeit respectful, approach will help to dissolve some of the negativity surrounding the change and help the individual make positive progress.

Sometimes the individual will say they simply don't know what to focus on and this confusion can feel uncomfortable, especially for seasoned, experienced individuals who are paid to 'know' what to do and what to focus on. It can be extremely confronting to realize that they don't know how to make changes so they can improve further. If the person going through the change initiative is a top performer they may not receive much feedback on how they can go to the next level, or they could be very self-assured and not see any opportunity or way they could be better. In this case the facilitator might hear, '*Well, obviously I'm not perfect but I don't know what I could do differently to get a better result with the new change proposed.*' It is the TLA facilitator's job to help them find out.

The facilitator must always let the individual know that it's OK not to know, reassure them that getting better may not be a radical departure from what they are already doing and perhaps a little tweak is all that's needed. There is actually power and possibility in admitting we don't know. Remember Peter Bregman's TEDx presentation we discussed in Chapter 5. Being able to admit that we don't know is actually part of the growth mindset and it's an extremely potent weapon in the process of change.

The idea behind the Panel of Three process is for the facilitator to help the participant take a bird's eye view of the situation so they can gain some objective, big-picture perspective on the change they are being asked to make. This altered perspective can help the individual to step into another vantage point that can allow them to see change in a new light.

How to use the Panel of Three process

1 Once the individual has explained that they don't know what to action next, the TLA facilitator summarizes the conversation and repeats back what they have heard so far. The facilitator might say, '*I'm hearing that you really feel that you've got everything covered or that you are unsure what else you could discuss in this conversation. Is that right?*'

2 Assuming permission is given the facilitator might say, '*Let's switch our minds slightly – who are three people that you really admire in the world of business? We want three people who are probably innovators in their fields, possibly business leaders – they may be people you have worked with in the past or people that you don't really know – perhaps Richard Branson or even someone with a fresh perspective like Nelson Mandela or the Dalai Lama – no problem if they are alive or dead. They just need to be people you admire and whose opinion you would respect on this change initiative. And of*

course you don't have to admire everything about this person, just an aspect of them. So who would your three people be?

Great, that's John your boss from your previous job, Michael Jordan the US basketball legend and Sir Richard Branson.'

3 The TLA facilitator then asks the questions: *'It's an unlikely mix but we are just playing here. Now imagine for whatever reason their diaries suddenly were free and they have been work-shadowing you for the last month. They have been seeing everything that has been happening in your role and what has been happening with the change project. They have seen every customer conversation, every interaction with your team and every meeting you have attended.'*

4 *'The panel of three have sat down and compared notes and are now ready to feed back to you. What would the panel say are the three key things that they see you doing well in your role that are helping contribute to the change project?'* As this is focused on the positive, most individuals can identify three things that are done well in the role. From this altered perspective, once the individual has created the list the facilitator would then repeat the three things back to the participant.

5 Once the facilitator has repeated the strengths and the individual has acknowledged them the facilitator might say, *'Now the panel of three really want you to do a great job and get the very best results for you and the company – so what three things might they feed back that could possibly be* **done slightly differently to get an even better result for this change project**? *I stress here it could be things that are already done well but could be done even better or it could be the smallest tweak that if changed a fraction would help the business get an even better result. What are the three things the panel would suggest?'* (Note here that the facilitator doesn't use the words 'doing badly' or 'doing anything wrong', it's just 'done differently to get an even better result'.)

6 Buoyed by the previous strengths the individual is much more likely to find a few things and move past 'I don't know.' Once the individual has identified the three things that could be done differently for better results the facilitator plays them back and asks the TLA participant to pick one item from the list of things that could add the most value and progress that point in the TLA conversation.

7 If the individual is undecided the facilitator simply gets them to rank the three items they identified in terms of easiest to hardest or what will add the most value and least value. The facilitator should always encourage the individual to work on the hardest issue or the one that will deliver most value. That way they are supported through those issues during the TLA process, gain the win and are then much more confident about handling the other less difficult issues on their own.

These techniques can be particularly useful for depersonalizing the feedback, which can minimize defensiveness and the reluctance to identify possible issues can fall away. This approach also massages their ego a little while providing them with a less confronting way to get past 'I don't know' so the facilitator can move forward and help the individual make behaviour change.

Example of the Panel of Three process in action

The Panel of Three process can really help to create a new perspective which can in turn allow the individual involved to find the gap that they want to work on and keep forward momentum in the change process.

I (EW) remember one TLA conversation where the individual was very resistant to the change initiative and the follow-up process to support real behavioural change. Whatever I asked him he continually replied with 'I don't know,' albeit said in a variety of different ways. So I quietly shifted into the Panel of Three process to see if I could move him forward.

I asked the participant who he respected in the industry, someone he had worked with or knew of personally or professionally, or maybe someone from elsewhere in another industry. Every time I asked for a name the individual then insisted that he didn't know anyone he respected.

Eventually after a little probing he admitted that he respected Nelson Mandela. So I used the technique above and said, 'So if Nelson Mandela had been work-shadowing you in your workplace for the last three weeks what would be the three things he would say you've done really well and what would he suggest you could have done differently to get a better result?'

Just by shifting his perspective and standing in the imaginary shoes of Nelson Mandela this person was able to rattle off suggestions which then led to the identification of a gap and we were able to move forward with the TLA conversations. Just taking a new perspective, even an imaginary one, made a huge difference to his ability to access his own innate intelligence and make constructive progress.

Although this might seem a little odd, when the facilitator encourages the individual to stand in someone else's shoes and look at their own situation from a different perspective it can be incredibly powerful. No one really understands why this type of guided imagery works but it is a recognized way to help people to connect with their innate wisdom and cognitive resources.

Science has already demonstrated that the brain processes about 400 billion bits of information per second and yet we are aware of about 2,000 of those bits (Csikszentmihalyi, 2002; Lipton, 2011). The vast majority of the information is therefore shunted to the subconscious mind without us being aware of it. What's amazing and slightly perturbing is not only that the subconscious mind knows things our conscious mind has forgotten, but that it knows things our conscious mind never even knew! It may be that shifting someone's perspective or viewpoint through guided imagery allows that individual to access different information that can provide innovative solutions. This type of process is a simple way to increase creativity and imagination which in turn helps to solve problems more effectively. By visualizing situations from different angles it's possible to source novel new insights that can lead to improved ideas and solutions.

If you would like to listen to an audio recording of the Panel of Three process in action please visit **http://transferoflearning.com/resources**.

OARBED, Off the Fence and the Panel of Three process are all designed to get the person going through the change process into a gap that they can then bridge to bring about effective behavioural change. The ACTION Conversation Model will not yield results unless the individual has been assisted to identify an issue they want to improve, calibrated a starting score for that issue, and created a target score so they appreciate the gap between where they are now and where they want to be. Without acknowledgement of that gap and a willingness to own the gap and do something constructive to close it nothing will change.

Successful change is possible when change is aligned to business needs and initiative alongside TLA. In the next chapter we will explore how to roll out TLA successfully for your own change initiatives.

Summary of key points

- The skill set is just part of making TLA work in reality. The other is how to guide the conversations toward behavioural change.

- A single conversation doesn't create change – it's the accountability that emerges from the series of conversations.

- What happens between the conversations is every bit as important as, if not more important than, what happens during the conversation.

- Personal accountability is created when the individual knows that in a matter of weeks another conversation is going to take place and they are going to have to account for their progress (or lack of progress) – then action and forward movement are much more likely.

- TLA is focused on creativity rather than compliance, curiosity rather than control and context rather than content. Creativity, curiosity and context further facilitate and drive self-accountability and are a much more powerful way to approach change than compliance, control and content.

- Even when the TLA facilitator understands the process through the ACTION Conversation Model, appreciates the crucial interplay between structure and flexibility and has a level of proficiency in the TLA skills that will guide every TLA conversation, it can sometimes take a few minutes to find the groove in the process. The most common obstacle to finding that groove is when the individual isn't genuinely 'in the gap'.

- The whole point of any change initiative is for something to change. The TLA process is designed to bridge the gap between the old behaviour and the new but unless the TLA facilitator can encourage the individual to identify that gap and own it, then progress can be slow.

- The individual involved in the change will have identified approximately three things they want to address and these will be documented in the TLA Action Plan. At the start of every follow-up conversation the facilitator needs to have the individual choose which issue they want to focus on for the next 20 minutes.

- The facilitator will have the person reaffirm their calibration regarding the issue they have chosen. In other words, they must state where they think they are in that moment against that target or issue on a scale of 1–10.

- Calibration is often used throughout the TLA process and acts as the transition from structure into flexibility. It allows the individual to put a stake in the ground about what they want to address and their current ability against that target – therefore identifying and getting into the gap they are seeking to bridge.

- Typically there are three things the individual will say when they have not identified or acknowledged a gap they wish to bridge.
- Scenario 1: Identify a gap and explain in detail why they can't fix it (solved by the OARBED technique).
- Scenario 2: Identify a gap but won't be able to decide whether it's something they want to address or not (solved by Off the Fence technique).
- Scenario 3: Say they can't identify a gap (solved by the Panel of Three process).
- OARBED, Off the Fence and the Panel of Three process are all designed to get the person going through the change process into a gap that they can then bridge to bring about effective behavioural change.
- The ACTION Conversation Model will not yield results unless the individual has been assisted to first identify an issue they want to improve, calibrated a starting score for that issue and created a target score so they appreciate the gap between where they are now and where they want to be. Without acknowledgement of that gap and a willingness to own the gap and do something constructive to close it nothing will change.

References

Csikszentmihalyi, M (2002) *Flow: The psychology of happiness: The classic work on how to achieve happiness* Paperback Rider, London

Lipton, B H (2011) *The Biology of Belief: Unleashing the power of consciousness, matter and miracles*, Hay House Publishing, London

How to roll out TLA in line with the alignment model

13

TLA is a series of follow-up conversations that facilitates behavioural change after the change initiative has been launched. Modern business operates in an incredibly competitive environment which means that the 'let a thousand flowers bloom' approach to change initiatives is over. In other words 'planting' thousands of change initiatives and hoping that at least some of them bloom or bear fruit is futile. They rarely do because the care and attention required to ensure the initiatives deliver are spread so thinly that nothing blooms. This chapter unpacks how to roll out TLA in line with the alignment model for maximum impact and minimum disruption.

You will remember from Chapter 2 that there are three key stages to business alignment for your change initiative:

1 defining stakeholder needs;

2 developing measurable objectives;

3 evaluating results.

Rolling out TLA happens *before* you evaluate results; TLA helps you *create* those results. Use your measurable objectives as a great place to start and assess what behavioural changes need to happen back in the business. These are the application objectives you have identified. These objectives will then drive business impact and create the ROI.

Organizations simply can't afford to waste time, money and effort pursuing change initiatives that come to nothing, fail outright or are only partially implemented. There are few change initiatives that do not require human beings to change their behaviour in some form or another. Those changes are expected to yield specific results that will have a direct impact on the P&L – whether in cost savings, greater efficiency or improved output and performance. So it follows that the only real indicator of success is whether or not the people who were expected to change have changed and therefore the expected benefit of the change has been realized.

Whilst this is all true, when people first hear about TLA it doesn't take long for them to put two and two together and make a bunch of assumptions about the feasibility and cost of the TLA process. After all, what we are advocating is an additional investment in both time and money on top of the change initiative itself. But remember, 70 per cent of all change initiatives fail to deliver on their promise. Wouldn't it be better to reduce the number of change initiatives your business implements and simply ensure the change that is initiated always delivers results and real-world behavioural change? Not only will you reduce change fatigue that can so massively impact employee engagement and creativity, but you will reduce your change costs and ensure that the benefits the change was hoping to deliver are delivered.

This chapter unpacks the logistics of how to make TLA happen, including:

- WHO rolls out TLA;
- WHEN TLA needs to support change;
- HOW to roll out TLA effectively.

WHO rolls out TLA?

The TLA roll-out will of course depend on how many people are involved in the change initiative and expected to make behavioural adjustments as a result. Plus it will also depend on how much change occurs in the business in any given year.

Managing the TLA process for 50 people is a very different logistical consideration to managing a roll-out of 250 or 2,000 people. The volume of TLA required and the relative importance of the change will clearly impact who is best placed to roll it out.

It is important to realize, however, that even if the roll-out runs into hundreds or even thousands of people it's all manageable and feasible through what is known as the cascade process. If 25 people are trained in TLA and they each give two hours a week for two months then those

25 people can effectively roll out TLA to 250 people. The big question of course is whether those people should be internal personnel trained in the TLA methodology or outsourced external TLA specialists brought into the business as and when they are needed.

There are two internal and two external options to choose from:

1 the manager of the individual (in the change process);

2 the internal specialist;

3 the subject matter expert;

4 the external specialist.

The manager of the individual

The first internal option for rolling out TLA is the manager of the individual. In other words the manager of the person who is expected to change their behaviour supports the individual through the change process.

The advantages of the manager

- A manager trained in the TLA follow-up methodology will massively increase their internal and external value. Change is the number one challenge in modern business so anyone who can consistently facilitate and execute successful change will be highly sought after inside and outside the business.

- Once a manager knows how to facilitate behavioural change through TLA follow-up they can use the same basic skills in a variety of different management roles and situations, such as meaningful performance review and following corporate learning and development initiatives. Learning TLA – which is fundamentally a behavioural change methodology – can make managers better managers.

- The TLA skill set stays inside the business for future use.

- The individual's manager is close to the business results so they can see the impact of the behavioural change first-hand.

- It's a very good way to get the managers engaged in the change process.

- The manager learns a proven methodology to successfully hold people accountable for their actions. It gives the managers greater confidence in their own skills as managers.

The disadvantages of the manager

- For TLA to be truly effective and transformational the person making the changes needs to be very honest and this requires a certain level of vulnerability about their weaknesses or shortcomings. Often it's hard to be that vulnerable and honest with the person who directly influences the individual's future position or salary.

- Managers are already time poor so finding three 20–30-minute sessions for each of their reports who are involved in the change over a two-month period can be difficult.

- Managers can lack the focus and discipline to invest in TLA, especially if they have numerous competing priorities.

- Managers may want TLA to happen through a casual conversation or they may want to tack the TLA follow-up conversation on to the end of an existing agenda, but that won't work. They need to 'change hats' from 'manager' to 'TLA facilitator' for the TLA conversation to be effective.

- Specialized behavioural change is a skill set that needs to be taught and practised and yet managers often assume they can automatically shepherd the change process without specific training. They can't. TLA will only be successful if the person facilitating and supporting behavioural change is trained in TLA or some other behaviour change methodology.

Consider using the individual's manager

- If there is a high level of skill within the management team and the manager is proficient in another change methodology, TLA, or is willing to be trained in a specific behavioural change methodology.

- When there is a large programme roll-out.

- When there are several important change initiatives in the pipeline over the coming years – each requiring real-world behaviour change to improve performance.

- When there is a trusting and productive relationship between the manager and their reports.

- When the manager is involved in the change programme, which means they will be close to it. Of course in such a situation someone else also needs to hold the manager accountable for change.

- When the manager understands the importance of 'changing hats' so they take off their manager's hat for the TLA conversation and replace it with their change hat.

The internal specialist

The next internal option is the internal specialist. The internal specialist is someone inside the business who may or may not be a manager of those going through the change process. This may be someone in the learning and development department, HR or someone identified as a 'high potential' in the business. Often senior managers will seek to identify individuals with high potential who they recognize as future managers or people who will drive the business forward.

If a business operates in a highly fluid environment where change is a near-constant reality then training an internal team in TLA follow-up can be an excellent way to implement TLA over the long term and bake change management capability into the business. This team may be cross-functional or reside inside the HR or learning and development department.

The advantages of the internal specialist

- An internal specialist trained in TLA will increase their internal and external value. The ability to consistently facilitate behavioural change and execute successful change will always be a highly sought-after skill both inside and outside the business.

- The TLA skill set stays inside the business for future use.

- Creating a team of internal TLA specialists can be a brilliant way of enrolling high potentials that need more from their role but are perhaps not fully ready for a managerial position.

- Facilitating TLA and supporting others through behavioural change can be very rewarding, which can also spill out into other areas of the specialist's work.

- If the internal specialist is not linked to the individual in their day-to-day working life the individual is much more likely to be honest and open during the conversation, which will always improve results.

- Using an internal specialist can help build cross-function relationships and reduce silos in an organization.

- Using an internal specialist can give both parties an experience and insight into different parts of the business which can often assist creativity, understanding and performance in their own role.

- If the internal specialist is within learning and development or Human Resources then issues of seniority are less important. Depending on the change initiative and the seniority of those involved it probably wouldn't be appropriate for a junior high potential to be conducting the TLA follow-up with a senior leader but the process would still work for an L&D internal specialist to facilitate TLA with that senior leader.

The disadvantages of the internal specialist

- Depending on the size of the organization, there could be an issue of trust between the internal specialist and the individual. Even with a confidentiality agreement in place, it may take a while to build a sufficient level of trust to get the individual to open up if the internal specialist frequently interacts with the individual in their normal working day.

- TLA requires a high level of skill so there will still be people who are naturally better at it than others. It's important to acknowledge this so that the internal specialists are all very proficient at TLA and can be picked to suit the process.

- Depending on how much change is done annually, being an internal TLA specialist could involve a big time commitment from people who already have other roles and responsibilities. Being a facilitator for TLA must become part of that person's role and responsibilities otherwise they may not prioritize it.

Consider using the internal specialist

- When the change initiative requires a large-scale programme roll-out.

- When the business has good internal people with the necessary time available, to learn and master TLA as a behavioural change methodology.

- When the business has internal people that are interested and want to learn the skill, use it and help grow the organization.

- When senior management wants to give their high potentials more responsibility without promoting them too early.

- When the internal specialist understands the importance of 'changing hats' so they take off the hat they usually wear in their day-to-day role and replace it with their TLA behavioural change hat.

The subject matter expert

The first external option for rolling out TLA is the subject matter expert who is assisting the organization through the change. That subject matter expert may take many forms, including the trainer of a new IT platform or an operations or logistics expert who is consulting on the change and helping the company through the transition.

The advantages of the subject matter expert

- It's useful for the subject matter expert because they become closer to the business and see the change through to completion, which will massively increase their value as someone capable of both devising and delivering change.

- Where the validity of change is being increasingly questioned incorporating a behavioural change methodology into the change can massively increase real-world results.

The disadvantages of the subject matter expert

- The subject matter expert is so familiar with the type of change they are implementing that it can be hard for them to ask questions instead of telling the people involved in the change how it should be done. Even if the subject matter expert is correct and the individual agrees with them, this situation makes it very hard for the person who needs to change to take ownership of the process and the necessary behavioural change. When we remove the autonomy from the process and stop the individual from working things out for themselves then we remove the possibility for intrinsic motivation which is essential for effective change.

- Even if the subject matter expert is conscious of this challenge and deliberately holds back from offering solutions, the person who needs to change may already be used to seeing that person in an educator/leader role which means they are still expecting them to do just that. As a result they often don't fully engage with the process because they assume if they get stuck the subject matter expert will step in and solve their challenge. When they don't, the person doing the changing can feel resentful as though they have been abandoned by the subject matter expert.

- It's often more expensive to have the subject matter expert conduct the TLA follow-up because they are used to calculating their costs based on a day rate where they work with, say, 15 people. TLA is a 1:1 process, not 1:15, and the danger is that the subject matter expert will cost the process based on high-end executive coaching which is not comparable or necessary in the behavioural change context.

- TLA is most effective when the conversations are conducted over the phone (we will discuss this in more detail shortly) rather than face to face, and yet subject matter experts are typically more experienced and proficient in the face-to-face environment.
- The TLA skills stay outside the business.

Consider using the subject matter expert

- When the subject matter expert is specifically skilled in behaviour change in addition to designing effective change.
- When the subject matter expert is providing TLA for a programme they did not personally deliver.

The external specialist

The final external option for delivering TLA is the external specialist.

The advantages of the external specialist

- The external TLA specialist is an expert in the field.
- They are highly proficient in supporting people through behavioural change because they are doing it all day every day.
- There is no pre-existing relationship or politics between an individual and the external TLA specialist which makes it easier for the person involved in the change process to be open, honest and vulnerable regarding what they want or need to change. The conversations are more focused and productive as a result.
- It means that the business doesn't have to invest any additional time to get the results it seeks. This is especially valuable if the people in the business are already time poor or when the business doesn't initiate change very often.

The disadvantages of the external specialist

- The manager of those people expected to change can feel as if it is their role to directly manage their team even though it is a specific initiative. They can feel as if they are being kept out of the loop and extra effort is necessary to make sure they are still engaged in the change process.

● Bringing in external TLA specialists to support behavioural change can be more costly over the long term than training an internal specialist so the skills remain in the business to be reutilized into the future. However, this is only an issue if there are several change initiatives each year. (We'll explore investment levels in more detail shortly.)

● The skills stay outside the business.

Consider using the external specialist

● When senior management has a highly visible change programme that is critical to the business and behavioural change needs to be guaranteed.

● When the internal people are already stretched for time and don't have the resources or capability to deliver TLA internally.

● When a business doesn't invest in a great deal of change each year and it's not worth up-skilling people internally but senior managers still want to ensure that what they do invest in delivers results.

● When a business is trialling the TLA process to see what results can be generated.

How to decide on the best roll-out strategy

When deciding who is going to be the best person to roll out TLA ask yourself the following questions:

1 Is this person proficient in a change methodology?

2 Is this person an effective coach?

3 Does this person have the time to effectively facilitate behaviour change? They will need three 20–30-minute sessions per participant over two months following the change initiative.

4 Does this person already have the skills?

5 Could this person learn the skills?

6 Does this person have the desire to support behavioural change?

7 Can they make behavioural change a priority in their schedule?

8 Do we have the resources within the organization?

9 Do we have access to a system that could be used to disseminate actions and outputs following the TLA follow-up conversations to keep everyone on track?

10 Will we be able to evaluate the success of the programme?

If the answer to these questions is mostly 'No' then it may be best to outsource TLA to an external specialist or train an internal specialist in TLA – especially if more change initiatives are in the pipeline.

TLA has already proven itself as a highly effective behavioural change methodology. If you are serious about getting business impact results from the change initiatives you instigate then someone in the business should be trained in TLA or the process should be outsourced to external TLA specialists. Even if you only do this once to get a sense of how effective TLA can be in facilitating behavioural change, it can help to get everyone enrolled in the process and the outcome.

WHEN TLA needs to support change

Not all change initiatives are created equally. For some change initiatives the fact that they never stick in the business is not that important. For example if a business initiates a new policy around 'manual handling' or 'fire safety', the changes in behaviour may still be required or hoped for but ultimately the purpose of the change may have been merely to comply with shifting regulations. Such changes are not necessarily seeking habitual behavioural change but rather to ensure that should a certain situation arise in the workplace everyone knows how to act or what to do – and to limit liability for the employer should someone ignore the guidelines and get injured.

The real value of TLA and when it should be applied to change initiatives is when the purpose of the change is to alter and improve habitual ongoing behaviour. It is therefore a vital component for any people-based change initiatives such as altering leadership skills, communication skills, management skills, sales skills, software implementation – anything that alters habitual behaviour or is seeking a change to the way participants operate or show up in their working life.

In an ideal world TLA could be used for every change initiative that is seeking to change behaviours in the workplace but that may not always be realistic depending on the size of the business and the size of the change budget. So this section explores when TLA is really needed and why.

When a change programme is highly visible or critically important to the business then invest in TLA to ensure success and real-world behavioural change. If it is absolutely essential that results are achieved and there has been little past success in achieving behavioural change from change initiatives then recruit the assistance of an experienced external TLA specialist to get the job done.

This is a cost-effective and logical approach that allows a business leader to experience the uplift in results and improved performance TLA can deliver before committing time and energy to training their own internal specialists. In addition it is also smart to choose a change initiative that will or could deliver fast results.

TLA works. But we appreciate that business leaders and senior managers must verify that for themselves. The best way to do that initially is to choose a suitable change programme and hire an experienced external specialist to facilitate behavioural change in the workplace. A suitable programme would be either one that will deliver fast and easily measurable results or one that is critical to the business. Once a business unit has confirmed the results then senior management can decide whether to train a dedicated internal TLA team or simply buy in the skills as and when they are needed depending on the importance and impact of the change programme.

The bottom line is that if we are seeking soft skill habitual behavioural change where the individuals are required to create new, better work practices and improve performance then we *must* support the change process with a follow-up methodology that ensures the individuals are held to account for the change that's required.

If we don't, there is a much higher likelihood that the change will fail for the vast majority of those involved. There is always a small percentage of any change programme participants who will naturally welcome the change and make the necessary behavioural shifts, but investing millions in the vain hope that a few individuals might make the necessary changes and miraculously 'infect' all the others is futile. It's bad for morale, creates change fatigue and it's extremely expensive and time consuming.

Investing in TLA after the change initiative is launched allows for a much more precise and targeted approach to behavioural change, which then allows us to finally reverse the dismal statistics around failed change.

If we are serious about seeking to change behaviour and elevate performance then change initiatives need to be backed by a robust behavioural change methodology to ensure the desired results actually materialize. And let's face it, if we are not seeking behavioural change and real-world application from the individuals involved then why are we starting the change process in the first place?

HOW to roll out TLA effectively

The secret weapon for supporting people through the change process, regardless of the numbers of people who are required to make behavioural change, is the telephone.

It's easy to dismiss the telephone as a productive coaching medium because a coach often assumes that they would miss important visual cues or lose out on rapport-building opportunities only available through face-to-face contact. However, using the telephone to facilitate behaviour change after the change initiative has been launched is infinitely more time efficient than face-to-face interactions. And that is true for the TLA facilitator and the individual who is being supported through the change process. There is no commute, no travel expenses and less time for chit chat, and it's easily scalable across diverse geographical locations. There is less opportunity to wander off topic, and perhaps more importantly it's more effective in the process of change.

Behavioural change, which is the driver of most change initiatives, is only really possible when we engage the individual in the process and get them to appreciate the need to change for their own benefit rather than that of the facilitator or the business. Change comes about through a process of self-reflection and personal contemplation. It is initiated from within and is facilitated by encouraging the individual to listen to their internal dialogue and allowing them to effectively have a conversation with themselves. This process is greatly assisted by the telephone because the questions and conversations go straight into the individual's ear. When we are having a face-to-face conversation with someone it can often bounce around the room, it's easier to ignore tough questions, and people get distracted more easily. Often the interactions are not as intense or focused because such exchanges can feel uncomfortable face to face. But that discomfort is greatly reduced when the conversation occurs over the phone. Using the telephone is like whispering in someone's ear, where the communication goes straight down the ear canal to the brain. It can't be deflected; it has nowhere else to go. As a result we get access to a greater level of truth because we talk directly to the person before they have had a moment to filter their thoughts and message.

Facilitating behavioural change is not about the TLA facilitator – it's about the individual doing the changing. The facilitator doesn't need to see visual cues because they have an effective structure instead. It's far harder to tell someone something difficult when we are face to face with that person, even if we don't know them personally. On the phone that discomfort is reduced because we are not in the same room. It can be really hard for someone who is very competent in their role to have to admit they are struggling in one particular area or have any vulnerabilities or opportunities to grow. That process is made much easier if the conversation occurs over the phone and the facilitator is not someone who is intimately involved in the individual's daily activity.

Many of us have had the experience of sitting next to someone on a long-haul flight and telling them things we hadn't even told our friends or partner. This openness comes from the anonymity fostered when we either won't see that person again or can't see them. And it is this 'not seeing' the other person that is so crucial in the telephone dialogue. Modern technology may have allowed us to conveniently forget that the communication we are sending out is read by other human beings, which has often led to career limiting 'over-sharing' on social network sites or in e-mails. But in a reflective conversation the honesty that comes from 'not seeing' the TLA facilitator can be a real bonus because honesty is imperative for successful change.

Using the telephone for TLA follow-up means that the individual can't see their facilitator, and may never even know what that person looks like if the TLA is delivered from an external specialist. As a result these conversations can feel a little like that long-haul discussion with a stranger – only more focused on results. The individual is much less self-conscious and more likely to open up and be honest. It can often feel as though the individual is actually having a conversation with themselves and the facilitator is simply steering the conversation and supporting the participant toward behavioural change. This idea is critical to the TLA methodology and telephone delivery of the follow-up conversations is not just more efficient but infinitely more effective because it allows the individual to be more honest with the facilitator and – perhaps more importantly – with themselves. It is the internal dialogue and internal conversations that we have with ourselves all the time that ultimately control our thoughts and feelings and it is then those thoughts and feelings that determine how we act and how we behave. So if we are looking for behaviour change we have to create a safe environment where the individual can access their own thinking and really bring that internal dialogue into awareness. The phone is the easiest way to access this state.

Pay attention to logistics

Regardless of who rolls out TLA that person needs to also be mindful of logistics. TLA can sound pretty straightforward and it is – three follow-up conversations over the course of a few weeks or months. But it's not always easy because of what's involved in making those calls happen.

Scheduling and managing the follow-up conversations are critical to the accountability of the whole process. In fact, we believe this is why so many change projects fail – because not enough thought or organization has gone into the logistics of the follow-up, after the change.

The key logistical considerations that you need to stay focused on are:

- **TLA Action Plans.** It is essential that you find a system for ensuring that the action plans that people commit to go somewhere. If you outsource the execution of TLA to external TLA experts then that execution comes with full access to an online system that facilitates collection and distribution. If you are delivering TLA internally then at the very least you need to take photocopies of the action plans and make sure the copy goes back to the person who is managing the behavioural change so they can ensure that the people involved action those plans and behaviour really does change. If copies are not made and the change agent is simply relying on the participants to execute what they committed to then they will be disappointed.

- **Scheduling and rescheduling calls.** As we've pointed out the telephone is absolutely the best way to execute the follow-up conversations and facilitate behavioural change but unless someone is in charge of scheduling those calls it can quickly became a major headache. Again, when outsourced all this is managed by the TLA expert but when this is done internally one person needs to be responsible for scheduling and rescheduling the calls otherwise they just won't happen. Remember, even if you are rolling out to a small group of 25, that requires the scheduling of 75 separate phone calls. Those people are usually already busy so chances are at least 20 per cent will have to be rescheduled. This can become a logistical nightmare very quickly so one person needs to manage the scheduling and rescheduling of calls.

- **Monitoring and evaluation.** There is no point getting to the end of the process and looking back only to find that you can't actually tell what, if anything, has happened. It is therefore essential that information is recorded about the outcome and progress of all three TLA conversations so that useful and meaningful evaluation can occur at the end. Otherwise it's just a guess.

The reason so many change initiatives are not followed up effectively, and ultimately fail, is because no one is managing the logistics of the follow-up process – the nuts and bolts of what has to happen to support someone through the change process and keep them on track. By staying mindful of the derailing potential of logistics on your change initiative you can take steps to ensure these details don't fall through the cracks.

When we bring all these component parts together we are finally in a position where failed change can be a thing of the past. When we start the change only when it's absolutely necessary, clearly and concretely aligned with the business needs and clear definable objectives, and marry that change to a behavioural change methodology such as TLA then real-world success is not just possible but almost guaranteed.

Summary of key points

- Organizations simply can't afford to waste time, money and effort pursuing change initiatives that come to nothing, fail outright or are only partially implemented.

- The only real measure that matters is whether or not the people who were expected to change have changed and therefore the expected benefit of the change has been realized.

- It doesn't take long for people to put two and two together and make a bunch of assumptions about the feasibility and cost of the TLA process. After all what we are advocating is an additional cost and investment in both time and money on top of the change initiative itself.

- But, considering that 70 per cent of all change initiatives fail to deliver on their promise, wouldn't it be better to reduce the number of change initiatives your business implements and simply ensure the change that is initiated always delivers results and real-world behavioural change?

- How TLA is rolled out will depend on how many people are involved in the change initiative and expected to make behavioural adjustments as a result. Plus it will also depend on how much change occurs in the business in any given year.

- Managing the TLA process for 50 people is a very different logistical consideration to managing a roll-out of 250 or 2,000 people. The volume of TLA required and the relative importance of the change will clearly impact who is best placed to roll it out.

- There are two internal and two external options to choose from, namely: the manager of the individual in the change process; the internal specialist; the subject matter expert; or the external specialist. Each have their own advantages and disadvantages.

- Not all change initiatives are created equally. For some, the fact that they never stick in the business is not that important. Such changes are not necessarily seeking habitual behavioural change but rather to ensure that should a certain situation arise in the workplace everyone knows how to act or what to do – and to limit liability for the employer should someone ignore the guidelines and get injured.

- The real value of TLA and when it should be applied to change initiatives is when the purpose of the change is to alter and improve habitual ongoing behaviour. It is therefore a vital component for any soft skill change initiatives such as altering leadership skills, communication skills, management skills, sales skills – anything that alters habitual behaviour or is seeking a change to the way participants operate or show up in their working life.

- When a change programme is highly visible or critically important to the business then invest in TLA to ensure success and real-world behavioural change. If it is absolutely essential that results are achieved and there has been little past success in achieving behavioural change from change initiatives then recruit the assistance of an experienced external TLA specialist to get the job done.

- TLA works. But we appreciate that business leaders and senior managers must verify that for themselves. The best way to do that initially is to choose a suitable change programme and hire an experienced external specialist to facilitate behavioural change in the workplace. A suitable programme would be either one that will deliver fast and easily measurable results or one that is critical to the business.

- Investing in TLA after the change initiative is launched allows for a much more precise and targeted approach to behavioural change, which allows us to finally reverse the dismal statistics around failed change.

- The secret weapon for supporting people through the change process, regardless of the numbers of people who are required to make behavioural change, is the telephone.

- Using the telephone for TLA follow-up means that the individual can't see their facilitator. As a result these conversations are much more focused and the individual is much less self-conscious and more likely to open up and be honest.

- Regardless of who rolls out TLA that person needs to also be mindful of logistics. TLA can sound pretty straightforward and it is – three follow-up conversations over the course of a few weeks or months. But it's not always easy because of what's involved in making those calls happen.

- The reason so many change initiatives are not followed up effectively, and ultimately fail, is because no one is managing the logistics of the follow-up process and keeping the participants on track. By staying mindful of the derailing potential of logistics on your change initiative you can take steps to ensure these details don't fall through the cracks.

- When we bring all these component parts together we are finally in a position where failed change can be a thing of the past.

Case study

UNSW
Innovations at
UNSW Australia

14

UNSW Innovations is the technology transfer and innovation office of UNSW Australia – one of Australia's leading research and teaching universities. Situated within the Division of Research, UNSW Innovations has pioneered new models for technology transfer and knowledge exchange to grow the research business of the university. UNSW Innovations is dedicated to channelling UNSW research outputs to external research users who can then create impact by tackling some of the biggest issues facing society today.

UNSW Innovations works in partnership with UNSW researchers, industry, government and the community to transform research discoveries into successful real-world innovations that will benefit society, the economy and future generations.

Named the most innovative university at the 2012 Thomson Reuters Citation and Innovations Awards, UNSW has influenced academic research on a global scale. From eco-friendly packaging made from banana tree waste, medical imaging, photovoltaics and clean drinking water, to developing lifesaving HIV drugs, UNSW Innovations works to help researchers engage with and translate research to use in society and the economy, encourages an entrepreneurial culture at UNSW and leads the way with innovation leadership.

Opportunity for change

At UNSW Innovations, there was an increased appreciation of the importance of data and knowledge management (ie information on interests of companies and points of contact, relationships between technologies managed in the portfolio) to conduct projects and measure outputs to deliver strategic objectives; information is at the heart of decisions, collaboration and client management. Although UNSW Innovations had a solid central database system, with recent advances in technology, changes in work practices and the business model, a world-class software solution was sought to meet business knowledge needs and wants. In addition, functionality in the existing system was underutilized and the system was not used by all 35 employees. While this didn't affect client outcomes, it did mean that the system couldn't be used for consistent, centralized reporting across the organization, nor was there optimization of knowledge sharing through an effective CRM system to grow and support more effective business partnerships. Some essential reports could be generated and a good level of visibility was available from the existing IT solution but a better option was available that would help UNSW Innovations future-proof the department to operate successfully in a fast-paced, fast-changing innovation landscape. With a 'best of breed' IT solution the system could further centralize reporting, progress development of the CRM system and improve corporate memory, which could in turn elevate decision making and help better manage business moving forward.

As with any IT system it was recognized that the new solution would only be as good as the data entered. As a consequence, one of the key aims was to attract all areas of the business to integrate all business processes with the system, not just the business-critical operational processes that were favoured in the existing system. This plan included the involvement of the marketing and business development teams and would facilitate even deeper business-critical insights by teams and across the business.

Corporate memory was also important to UNSW Innovations. When employees moved on, the knowledge they held was too easily lost. Encouraging improved centralized record keeping rather than personal systems or information existing inside key individuals' heads was considered another key priority to support reporting and development of the CRM.

UNSW Innovations recognized that reticence to use the existing system was in part due to difficulties with remote access and ability to use the system effectively on different platforms. Often staff worked remotely whether on campus or offsite and did not have easy access to the central office system to make real-time updates to records. This meant that staff would need to update the system once they were back in the office. Understandably, especially considering the fast-paced, dynamic commercial environment in which knowledge exchange and technology transfer occur, updating the system was often bumped to the bottom of the 'to do' list and the details stayed with the individual client manager.

The accessibility issue was going to become increasingly important as more UNSW Innovations employees travelled more frequently to develop external partnerships, and in the present-day work environment where employees increasingly work flexible hours, virtually and remotely. Hence a significant factor influencing the change was the need for an immediate, effective cloud-based software solution. Other reasons driving the need for change were:

- the need to have all UNSW operations managed from one system to the greatest extent allowed by business needs, including development of a more effective CRM system;
- to have a system that was more intuitive and user friendly, including intuitive reporting tools; and
- better integrated workflow and project management tools to improve efficiencies with existing business processes.

Although additional training and a concerted effort to engage employees in the current system may have in time potentially solved the problem, UNSW Innovations decided that a fresh start was preferable. As a leader in the field of innovation they needed to have a system that could meet present and future business knowledge needs and wants and engage the key stakeholders in the change right from the start.

Additionally, a new, world-class knowledge management system could address the accessibility issues and, through improved metrics and reporting, give increased visibility across the organization. If it was possible to update records anytime, anywhere on a cloud-based system then employees would be much more likely to access information and update the system directly. This would therefore expand the use of business information systems and allow metrics and useful reporting to be drawn from one central source.

Increasingly, as different members of the team would be working across client projects on different aspects of those projects, the system would enable a central repository for client information and exponentially add to the reservoir of corporate memory from which to draw additional insights.

The change: a new IT solution

A working group of diverse stakeholders was created within UNSW Innovations to evaluate whether they needed and wanted to make a change to the existing IT system. The working group also obtained feedback from broader staff surveys and from users of potential new systems from outside the university. Those stakeholders then advocated in favour of the nominated new system to the management team. The proposal for a new software solution was accepted by the management team.

After a thorough analysis of the various systems on the market the system chosen by UNSW Innovations was Wellspring's Knowledge Supply Chain™ software called Sophia, which was considered to be the best available off-the-shelf software solution to meet the organization's knowledge needs and wants.

Specifically, Sophia is enterprise software that manages an organization's knowledge assets and network of innovation partnerships. Leading innovators actively develop and manage their knowledge assets, from test data, to patents, publications and expertise. In Sophia, each type of knowledge asset is managed in a specific module. Additional modules could be added to the core system to meet specific organizational requirements.

Each module in turn catalogues and tracks knowledge assets through their life. Sophia's intuitive user interface and extensive analysis tools empower the user to search, identify, manage, and exploit their knowledge assets and networks.

Business alignment and the approach to change

Change implementation was aligned to the business using the three phases of business alignment, namely defining stakeholders' needs, developing measurable objectives, and evaluating the results.

Defining stakeholder needs was quite clear. The key payoff needs were the reporting, visibility and need to increase user engagement and related data input to build a more comprehensive CRM and data-management system. This would enable easier and more streamlined management and greater transparency across the business. Another payoff need was the anticipated increase in partnerships with new and existing clients and related transactions to support achievement of organizational strategic goals.

Business needs included the increase in reporting, increase in communication across clients, and the improvement in knowledge management when staff left the organization.

Performance needs were anticipated from simply using the system and inputting the correct data in a timely manner to enable the reporting and improved communication.

Learning needs were identified and developed by close collaboration between the project team including the UNSW Innovations Learning and Development coordinator and Wellspring, the US-based software provider. Exactly what needed to be learnt by the participants for the change project to be successful and for the audience to use the system effectively was detailed clearly. This was extensive and included how to input data and update project records. Learning needs are often the easiest to articulate, particularly if you partner with a provider in the learning and development space, engage effectively with stakeholders within the organization and have well-developed business processes to implement through a system.

Preference needs included needing the system to have all necessary staff using the new knowledge management software for the operational functions that were facilitated through the old system, within three months of data migration to the new system.

Input needs included the two-day workshop from the US provider as a start point. The management team were conscious that they needed to get good traction in the first three months otherwise the momentum might slip and, as human nature would suggest, people would start to lose faith in the change. If data integrity was not significantly achieved in the first three months, and the value of the new system was not demonstrated through better analytics and insightful reporting that helped to identify further business opportunities and provide the metrics required to measure business impact, then that failure could give ammunition to those that did not see the full benefits the change could bring.

To help create a strong initial momentum, UNSW Innovations decided to involve Lever – Transfer of Learning in the project to deliver TLA sessions as part of the change initiative.

The second phase of business alignment is to develop measurable objectives. Depending on the scale and size of the project, measurable objectives may or may not be set at all levels. As an overview, UNSW Innovations set the application objective of 100 per cent of reporting (where feasible from a central database management system)* to be driven from the new system within three months.

*Not all operational functions are managed from the UNSW Innovations central database management system, as due to alignment and integration with UNSW, other software systems are also used for specific functions such as finance.

They also had the application objective of the data being at least 75 per cent accurate in the new system.

The reaction objectives centred on people being satisfied with the TLA workshop, with learning objectives detailing what people needed to learn from the workshop.

The impact and ROI objectives were difficult to identify for this programme and given the high level of stakeholder engagement it was not considered necessary. It was going to be pretty clear reasonably early in the change initiative if employees were using the system or not and therefore whether the change was successful or not.

Installation and training

With strong support from UNSW Innovations employees Sophia was purchased and installed. Wellspring sent a trainer out to Australia to give a two-day training and overview following the go live date. A project team was assigned to UNSW Innovations at Wellspring, and they offered direct support during the initial weeks of implementation and through a help centre in the later stages of implementation. Basecamp, a web-based project management tool, was used to manage any outstanding implementation issues. Post-implementation support was through the Wellspring help centre only.

At the launch and immediately afterwards UNSW Innovations employees were very responsive as were the Wellspring support team, who also assisted with data migration from the old system to the new system. They were given good support from the software provider. Some of the internal stakeholders worked one-on-one with the trainer, and there were also group sessions. Importantly there was significant senior management buy-in to support the implementation process.

At the time of purchase, staff support was towards the top end of the engagement spectrum and there was enthusiasm about the change or at least a 'happy to go along with the change' attitude. Inevitably, as with most change projects, once change was actually required by people at an individual, daily level that enthusiasm started to wane in some quarters. In a change project this is where the rubber hits the road and change can become harder to sustain.

It was crucial for UNSW Innovations' management that people stayed with the change, were encouraged to use the new system and were not allowed to get away with going back to old habits when the going got tough or they came up against barriers to implementation. It would have been all too easy for people to go back to using spreadsheets, come up with a bespoke shortcut or continue to use their own information gathering methods so as to avoid the system. This would have hampered the ironing out of any potential teething problems and would not have aligned to the overall organizational objectives, therefore minimizing data visibility and the improved reporting capabilities they envisaged.

In order to ensure that the goodwill stayed in the change process and early wins were celebrated and built on to maintain the forward momentum, the TLA change approach was implemented three weeks after the initial briefing to ensure behavioural change across the organization.

TLA after the change

Out of a possible 35 employees in UNSW Innovations, 15 were selected for the TLA follow-up process. These 15 individuals represented at least one person from key teams, all the business development team who did not always use the old system but were keen to get the added value from the new system, as well as a couple of other key contributors who were finding the initial integration with the new system difficult. The project manager and IT manager were also participants.

The process was kicked off with a 'lunch and learn' briefing session that lasted 90 minutes. When I (EW) introduced the 15 to TLA, I was clear that this process was not about revving them up to push through the change but rather giving them the choice about how they wanted to experience the change. I set the scene, using reflection to get participants to think about why the change would be useful to them individually and why it was useful for the department as a whole.

Although it was clear that some attendees were expecting me to reiterate the benefits of the change or try to convince them of the merits of change, I took a different tack. Instead I highlighted that it was down to each individual to choose how they wanted to experience and contribute to the change.

This TLA planning session took place three weeks after the training from the US Wellspring representative. All the participants had therefore had three weeks to get to know the system and investigate what it meant to them so that they were in a position to create a personalized action plan and commitment to what they were actually going to do.

Each individual created a TLA Action Plan that was relevant to them (you can see a sample TLA Plan in Appendix 1). As with any TLA intervention the action plan is the base document that each individual creates.

Example actions included:

- Use system to track all UNSW Innovations marketing campaigns including impact and metrics.
- Implement the Advanced Workflow process in the invention module in Sophia.
- Integrate Sophia and Constant Contact records and create processes/systems.
- Transfer all technology info from e-mails onto Sophia.
- Revise or develop processes to do my work in Sophia.
- Set up nominated metrics as queries and direct queries in Wellspring.
- Implement system to track 'Easy Access IP' technologies through their full life-cycle – Invention, Engagement and Input.
- Update previous tech records relating to current projects by end of May.
- Engage more academics.
- Use Sophia for all elements of the 'commercialization' of technologies.

Underneath each goal individuals detailed why it was important to them, what success looked liked, and calibrated on a scale of 1–10 where they were with the particular objective at the set-up stage. Finally they captured immediate next steps.

The 15 key change leaders were each to have three specific TLA follow-up conversations to support the implementation of the change over the coming weeks. The first would take place three weeks after the planning session and the second session would be four weeks later. The final TLA follow-up call would be four weeks after the second.

Making time for the follow-up calls can be tricky when competing priorities emerge. When someone is looking at their diary and they have 20 other things they really need to be doing that day it can be really easy to reschedule or cancel the call and really hard to prioritize their learning. So what we do is encourage participants to prioritize their learning/implementation of the action plan; subsequent implementation draws a link between their learning and the learning of a child in India. Every time the participant calls in on time for the TLA follow-up conversation as scheduled we make a donation to a charity that provides midday meals to children in India. Each completed call feeds one child for a month.

This connection has been really powerful for helping keep people on track. It's a win–win – the child in India gets fed for a month and the TLA participant maintains forward momentum through the change and is able to feel good about what their commitment is doing for someone in a disadvantaged part of the world.

Common barriers that TLA helped overcome

The 15 key people involved in the follow-up change conversations had three conversations each over a 12-week period. They used the sessions to help keep the process on track and keep the momentum of the change process. These sessions also helped overcome barriers and obstacles.

This change project was no different to the majority of change initiatives that take place in businesses around the globe on a daily basis. At times it was hard going and frustrating for participants. Not everything went smoothly. In some TLA sessions it became important for people to let off steam and vent their frustrations with the change process, in a safe, non-judgemental environment. Once their issues had been aired then there was space for a constructive conversation around what needed to happen. This journey is a normal part of the change process.

The other common barrier was finding time and prioritizing the implementation of the new system. Like most busy workplaces, employees had competing priorities and a day job to do. The conversations helped to break down what needed to be achieved with the new system into small workable pieces that they could commit to. For this project the important factor was maintaining forward momentum and holding the individuals accountable to themselves for the successful outcome of the project.

Below is a sample of comments that participants made following the end of the TLA follow-up in relation to the changes they had made as a result of the TLA:

'I allocated time to backtrack through projects and organize the associated documents/information in a useful way in Sophia. I clarified marketing issues with our marketing manager and corrected the information accordingly and I have approached a team member who helped design where the metrics would be pulled from and clarified I was inputting the metric data in the correct place.'

'[The business benefits included] focus on action and arbitrary deadlines which have driven an outcome rather than inaction.'

'Benefits to me: Some of the team members talk about the calls (and issues they brought up) over lunch. This has helped me to understand what others are having issues with and how they've dealt with them (or are dealing with them), and we've frequently discussed how to address issues together.

For the company: Everyone seems to be using Sophia as they've been asked to do. Metrics reporting should therefore be easier and monitoring of projects/technologies/activities should be easier for senior management.

The CRM function of Sophia should also be taking shape.'

'The new system is now part of our standard operating procedures.'

Outcomes and evaluation

The TLA process helped to facilitate the change much quicker than would otherwise have been achieved. Anecdotally we know this because UNSW Innovations was further along in terms of usage and application of the Sophia system just six months after installation than another university that had been using the same software for a few years. Although not everyone expected to make behavioural change was involved in the TLA follow-up, at least one person from every team was, so that person was then able to support their colleagues and the change took hold faster. The outcomes were a testament to the groundwork that the UNSW Innovations team had put in place and the commitment that they had to driving the implementation forward within the business.

Six months on, systems are now in place for all new proposals and projects to be managed through Sophia. User engagement with the database has increased, evident through more widespread use of reporting tools and greater data input into underutilized modules in the old system. The accuracy of the data has increased to around 80 per cent (above the planned 75 per cent), and there has been a 40 per cent increase in organizational performance reporting from Sophia. There has been a clear shift in culture and acceptance of the database as the central knowledge management system for business information.

Full evaluation of the transition and performance of Sophia in terms of its effectiveness in relation to operational functions, whether or not it has led to greater efficiency in business processes and whether the increased use of the database will be sustained over time requires a time lag. Impacts on the business through improved reporting for metrics, progressive development of the CRM system and implementation of workflows in relation to delivery of the strategic goals of UNSW Innovations would also only be demonstrated in time.

Plus, 14 participants kept all three TLA follow-up conversations, with 93 per cent completed on time. One participant left the business part way through. Forty-two children in India were fed for a month as a result of the programme.

Case study
Successfully managing a mature workforce

15

WCD – Workers' Compensation Solutions – is Australia's largest national workers' compensation management service. At its heart, the vision of WCD is to help organizations avoid damage to their people and, in the event of that damage occurring, help them back into the workforce and their normal lifestyle in a manner that is cost efficient and compassionate. WCD supports businesses to ensure the best possible financial and social outcome through their range of practical, cost-efficient, innovative support services to the Australian and Pacific Rim business community.

This case study details what happened when WCD were approached by a small but important division of a well-known Australian company to help them better manage an ageing workforce.

Opportunity for change

Sixty per cent of the company's population is over 45 years of age (not uncommon in Australian industry at present). In one division, across all occupation types of those with greater than five years' service, 24 of 38 employees are over 45 years of age. Of these 24 employees, 20 of them have more than 10 years of service and 11 of them have over 20 years of service in manual work. There was concern about the rising injury rates and the risk profile of the employees.

Increased injury was not only bad for the individual who was hurt but it affected productivity, increased compensation claims and increased insurance premiums. Claim costs had spiralled up in the previous two years and premiums had doubled. From the previous four years of data, the over-45 cohort account for 92 per cent of the cost of claims. The average cost of a claim when 45 years of age is reached quadruples compared to any other age cohort.

Looking at the broader context for this change, in Australia, like many developed countries around the world, there is a growing realization that as the baby boomers retire in large numbers there will be fewer tax-paying adults to support their pension demands, which is putting significant pressure on government budgets.

An ageing workforce creates new challenges that every business has to manage, whether in the manufacturing, professional or service industries. Ageing employees are often perceived as not being as productive as their younger counterparts, they usually incur higher workers' compensation costs when injured, they are more likely to suffer secondary claims as a result of wear and tear, and failing health can lead to increased absenteeism.

These challenges are often further exacerbated because no one is talking about them and most employers are doing little to support their older colleagues. Employers acknowledge there is a problem but few are planning to offset looming challenges. Those in the latter years of their working life are often reluctant to discuss plans with employers in case that information is used against them and they are moved on earlier than they want. Plus, many simply don't have a plan and often events such as failing health are the trigger for those individuals to start thinking about retirement or insurance claim options. Over 30 per cent of retirees have a chronic health condition at the time of retirement and this plays a part in the retirement decision.

This makes retirement planning harder for the employer who is also keen to ensure that knowledge is captured before retirement but again may be reluctant to discuss that with the ageing employee. The employee may feel threatened if they are asked to document their knowledge.

What tends to happen therefore is that plans for the later working years are not considered until after an event, either an illness or failing health when retirement or even early retirement arrives on the agenda – often with insufficient time to plan on either side. It is a fact that 'half of female "boomers" between 50 and 64 have less than $30,000 Australian dollars in superannuation' (Butler, 2015).

Recognizing this, WCD wanted to support its clients through a change initiative that would not only create awareness and conversation but would directly influence the area of retirement planning.

The change: workshops for mature staff

The aim of this change intervention was to help the company to create an environment where individuals could consider their current situation regarding their later working years and put in place a plan to help them achieve their longer-term goals without resorting to long-term absenteeism or insurance claims. It would also allow the business to identify in advance individuals' retirement intentions so that an appropriate resource plan could be put in place to accommodate the needs of both employees and the business, allowing the employees to finalize their working life with dignity.

The initial intervention and pilot for the programme consisted of a business case development, benefit–cost analysis, workshops and information-planning sessions, and all elements were deemed to be successful. There was no follow-through planned. The intervention did a lot to create awareness but it soon became clear that plans were not being actioned and therefore the intervention delivered limited tangible results. The WCD therefore proposed to the client a more thorough approach, keeping all the elements in place and adding follow-up TLA conversations to ensure that the plans created by the mature workers were executed.

The components of this adapted WCD process, through to follow-up and beyond, are outlined below and have become the framework for developing the programme following discussion with the organization's representatives.

The company will now use this process to define their workforce management strategy and incorporate this into future business plans.

The model for the WCD programme is shown in Figure 15.1.

Aligning with the business

Change implementation was again aligned to the business using the three phases of business alignment: defining stakeholders' needs, developing measurable objectives and evaluating the results.

As part of defining stakeholder needs, WCD identified several business risks caused by an ageing workforce. These risks need risk mitigation strategies.

During this investigation various needs were identified.

Business needs

It was clear that the business needed to create a strategy for the management of their mature staff. The process described below enables this organization to set their strategy for the achievement of successful outcomes.

FIGURE 15.1 WCD programme model

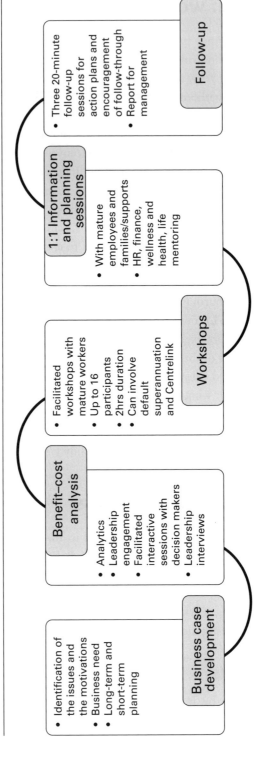

A business case was also needed to communicate the resulting strategy to all stakeholders and identify further business needs.

It was hoped that the strategy would reduce injuries, reduce compensation claims and therefore potentially reduce the cost of insurance cover. In addition, the business had a clear mandate to retain the intellect, knowledge and experience of mature employees that was often not easily transferred in a short time frame. The industry is struggling to attract younger employees into this type of work and if it does attract them, it is unlikely they want to stay for long durations of employment.

Performance needs

The performance needs identified were that mature workers would take constructive action in areas of finance, health and wellbeing as well as planning for their eventual retirement. This would include the creation and execution of personalized plans for transition, allowing management much greater insight from which to plan effectively around mature workers and resourcing needs.

Learning needs

The learning needs of the change initiative were to allow the organization to gain an understanding of the attitudes and expectations of mature employees towards their work and retirement for planning purposes.

The initiative would introduce mature employees to a framework and meaningful strategy for successful transitions, and ensure that the leaders, managers and relevant stakeholders were behind the business case for change.

Preference needs

The preference needs were identified as short, bite-sized learning and reflection initiatives that would encourage engagement and interaction by the mature workers. Plus, ideally the programme would mean that mature workers were only away from frontline duties for a limited time.

Input needs

The input need of the initiative was a workshop with a cross-section of staff over the age of 55 (15 attendees).

In addition, there would be one-on-one follow up sessions addressing finance, life mentoring, wellness and HR information.

There was also a workforce management business risk presentation with senior management team and other key staff, as well as action planning with follow-up to embed the changes.

As part of the alignment of the business it was useful to consider the output from each part of the alignment process (Table 15.1).

TABLE 15.1   Output of the alignment process

Activity undertaken	Output
Analysis of workforce demographics including workers' compensation data.	Graphically presented information to assist forward planning. Identification of potential liabilities and risks.
A workshop with a cross-section of staff over the age of 55 (15 attendees).	Gained insights into attitudes and expectations of mature employees towards work and retirement. Identified key themes, needs and intentions.
One-on-one follow-up sessions addressing finance, life mentoring, wellness and HR information.	Individual plans developed. De-identified business report to assist management planning.
Workforce management business risk presentation with senior management team and other key staff.	Identification of key business risks; reported.
Action planning.	Stage 2 to address concerns and wellbeing developed.

The workshop

Following an examination of the analytics for the business, a workshop was facilitated by an experienced occupational therapist and HR professional with years of expertise and interest in this field. A finance professional with a specific interest in mature workers, knowledge of government benefits and superannuation was also in attendance.

The workshop was very interactive and attendees were asked to start thinking about their circumstances, the role work played in their lives and what realistic planning they had done, or needed to do, for the future. Discussion was facilitated in relation to their current employer and employment – many openly shared their thoughts and concerns about the future.

During the workshop, WCD followed Kielhofner's model of human occupation (2007) addressing working life, social and community engagement, family and leisure, and also added financial literacy and the health benefits of work to the discussion.

All the participants were forthcoming with their recommendations for the business to improve interaction with mature employees, and business insights into attitudes and expectations of these mature employees towards work and retirement were also gathered.

'Finance' in the workshop

The finance section of the workshop attracted a lot of interest from attendees and generated the most discussion and conversation. The finance representative addressed:

- life stages in relation to saving, superannuation and planning;
- realistic financial developments/needs;
- considerations for the financial future.

From this point WCD encouraged individuals to seek further information and advice, and on the back of this the management team arranged for one-to-one finance and wellbeing mentoring sessions.

Health benefits of good work

Those employees who participated in the workshop were also provided with specific mentoring sessions with an HR specialist, a life coach to assist with the development of conversations, a wellbeing mentor, and a finance specialist on transition to retirement.

They all received the opportunity to participate in the creation of a health programme tailored to their individual needs. Discussions included information about the health benefits of work. Each plan was specific to the individual but considered aspects including:

- maintenance of mental wellbeing;
- exercise physiology needs;

- occupational therapy needs;
- improved ergonomics;
- work design elements.

As a result of the workshops other employees also voiced their interest in participating in any future workshops.

TLA after the change

As discussed, the pilot ran without any follow-up and as with many change initiatives, the process had begun well with great consideration being given to the aims, business alignment and learning that the group needed to move forward. Despite the sensitive nature of the change, after the workshops the group had a clear idea of what needed to be done, awareness was raised and conversations were started. However, immediate traction was hard to see and, despite best intentions, little change was actually taking place. It was at this stage that WCD and their client decided they needed to add TLA to the process.

The easiest way to integrate TLA into the process of change was to create a brief two-hour review workshop where the group reconvened to discuss progress and make concrete action plans for the next steps.

These specific action plans formed the basis of the TLA conversations that would create the momentum around the change and the planning.

Typical actions for this type of intervention included:

- creating a solid financial plan and documenting with a financial planner;
- speaking with my manager and creating a plan for transitioning to an alternative role;
- investigating what my later work years could look like, and getting clear on what I want.

The TLA conversations for this type of change were particularly relevant due to the sensitive nature of the change. The employees in some cases had significant conversations to have and decisions to make. They could all be classed as important but not urgent, so it was very easy to ignore or procrastinate. Of course the whole idea of the change initiative was to ensure that the conversations were started and decisions considered before they became urgent. Under the guidance of a TLA specialist to support the change employees could follow through on planning for a financially secure future and fulfilling later working years.

Unfortunately the TLA follow-up conversations were not completed by the time this book went to publication. For information on the results of the TLA follow-up, visit **http://transferoflearning.com/resources**.

Outcomes and evaluation of the initiative

At this time the learning outcomes are confirmed. The outcomes from the workshop were presented back to the management team and revealed a number of measures for them to actively consider and implement.

They included an in-depth understanding of motivations for working and considerations for the future such as:

- Concerns around keeping fit and active – this was a frequent theme throughout and whilst several participants seemed to carry excess weight, they were not interested in weight control information. Their preparedness to change was assessed as low.

- Recognition that there is a need to plan for the future.

- A focus on the importance of strong relationships outside work being important to wellbeing and happiness.

- Financial awareness was considered fairly low with only one attendee able to state their partial superannuation balance. All expressed a need to do further research.

- Loving the job continued to be important and attendees expressed how much they liked working but their physical limitations were a concern as they aged.

- A desire for further discussion about part-time opportunities within the operation was shared.

- These outcomes also created awareness around next steps.

- Application objectives and business impact are in the process of being realized.

- TLA follow-up support to help the participants follow through on their action plans and transfer the learning from the workshop to their working lives and beyond was considered an essential component to this programme.

- The management team have agreed that they now need to incorporate some of the programme findings into the HR and operational requirements of the business.
- A wellness initiative is now being considered for the business overall.

References

Butler, M (2015) *Advanced Australia: The politics of ageing*, Melbourne University Publishing, Melbourne

Kielhofner, G (2007) *Model of Human Occupation: Theory and application, 4th edition*, Lippincott, Williams and Wilkins, Baltimore

APPENDIX 1
Sample TLA Plan

Action Plan – IT client, Change Programme

Participant Name: <u>John Bloggs</u>   Course Date: <u>23rd May 2015</u>

TARGET	SEE SUCCESS	CALIBRATE	MOTIVATION	NEXT STEPS
What specifically will you implement from the programme and by when?	How will you know you have been successful in implementing this target? What will you see happening around you? What will people be saying? How will you feel?	Where are you now with this target on a scale of 1 (low) to 10 (high)?	Why do you want to achieve this? What does it mean to you personally? Why is that important for you?	What actions can you take within the next 48 hours? What other steps will you take before your first TLA session?
Implement system to track our technologies through their full life cycle – Invention, Engagement and Impact.	External recognition by others that I have achieved success. Smiles all round.	2 – Basic system in place but needs lots of work.	The system can be a key portfolio to me and the company. I need to demonstrate my ability and raise my self-confidence and others' confidence in me.	Prepare high-level process/system map.
System to track all marketing campaigns including impact and metrics.	All campaigns in the system being updated on an ongoing basis.	0 – company has a very poor record of tracking marketing campaigns.	Similar to above. It's about demonstrating my ability and raising my confidence and worth.	Research capability of new system marketing campaign records.
Integrate the new system and constant contact records, and create processes/ systems.	All data kept in one place.	0 – no system at present.	Demonstrates strength/value of 'constant contact' and value to department. I feel good.	Create high-level plan.

APPENDIX 2
Turning Learning into Action™ Change Agreement

Name:	
Position:	
Telephone office / mobile	
Email	

This agreement covers the relationship which is being entered into between you, the client, and your TLA facilitator with the intended outcome of implementing into your role the action plan created to support your company's change initiative. The sessions will be tailored to your individual objectives. TLA, which is not consulting, advice or counselling, will address the specific outcomes detailed by you in your TLA Plan. The telephone sessions will cover any issues that directly or indirectly affect your ability to follow through or implement your action plan. You need to enter into the sessions with the full understanding that you create your own results.

CONFIDENTIALITY
Confidentiality is at the cornerstone of TLA. Essentially, everything you share with me within the session is confidential, whether it is business or personal information. I undertake not to, at any time, either directly or indirectly use or disclose any information you share with me during our sessions. In the unlikely event that you bring to my attention a matter that would constitute gross misconduct or a serious contractual breach your change sponsor will be informed.

SESSIONS
Sessions will last [enter session length, usually 20 minutes] and will be conducted over the telephone. The programme runs for a series of three sessions.

You call me, your facilitator, at the scheduled time for the session on [enter telephone number]. Missed sessions will be forfeited. [Company name] will be notifed as to missed sessions. In the event of you calling late for a session, then the prearranged scheduled finish time will remain.

ENVIRONMENT FOR SESSIONS

It is your responsibility to ensure the environment that you are calling from is suitable for a TLA conversation. Ideally, it is a quiet, private area away from your personal office space, on a landline phone with a phone handset. You must ensure that you can speak freely and are not interrupted or distracted during the conversation. Mobile phones and computers should be switched off for the session.

DOCUMENTATION/NOTES

It is your responsibility to document your own action points from sessions. Most clients also take notes during the session. Using your own language and emphasizing what is important to you increase the level of ownership and your results.

EXPECTATIONS

You can expect your TLA facilitator to:
- Be honest with you at all times
- Maintain confidentiality
- Encourage and support you
- Be punctual
- Keep your appointment in high priority
- Respect your decisions, skills and knowledge
- Put your interests first

Your TLA facilitator expects you to:
- Be honest with the facilitator and yourself
- Maintain confidentiality of all on the call
- Be punctual
- Keep your appointment in high priority
- Be prepared to experiment and do things
- Offer feedback at the end of the process

Our signatures on this agreement indicate full understanding of, and agreement with, the information outlined:

Client: _____   Date: _____
TLA Specialist: _____   Date: _____

APPENDIX 3
Sample conversation to illustrate the flexible TION part of the ACTION model

Context: In this sample the participant wanted to tick the box and talk through how he knew how to build trust but he had clearly identified it as being difficult. The TLA facilitator needs to find out which bit is difficult and where they can add the most value.

	The TLA conversation	Commentary	Model
Facilitator	*Which target would you like us to work on today, John? I often suggest people choose the one that will be hardest or trickiest to implement so we can add the most value with our time.*	Use this question to gauge where the most value will be gained.	Target.
Participant	*Number 2.*		
Facilitator	*Ok, so looking at your action plan, number 2 was to use the new system to track all marketing campaigns including impact and metrics?*	The facilitator will have got this usually in the very beginning of the call.	Clarifying gap/ target (plus calibration).
Participant	*Yes.*		

	The TLA conversation	Commentary	Model
Facilitator	*Great – so I can see that you started that on '0', knowing that it wasn't really happening. Now the end of the briefing was about three weeks ago, have you made any progress so far?*	Using the action plan projecting forward.	Target.
Participant	*Yes. I'd say I'm on about a 2 and a half now.*		
Facilitator	*Well done on getting some traction; so what's happened to start to shift it up that scale to a 2 and a half?*	Congratulate/ celebrate/reflect.	
Participant	*Well, I've started to research and get a sense of the capability and what is possible within the system and I know now what we need to start to include.*		
Facilitator	*Wonderful, so we've got some traction. You and I are going to be speaking again in three weeks' time, so if you really put effort into it over the next three weeks, where do you feel you could get it to on your scale of 1–10?*	Identifying the gap.	Target.
Participant	*Well, at a push within three weeks I think I could get it to a 6.*		Target.

	The TLA conversation	Commentary	Model
Facilitator	*And would you be happy with getting it to a 6, John?*		Target.
Participant	*Yeah, I'd be happy with getting to a 6 and then within another month from then I'd really like to get it to an 8.*	Confirming what number he wants to go for.	Target.
Facilitator	*Excellent, so we've got in our minds then within three weeks we want to get it to a 6 and then within another month we want to get it up to an 8. And so let's just look at that 6. Where are you when you've got to the stage of being a 6?*	Narrowing the time frame to something immediate.	Target.
Participant	*So at a 6 I will have around half of my current marketing campaigns in the system, I will have all of my metrics updated for those campaigns, and I'll have clear next steps in the system for those campaigns.*		Target.
Facilitator	*It sounds as if you've got a really clear view of what that looks like at a 6 – if you were to project yourself forward, let's just check in – how easy is that going to be to implement? 10 is really easy, 1 is you've got no chance.*	Gap, gathering info. The facilitator may think they have a gap so they start to gather information.	Target.
Participant	*Well, in theory it sounds easy, but if it were that easy I could actually just sit down and do it! Part of the truth is I can sit down and do it, but there is a reluctance.*		Info.

	The TLA conversation	Commentary	Model
Facilitator	*I can hear the reluctance in your voice, John, and that's absolutely fine because we can brainstorm this out together. What is it that's making you reluctant in terms of your ease of following through on this?*	Further identification of the gap.	Info.
Participant	*Well, there's two things – one is just finding the time to do it, and two, I'm going to need to get some additional information from a colleague to be able to do this. They have some of the metrics I need, and I don't have access to all of them. And I'm just wondering if they're going to be able to give those across to me.*		Options.
Facilitator	*Great – so we know that the real barriers are finding the time, and getting these metrics. Which of those do we need to tackle first? Time or metrics?*	Identification of the gap.	Info on the target.
Participant	*I think... the metrics.*		
Facilitator	*OK, let's think about those metrics – what's the barrier or challenge to that happening?*	Identification of specific gap.	Target.
Participant	*Well, in truth it's a colleague I haven't got the best relationship with – there's mutual respect there, but we aren't the closest of colleagues.*		Info

	The TLA conversation	Commentary	Model
Facilitator	OK, so given that you haven't got the best relationship but you need to get these metrics from them, what are your thoughts around that?	Reflection.	Info/options.
Participant	Well, he's a reasonable guy, I think if I just explain to him why they're important, and how much I'd appreciate it, I'm sure he would help me out.		Options.
Facilitator	So let's have a think about this; if you took that action and explained to him why it was important to you – what do you feel – is that going to get you those metrics?		Next steps.
Participant	Yes, I'm pretty confident it would.		
Facilitator	And sometimes when we set a deadline for ourselves it just helps us move forward, so when will you approach your colleague?	Gaining commitment to a time.	Next steps.
Participant	I think I need to do it sooner rather than later.		
Facilitator	And when's sooner in your calendar?		
Participant	Well, today's Wednesday – if I did it by the end of day Friday that would be great.	Gaining commitment to a time.	

	The TLA conversation	Commentary	Model
Facilitator	*OK, so are you happy with that as a plan – to speak to this colleague before the end of day Friday to get that moving forward?*		Next steps.
Participant	*Yeah, that sounds good.*		
Facilitator	*So let's also then just tackle this piece around the time – just finding time to do it. So to get 50 per cent of these marketing campaigns, how much time do you think that is going to take you?*		Target/info.
Participant	*I think it's a good four-hour job. It's a half day.*		Info.
Facilitator	*And when you look at your calendar in the next three weeks, how could you make that happen?*		Info/options.
Participant	*Well, if I look in my calendar over the next three weeks half a day just isn't available.*		
Facilitator	*So imagine you're chatting with a friend, and they say 'Look, I need half a day to do a project, but there's just no room in the diary' – what would you say to that friend?*	Encouraging conversation with themselves.	Options.
Participant	*Well, I'd say is it important or not?*		

	The TLA conversation	Commentary	Model
Facilitator	*And so let's look at that – is it important or not to you?*		
Participant	*It is important, I want to find time to do it.*		
Facilitator	*So if your friend says yes, it is important, what advice would you give to them then?*	Further reflection.	
Participant	*I'd say you're going to need to chunk it down.*		Options.
Facilitator	*And what could you chunk it down into?*		
Participant	*Well, I think really it's got to be chunked down into two two-hour blocks, and I think really I need to get away from my desk... which is going to be tricky... although actually I could take my laptop.*		
Facilitator	*Great, so we're thinking two two-hour chunks and taking your laptop. Where would you take your laptop to?*		Options/next steps.
Participant	*In my mind I just thought I would book a meeting room, and book both two-hour slots in that meeting room, and actually just get away and update the system then.*		Options/next steps.

	The TLA conversation	Commentary	Model
Facilitator	*Great, so that sounds like a plan. When do you feel you can get those two two-hour chunks in your diary?*	Breaking down the next steps.	Next steps.
Participant	*Well, that's actually quite easy to do, because I can do that first thing on a couple of different mornings before anything else is happening.*		
Facilitator	*So, John, we've got a couple of pieces planned there – do you want to play back to me what the actions are that you're taking away?*	The facilitator prompts a quick summary to remind the participant what path they are taking.	Summary, next steps.
Participant	*Sure, I'm going to book the two two-hour blocks in my diary and also get the meeting room sorted for those blocks. I'm also going to speak to my colleague before end of day Friday.*		Next steps.
Facilitator	*Great. So John, if we look at those actions – what we're trying to do is get yourself to a 6 in the next three weeks does – that feel workable?*		
Participant	*Yeah, that works for me.*		

	The TLA conversation	Commentary	Model
Facilitator	*OK, so let's just check in – on a scale of 1–10, how confident are you that you can follow through on that?*	The facilitator can gauge the certainty here by using the structure of calibration – *'On a scale of 1 to 10 how confident are you on following through?'* – the facilitator will probably be able to tell confidence by the participant's voice.	Next steps.
Participant	*I'm an 8 in confidence that I will action those things.*		
Facilitator	*And I know I'm obsessed with my scale of 1–10! What could we do to shift that from an 8 to a 9 or 10 in terms of confidence that you can get these actions to a 6, to get these things happening?*		
Participant	*Well, I think to make those two hours really productive I actually need to leave my mobile phone in my desk.*		Next steps.
Facilitator	*Great, if we did that – is that going to raise your confidence?*		
Participant	*Yes. I'd be a 9 out of 10 then. 10 never really happens completely in my world!*		

	The TLA conversation	Commentary	Model
Facilitator	*Wonderful, so when we next check in – we'll check in on how you've gone with those activities, and our next call is scheduled for Wednesday 15th November at 2pm. Thanks for that, John, really glad you're going to be making that progress.*		
Participant	*Thank you.*		

INDEX

Note: *Italics* indicate a Figure or Table.